D1475572

JUST
THE WORKING LIFE

JUST
THE WORKING LIFE

OPPOSITION AND ACCOMMODATION
IN DAILY INDUSTRIAL LIFE

MARC LENDLER

HD
4904
.L365
1990
WEST

M. E. Sharpe, Inc.

ARMONK, NEW YORK
LONDON, ENGLAND

Copyright © 1990 by M. E. Sharpe, Inc.

All rights reserved. No part of this book may be reproduced in any
form without written permission from the publisher, M. E. Sharpe, Inc.,
80 Business Park Drive, Armonk, New York 10504.

Available in the United Kingdom and Europe from M. E. Sharpe, Publishers,
3 Henrietta Street, London WC2E 8LU.

Library of Congress Cataloging-in-Publication Data

Lendler, Marc.
    Just the working life: opposition and accommodation in daily industrial life /
by Marc Lendler.
      p. cm.
    Includes bibliographical references.
    ISBN 0-87332-608-3
    1. Working class—Psychology. 2. Adjustment (Psychology)
    3. Acquiescence (Psychology) I. Title.
    HD4904.L365 1990
    158.7—dc20   89–70267
                                                                    CIP

Printed in the United States of America.

MV   10 9 8 7 6 5 4 3 2 1

To Ron, Mary Lou, Mary Beth, Bob, Nan, and Barry

We all tried.

Contents

Acknowledgments

This project worked its way onto paper slowly, starting in embryo with questions I developed while I was working at Diamond International in the mid-1970s. At that point, writing a book was the farthest thing from my mind. I moved from formulating questions to a book where I try to answer some of them in stages, and I received help from several sources along the way.

First and foremost, I want to thank the thirty-three men and women who work at "NEC" who took part in these interviews. Some were enthusiastic; some were bewildered, but all were helpful. I would like to be able to identify the leadership of the "UCW," the union at NEC, but of course I cannot do that. One person I can mention who aided me in locating a research site is John Sartori of the United Steel Workers. The management at NEC was also cooperative.

I want to thank the Political Science Department at the University of Cincinnati, where I spent my first year of graduate school, for taking a chance on someone who had been out of academics for ten years. In particular, Stephen Bennett alerted me to the possibility that the study of public opinion might help answer some of the questions I had been left with, as well as raising some new ones. When this book was in dissertation form, I received advice and counsel from Robert Dahl, David Mayhew, and James Scott. I think I should point out that contrary to the impression which may be created in these pages, Jim Scott's writings as well as advice have been important in helping me formulate my ideas.

As this work proceeded on the path from dissertation to book, Barbara Leffel, then social science editor at M. E. Sharpe, was more than helpful. When we first met to discuss the manuscript, she knew more about some of the characters in it than I remembered.

A special note of thanks is due to Mary O'Neil, a teacher at Choate Rosemary Hall, for providing me with enormous last-minute, panic-time computer help.

Finally, as will be obvious, I often turned for inspiration to the songs of Bruce Springsteen, whose understanding of the hopes and disappointments of working people in late twentieth-century America reaches into areas of the heart that social science may still be unable to enter. It should not be surprising that there were times when the insights of an artist about the ambiguities in people's perceptions helped me past points where more conventional approaches temporarily left me stuck.

JUST
THE WORKING LIFE

1

Introduction

*The wonder, then, is not that men are revolted. The wonder is that there is a
stone left standing.*

—Carl Oglesby[1]

These lines, spoken in 1966, were representative of several currents of thought at
the time. The world would soon be turned right side up as people rebelled against
centuries of insult and injury. The terms of the struggle were straightforward.
Some were born to sweet delight, some were born to endless night. This unshak-
able fact would in short order come to overshadow all others. Further, this
assumption implied a criticism of contemporary social science: it was nose-to-
the-ground, not ear-to-the-wind. It concentrated on (and perhaps favored) continuity, "normal" times, stability in social systems. It overlooked inequality,
poverty, glaring injustices; it did not spend much time on, predict, or particularly
care for popular protest or revolution.

There was, and is, no trouble in locating misuse of power or inequality. But
dominated groups do not always seem to be rebellious or even quarrelsome. Theorists
of revolution have tried to create models to explain when and how suffering translates
into broad popular activity. Most of these models revolve around some variation of
relative deprivation.[2] But no one ever has seriously contended that inequality or even
perceived injustice would everywhere give rise to revolutionary movements. Marx
even at his most optimistic saw countervailing forces.

This book does not examine those abnormal moments of high-intensity conflict. Rather, it looks at the varying responses people have to unremarkable, daily
situations of hierarchical authority and inequality. When and why is legitimacy
granted to superior authority? To what extent—and when—are inequalities that
define a hierarchical structure seen as unjust? What is the relationship between
perceived injustice and compliance? In some ways, these questions inquire about
and even imply the opposite of Oglesby's statement, quoted above. Subordination is not always seen as unjust, *nor is it always even seen as subordination.* In

3

addition, even deeply felt grievances do not always, or usually, move people to regard relevant authorities as illegitimate. A popular distillation of the thrust of Oglesby's words was in Mao Tse-tung's dictum, "Where there is oppression, there is resistance." Some social scientists[3] took the contrapositive of this claim, saw situations of little or no resistance,[4] and found, therefore, no oppression. My intention here is in some ways the opposite—to examine the ways in which oppression comes to be seen as inevitable and in which the fact of subordination blunts or limits the possibility of responses to it.

The Setting of the Question

> All societies are inegalitarian. But what is the relation between the inequalities in a society and the feelings of acquiescence or resentment to which they give rise?[5]

This question is certainly not a new one. One of Aristotle's central political projects was to find a governmental means to preserve inequality while preventing faction-class struggle-revolution (the various translations of "stasis").[6] Perhaps a more relevant way of writing the same sentence would be that Aristotle was attempting to preserve privilege by preventing "factional" strife. Machiavelli was more sympathetic to the populace as claimants to power,[7] but in advising those who wished to rule over it, he argued that quick and efficient use of coercion ("good arms") would lay the basis for creating public order ("good laws").[8] The prescriptions of Aristotle and Machiavelli differ sharply, but there is a common denominator—the concern that popular perception of injustice might result in unwelcome instability and that this situation must be carefully managed.

Nonetheless, it is not intuitively obvious why one would look for or try to explain passivity and obedience among subordinate groups. The prisoners of starvation will arise; to the extent that they are not starving, they will negotiate rather than arise; to the extent that they have not arisen, they must not be starving. How should one view social relations that include hierarchy and inequality if those who are subjects seem to have reached a degree of accommodation with those conditions? Several strands of literature have converged in discussing and proposing answers to this question. The genesis of the formulation of the question is in itself instructive. I am going to look briefly at four sets of literature in which this topic came to be near the top of the differing agendas. This review is intentionally fast-paced and the categories are by no means mutually exclusive. My purpose is to look at how a question came to be formulated, rather than to discuss the various answers in depth. Most of the authors mentioned will reemerge in later pages.

Marxism

One of the most vexing problems in the theory and practice of Marxism over the years has been understanding the process by which the international working class shall become the human race. Marx, of course, placed the very highest tasks on the working-class agenda—to be the gravediggers of capitalism, the first nonexploitative ruling class in history, the class that would "substitute for the old civil society an association which will exclude classes and their antagonism" and in which association "there will be no more political power, properly so called."[9] While Marx and Engels may have grown somewhat less optimistic in their later years regarding the immediacy of a revolutionary workers' movement in the more advanced industrial societies, both continued to see these most monumental of goals as practical historical possibilities. The strongest claim that is sometimes drawn from this agenda about Marxism[10] and by Marxists[11] holds that all or most workers must and will at some point become as conscious of history as Marx was himself.

But running simultaneous with the description of a world-changing working class, and in fact impelling it, is an account of the misery and degradation that was its fate in the capitalism of Marx's time. He was quite specific and emphatic that the capitalist division of labor, factory despotism, and poor living and working conditions affected not just the workers' physical lives, but their mental lives as well.

> It is true that labor produces for the rich wonderful things—but for the worker it produces privation. It produces palaces—but for the worker, hovels. It produces beauty—but for the worker, deformity. It replaces labor by machinery—but some of the workers it throws back into a barbarous type of labor, and the other workers it turns into machines. It produces intelligence—but for the worker, idiocy, cretinism.[12]

> Time for education, for intellectual development, for the fulfillment of social functions, and for social intercourse, for the free play of his bodily and mental activity, even the rest-time of Sunday—moonshine.[13]

> [Manufacture] converts the laborer into a crippled monstrosity by forcing his detail dexterity at the expense of a world of productive capabilities and instincts—just as in the States of La Plata they butcher a whole beast for the sake of his hide or his tallow.[14]

> [The factory] confiscates every atom of freedom both in bodily and intellectual activity.[15]

> [M]ore than any other mode of production, it [capitalist production] squanders human lives and not only blood and flesh, but also nerve and brain.[16]

The indictment of capitalism suggested in these passages is surely one of the important reasons for the continued appeal of Marxism. But the working class depicted here is a considerable distance from the politically active, conscious, mobilized, and altruistic[17] working class needed to meet its tasks as described earlier. If the legacy of capitalism to workers is their "misery, agony, toil, slavery, ignorance, brutality, mental degradation" (from one of the most quoted lines of *Capital*, vol. I), would not a revolutionary—or even a reformer—be better off looking elsewhere for gravediggers? Michael Burawoy, writing about the tensions implicit in Marx's description of a working class both beaten down and lifted up, put the dilemma well:

> But how does one get from one to the other—from competition, isolation, misery, oppression, slavery and exploitation to combination, association and struggle?[18]

Two frequently given answers would put that question outside the specific line of inquiry of this study. The first is that you *can't* get there from here; Marx has been proven wrong. As just one of many such assertions, consider this:

> In the long run, however, Marx believed that the experience of factory conditions, collective urban life, impoverished standards of living and the constant threat of unemployment would gradually make members of the proletariat conscious of their common and exploited situation. As a result Marx argued that the class in itself would become a class for itself and trade union activity together with participation in reformist political movements were seen as interim stages in the making of a revolutionary proletariat. Obviously enough, this has not yet happened. Capitalism is still with us and the workers are not yet manning the barricades.[19]

It is only in its strongest form that Marx's prediction is largely—and even then not wholly—wrong. Several recent studies of the Russian revolution, far from agreeing with Antonio Gramsci's description of it as a "revolution against *Capital*," have stressed the significant role of the working class and the way in which the working class gravitated toward the Bolsheviks *by virtue of its radicalism* from 1913 on—that is, before the impact of the war.[20] Workers before and since have been manning barricades, voting for Communist and Labor parties, striking for regime changes (in Iran and Poland for example) and adopting syndicalist programs (as in Denmark and Sweden). These activities have not been consistent or decisive, nor, as Marx and Engels expected early in their lives, part of a movement of the largest class. But these activities have been enough a part of the history of the working class that it makes the assertion that Marx was "obviously wrong" obviously wrong. If there has been no final conflict, there has at least been a fine old conflict.[21]

The second answer to Burawoy's question that makes pursuing it uninteresting for our purposes is the possibility that what took Marx's working class from misery to revolution was a simple assertion of historical agency, the creation of a "hypothetical proletariat."[22] At crucial moments, this argument goes, Marx was always a Hegelian, and the proletariat was a substitute for Hegel's universal class of bureaucrats—the class with no private or sectoral interests. Flesh-and-blood workers had no properties to propel Marx toward assigning them such a role. Andre Gorz has recently made this case: "Marx's theory of the proletariat is not based upon either empirical observation of class conflict or practical involvement in proletarian struggle."[23] And Gorz has a point. Marx wrote confidently about the future of the working class, in part because of the Hegel-derived assurance that essence was buried beneath appearance and would come to assert itself. If this were all Marx had to say on this matter, there would be little point in continuing the discussion, because one either is or is not a Hegelian.[24]

But Marx's approach to the working class drew from several different perspectives. I will mention six, briefly:

1. *The suffering described above must eventually draw the workers into concerted action against its cause.* This does not specify why the working class was uniquely in this position. Marx recognized the terrible conditions of the lumpenproletariat and some of the peasantry and drew different conclusions about their future.

2. *The "species-essential" character of humankind is to create, specifically through labor.* This argument drew heavily on what Marx saw as the revolutionizing aspects of capitalism, especially from the *Grundrisse* rather than the *Manifesto*. Until capitalism divorced the laborer from the means of production, individualization—essential for socialism and the realm of freedom—was inconceivable.[25]

3. *The labor theory of value showed all value creation to be directly or indirectly the product of workers.* This lent a moral dimension to the claims of the working class. These last two arguments would make a specifically working-class movement more legitimate, and would clarify the shape of the final goal, but they do not contribute to a theory of how that movement would arise.

4. *The battle had already been joined.* The working class of Marx's time often engaged in militant protest activities. Marx and Engels were participants in those movements and drew constantly from them in their writings. Luddites, Chartists, and Parisian communards marched around in defiance of capital, both in the streets and in the pages of Marx and Engels. English sociologist Richard Hyman felt that Gorz may have actually inverted the real case against Marx's proletariat:

> What *can* plausibly be argued is that the time and place in which Marx and Engels encountered the working class were exceptional; and that they were encouraged to treat the militant socialist worker as prototypical because the stereotype meshed so neatly with their unfolding world-historical analysis.[26]

5. *Struggle is the teaching process.* Marx accorded this a very important role. In the course of fighting an individual employer or for a particular reform on

the national level, those who took part would themselves be transformed:

> Both for the production on a mass scale of this communist consciousness and for the success of the cause itself, the alteration of men on a mass scale is necessary, an alteration which can only take place in a practical movement, a *revolution;* which is necessary, therefore, not only because the ruling class cannot be overthrown in any other way, but also because the class *overthrowing* it can only in a revolution succeed in ridding itself of all the muck of ages and become fitted to found society anew.[27]

"Learning through struggle" was one of the aspects of Marxism which most strongly influenced the New Left activists of the 1960s. It showed up also in the Fanon-Sartre scenario of a slave killing his own slavish aspects by killing his master.[28] But Marx went beyond this. Struggle would teach people *specific* lessons, leading them toward an understanding of their role as the next ruling class. This answer to Burawoy's question, thus, is a combination of observation and Hegel—an actual struggle of actual people producing real changes, revealing an idea-coming-into-being.

6. *Social being determines social consciousness.* Perhaps the most widely discussed of the ways Marx described the development of working-class consciousness is what I will call the sociological argument. This argument does not rely on the immiserization of the working class—either absolute or relative—but on its existence as a collective entity. The capitalists brought the working class into existence and gave them a certain commonly shared life—taking away skills and the land of newly proletarianized peasants, and forcing people to work together in huge factories.[29] This collective existence made cooperation a norm for those who had no choice. Cooperation took the political form of combination and collective resistance; it also foreshadowed the potential communal—communist—organization of society.

Debates have ensued, of course. The most familiar one revolves around the allegation that Marx mistook the cause of early resistance to capitalism; that the root of resistance was the dispossession of former small landowners and the deskilling of former craftsmen.[30] Historians of the Russian revolution have debated the relative importance of newly urbanized workers as opposed to more fully urbanized artisans in the pre-revolution radicalization.[31] Both those views are partly supportive of Marx's sociological argument, but neither would describe concentration under one roof as the determining variable. In trying to answer his own question about the hypothesized passage of workers from isolation to association, Burawoy raised the possibility that the socialization process varied by the form of "factory regime." There are several "regime" types, not just the market despotism described in *Capital*. Each gives rise to very specific forms of resistance.[32]

Marxism appears to leave an imposing gap between impoverishment and salva-
tion, all the while suggesting the two are inextricably intertwined. I have pointed
out that Marx saw the working class bridging the gap in a variety of ways. They
differ as to how rooted they are in philosophy, history, and sociology; most are
some combination of each. None is a flawless predictor—but this demand for
infallibility is made more often of Marx than of other writers. To the extent that
the predictions fail or the arguments themselves are not convincing—which at
times I have tried to indicate—Marxists and others who draw from the Marxist
tradition are faced with the problem of explaining varied responses to oppression
on the part of the oppressed. A potpourri of theories has grown up to explain
these responses—so much so that even overviews now are spawning overviews.[33] My purpose here has been twofold: to outline briefly how Marx saw the
fact of subordination reflected in the attitudes and actions of at least this one
subordinate class; and to indicate a pile of problems that his analysis and the
passage of time have left for those who share some of his broad premises. The
next subsection looks at some who fall in that category.

British Sociology

An important preoccupation of British sociology has been with accounting
for the relative stability in industrial relations in contradistinction to Marx,
but without denying the Marx-influenced understanding of ''the precarious nature of industrial peace given the ineradicable opposition of certain interests.''[34]
At times this inquiry has led sociologists to look to the concept of ''deference''
that Bagehot discussed and that Disraeli made into a political rallying cry. At
other times, writers try to fuse these two traditions, an improbable combination
that I hope will begin to look better by the end of this chapter and more so by
the end of the book. The British working class has served as the historical
basis for contrasting theories of revolutionary millenialism and conservative
incorporation.

David Lockwood found a three-part division of the modern British working class
into ''proletarian,'' ''privatized,'' and ''deferential'' to be a useful conceptual tool.[35]
Proletarian and deferential working-class images were variants of traditional class
images, contrasted by Lockwood with the more modern privatization. Of
Lockwood's three images, I find ''privatized'' and ''deferential'' especially
interesting, since the ''proletarian'' category is the traditional standard-bearer
for the revolted, while the other two may be able to explain the stones left
standing.

According to Martin and Fryer, deference is ''commitment by lower social
groups to a moral order which legitimates their own subordination.''[36] The usefulness of this concept assumes a hierarchical order and that those in subordinate

positions recognize that there is in fact a hierarchy. Lockwood drew on previous attempts to explain why some English workers voted Conservative. Subsequent efforts have been made to limit the range of ideas and behavior regarded as "deferent." McKenzie and Silver, for instance, argued that there are "secular" as well as deferent working-class conservatives—those whose reasons for voting that way center on assessment of the Conservatives' policies and performance in office.[37] Jessop teased out different domains that deference theorists have claimed for their product and found only "ascriptive socio-political deference"—a belief in an ascribed elite naturally qualified for governance—to be usefully covered by that term. Other belief structures that contain support for superiors are subsets of traditionalism, which can change as the dominant culture changes.[38] Newby wanted to separate out even from that grouping ritual acts that may seem to imply deference—bowing and saluting, for example—since these may be explained as either devoid of meaning or as the product of coercion.[39] Finally, Roberts et al., in *Fragmentary Class Structure*, asked researchers to call off the hunt for the deferent worker completely.[40] Lockwood's categories run into the most trouble when they are seen or used as explanatory variables. They are useful names and organizing devices for constellations of attitudes and behavior. "Affluence" can in some situations be viewed as exogenous; "deference" probably should not be. Nevertheless, McKenzie and Silver, Jessop, and Newby all found sets of attitudes—and people who hold them—even in the carefully delimited cells they constructed. For the purposes of my investigation, there is no reason not to allow "deference" the freedom afforded by Martin and Fryer's definition, quoted above.

The concept of "privatization" is a derivative of "instrumentalism," the central approach of Goldthorpe and Lockwood's *Affluent Worker* series to working-class imagery. The structure of work has not been altered fundamentally, the authors argued, nor has affluence led to *embourgeoisiment*. But they found that the two older methods of responding to inequality—proletarian and deferential—were not typical of modern workers. The modern orientation to work was to regard it as instrumental: "Work is regarded as a means of acquiring the income necessary to support a valued way of life of which work itself is not an integral part."[41] This modern view, according to the authors, has eliminated the need to see work as an appropriate venue for fulfillment. Alisdair Clayre argued that while instrumentalism may be an accurate term to describe contemporary working-class imagery, it is not a particularly recent development. There have always been important distinctions between craftsmanship and work.[42] Westergaard and Resler offer a competing interpretation of the findings of *The Affluent Worker,* arguing that instrumentalism could lay the basis for a thoroughgoing radicalization of the work force.[43] If the modern working class is *increasingly* instrumental, this confirms Marx in predicting that capitalism progressively reduces all social relations to a cash nexus. If all satisfaction from work is derived from the paycheck, what happens, ask these authors, if the cash nexus breaks—that is, if there is a severe economic dislocation?

Neither critique challenged the essential findings of *The Affluent Worker*. The central challenge to these findings has been that *The Affluent Worker* predicted increasing passivity on the part of the British working class and that the rank-and-file militancy of the 1970s left the book outdated. The general findings of the book were "cruelly put to the test" when the very workers they had interviewed some months before went on a rampage at the Vauxhall plant, "singing the Red Flag and calling 'string him up' whenever a director's name was mentioned."[44] The reason for introducing the concepts "deference" and "instrumentalism" here is that they have arisen within a defined body of literature to try to explain the acquiescence of a subordinate group to its superiors. But neither category singlemindedly predicted passivity.[45] *The Affluent Worker*, after all, was written to disprove the claims that the working class had merged into larger society.[46] Instrumentalism could mean a greater degree of satisfaction with work given the limited goals which it implies, or it could mean extreme alienation for eight hours, with the paycheck as the only solace. The authors conceded that both interpretations of their evidence were possible.[47]

Another area some British sociologists have investigated to explain the varied responses of blue-collar workers to inequality is relative deprivation and reference group theory. Of course, there is nothing intrinsic about relative deprivation to make it a candidate for predicting acquiescence. One of the prominent uses of relative deprivation theory is as a guide to understanding revolution.[48] But workers' understanding of "fairness" in pay and status is necessarily mediated by their comparisons with relevant reference groups. W. G. Runciman conducted a survey in which he found that manual workers rarely compared themselves with any group other than manual workers.[49] Hyman and Brough, in a review of various sets of blue-collar reference group data, proposed as the most informative finding the limited range of choices of groups for comparisons:

> [T]he choice of pay comparisons is typically unambitious and powerfully shaped by custom: major inequalities which form an established part of the incomes hierarchy are rarely a focus of contention.[50]

As with the two concepts taken from Lockwood and *The Affluent Worker*, even this broad view of relative deprivation did not uniformly predict passivity. While choice of groups for comparison may obscure some inequalities, those inequalities that remain visible can provoke anger. Hyman and Brough pointed out that the same studies which suggested narrow reference group comparisons found that "pay comparisons can generate discontent and conflict even when their focus is relatively narrow."[51]

These three approaches—deference, instrumentalism, and relative deprivation—start from the assumption that there is something to be explained, some support for a status quo which may be unfavorable to those doing the supporting, perhaps some lack of oppositional activity when opposition would seem warranted. Some others have disputed that there is much to be explained. There is, according to this school of thought, a somewhat unified set of ideas particular to subordinate classes, opposed to certain aspects of the dominant culture. Michael Mann calls this situation "deviant consensus within the lower class."[52] In *The Dominant Ideology Thesis,* the strongest formulation of this position, Abercrombie, Hill, and Turner wrote: "There is a sense in which it is foolish to ask how societies cohere, for the answer is that they do not."[53] Their survey of surveys indicated very little support for the theory that quiescence was the result of a coherent dominant ideology transmitted to and accepted by the lower classes. Moorehouse and Chamberlain in particular found lower-class respondents differing from norms commonly attributed to higher classes on such questions as the sanctity of private property and the legitimacy of profits.[54] As a corollary, these writers saw instability lurking closer to the surface of events than did the previous authors. But it is instructive to note that one of the authors of *The Dominant Ideology Thesis* had to spend much more time in his subsequent book describing the "pragmatic acceptance" of inequality even by those who do not accept it in principle.[55] If one acknowledges hardships in working-class existence—as these authors do—the degree of stability seems to require more explanation than simple coercion.

There is one variation of this "deviant consensus" theme that suggests a countersocialization process through which a working-class culture is transmitted, and argues that this can paradoxically result in behavior helpful to the dominant strata.[56] Richard Hoggart probably began this trend in his somewhat impressionistic account of the emphasis on physical immediacy in English working-class culture.[57] While not proposing a formal social-psychological theory, Hoggart's account verged on a reworking of the older hypothesis that the lower classes are unable or unwilling to delay gratification for future gain. Paul Willis extended this theme through interviews conducted at a working-class high school.[58] Nonconformist "lads" formed themselves into a self-conscious alternative to the school administration and the norms which it promoted. Their rebelliousness, according to Willis, allowed them to see through the false hopes for advancement the school held out for everyone and in which the "conformists" believed. The nonconformists knew these hopes were lies, and their rebelliousness led them enthusiastically from school through the factory gates, which, at the most intriguing point in the book, Willis shuts behind them, offering only a glimpse of the lads' future.[59]

Each of the above studies concentrated on exposing and explaining a set of attitudes believed to represent sections of subordinate classes. But what is the more important question: what attitudes do people hold, or under what conditions might they be changed? Another group of writers explored the second question after discussing possible limitations on the ability of subordinate groups to formulate alternatives on their own. This is a kind of soft-shoe Leninism, and not a school of thought at all, but a number of authors who emphasize some form of outside intervention in consciousness formation. Parkin argued that the life experience of the working class has at best given rise to a "negotiated" version of the dominant ideology, in which some nonthreatening elements of a self-generated subordinate culture are combined with the dominant value system.[60] On their own, this is as far as workers can go in creating an oppositional value system. The task of creating a fuller opposition—a socialist one in Parkin's account—is up to a mass labor party. He is explicit in calling the existence of such a party more cause than effect in determining the extent of working-class "radicalization."[61] Duncan Gallie compared English and French workers to establish that both political parties and the historical and institutional framework for including these parties in governing must be part of any generalization about causes for working-class attitudes. While industry is organized in roughly the same way in those two countries, industrial politics is not; the widely noted "higher class consciousness" of French workers may be a product of more forceful working-class parties, combined with less political inclusion.[62] Michael Mann did not emphasize parties as much as Gallie or Parkin, but his insistence on the importance of revolutionary traditions "as an important force in class consciousness" is not terribly clear outside the context of parties.[63]

This quick tour of some research in British sociology has been intended primarily to highlight the questions addressed, not the answers given. Certainly some of the themes contend with each other (and some of the writers might object to the company they keep in my loose subgroupings). It is precisely the variation that allows some common elements to assume importance. While I would not want to underestimate the differences within the literature in this section, I think that most of the writers would agree with the following as a general characterization of the motivation for their line of inquiry:

> The problem posed is that of the compatibility of consensus with persistent, socially structured inequality. . . . Why is it that individuals who so obviously differ in their command over power and resources none the less share certain values and manage to co-operate in the maintenance of society so that these inequalities are continually reproduced and often intensified?[64]

Reciprocity Theorists

The above name for this next grouping is not self-explanatory. I would have preferred to use the term "social contract theorists" for this section, but it has acquired an unshakably specific meaning in political philosophy. Nor are the boundaries of this grouping as clear as the previous two; it is a group without much groupness. Nevertheless, I proceed.

Included in this short overview are Alvin Gouldner, Barrington Moore, Eugene Genovese, and James Scott,[65] all writers from several academic disciplines who directly address my central question by rephrasing it somewhat. An intersection and distillation of their inquiry might produce the following question: what are the mutual obligations which actors in an unequal relationship impose on each other and where and to what degree does autonomy exist for actors in such a relationship? Each arrived at that question through investigation of a group which in any commonsense parlance is understood to be subordinate: Gouldner studied industrial workers; Scott, the peasantry; Genovese, slaves; and Moore, the German working class.[66]

The unifying theme is that inequality tends to become translated into an inescapable fact of life when it is persistent and widespread. The powerless create a "social contract" as the basis for relations with their superordinates. That "contract" imposes obligations and sets limits on their superiors, violations of which can lead to resistance. This is sometimes called the "moral economy" approach.[67] In return for the performance of these (quite small) duties, the subordinates reach an accommodation with the prevailing order—hence, the term "reciprocity."

There are, of course, precedents for this kind of investigation. In at least one respect, one of the more conventionally named social contract writers, John Locke, looked at similar questions. His contract was essentially defensive, a political means to protect certain well-defined social and economic relationships preexistent in the state of nature.[68] Rebellion was a right that could be asserted when a particular government violated its covenant—i.e., when it became "anarchic." Locke's citizens were a great deal more equal to each other than those in the above relationships, but they parallel their contemporaries in at least one respect: people would willingly put up with abuses over a long period of time, until certain basic norms were violated.[69]

A more direct influence on this writing was Hegel's description of master-slave relationships in *Phenomenology of the Spirit*. Although Hegel's purpose was to demonstrate opposing "modes of consciousness" and not principally to explore the nature of slavery, some of his observations along the way influenced Marx and became important in future studies of "slave"-type relationships, including the ones at hand. The master-slave pairing was not a relationship of reciprocity but of dependence. The modes of consciousness generated were not just different but opposed to each other; the master was essentially unfree because his creative ability depended on the slave; the slave, unfree in body, created through labor a sense of his own mind and therefore some autonomy in that relationship. It was Hegel's projection of the interweaving of subordination with autonomy which has proved useful to several of these current writers.

Gouldner's early work on industry was not as broadly comparative as that of the other three authors mentioned above, but it perhaps overturned a spade or two of theoretical earth for the others to explore. Gouldner explicitly sought to explain the tensions evoked by bureaucracy. He contrasted these underlying tensions and shifting instabilities to the "Gibraltar-like stability" which seemed to characterize industrial relations externally. In the industrial setting that he studied, a managerial decision to increase and streamline its control provoked widespread resentment and eventually a wildcat strike. Gouldner's diagnosis was that the move toward rational administration had disrupted long-standing "indulgency patterns" which had given it legitimacy in the eyes of hourly employees. These indulgency patterns were areas in which privileges had been extended to employees outside the negotiated contract. These unofficial rights softened the edges of plant authority and went some distance toward transforming "obeying" into "cooperating."[70] Gouldner did not discuss the significance of inequality in this relationship[71] but in a later article generalized from these indulgencies a "norm of reciprocity" that he called a "plastic filler," capable of acting as an "all purpose moral cement."[72]

Reciprocity in this last sense is the takeoff point for the other three writers. Each tried to explain when and why people comply with authority which seems, to the outside observer, to be patently unjust and exploitative. Moore and Genovese argued that there is some comfort for the lower classes in the stability of an unequal power relationship. "Protection" is the central contribution of authorities. The anger of the lower class principally stems from a failure on the part of the dominant authorities to provide that protection or from a new assertion of prerogatives from above. Injustice is so widespread that it becomes part of the environment, an inevitable condition of human existence. Both writers saw the powerless as engaged in a struggle for self-definition which necessarily preceded forays against their oppressive surroundings. They pursued Stanley Elkins's famous question, "What did slavery do to the slaves?"[73] Moore found injustice so all encompassing that it becomes internalized, even seen as just. Only under very unusual conditions can human beings overcome the "perilous capacity for getting used to things." Genovese was somewhat more optimistic, finding in the legitimating ideologies of the slave masters a reluctant but necessary affirmation of the humanity of the supposed chattels, a tool which the slaves themselves were quick to seize. To Genovese, fatalism—exemplified among slaves by Christianity—is a denial of the rights of the masters.[74]

Scott is more optimistic still. He described peasant relationships in which injustice was as pervasive as it was in the institutions studied by Moore and Genovese.[75] In his earlier book, *The Moral Economy of the Peasantry,* the peasants seemed to be restrained from revolt only by repression and memories of repression. When the cost of revolt was too high, the potential revolted created an oppositional culture of folk songs and poetry, religious millinerianism, and communitarian self-help associations. Scott did not see these efforts as an admission of defeat but rather as "an alternative moral universe in embryo."[76] In

Weapons of the Weak, he went beyond this position of a dissident subculture held at bay by repression to describe the operative legitimating ideologies of the superordinate strata as containing *within* them the basis for oppositional activity. "Everyday resistance"—small acts of noncompliance—was a negotiating strategy and, he strongly implied, was the best means to the best deal a subordinate group could get. Here, slavery does very little to the slaves.[77] There is a strong fatalistic element in this script.

Thus, the analysis of inequality as presented by this nongroup has to some degree—and probably contrary to Scott's intention—come full circle. The strongest claim that emerged was that the process by which subordinate groups forge areas of autonomy was one of negotiation—so much of obligation for us, so much for our masters. Injustice as perceived from below occurred at times when those above did not keep their part of this bargain. Moore especially felt that this left the lower classes with severely limited weapons with which to fight or even to comprehend their situation, leading to a state of perpetual acceptance of "exploitative reciprocity." Scott found those weapons to be quite sharp and effective and not easily taken away by the powerful. That they have not been wielded in a final conflagration is understandable given the remote likelihood that any worthwhile alternative could be created. But they were and are sufficient to achieve "minor humanities." The potential revolted have not overturned the stones, nor are they likely to do so. But they have moved them around to locations where they are less prominent obstacles and perhaps part of the landscape.

American Political Science

So far the list of contributors to theories of hierarchy, inequality, and its effects has been comprised of sociologists, philosophers, and historians. There is another contributing stream to these inquiries which comes directly from the field of political science.[78] The development of the question may in this case be even more informative than the substance of the contributions. Political science is intrinsically the study of power exercised at the level of government. The study of the *powerless* fits rather disjointedly into the field. This can be attributed in part to a simple division of academic labor. The study of subjects (particularly the study of their "subject-ness" as opposed to their indirect influence on policy) would seem to belong to anthropologists, sociologists, and—when the powerless leave visible footprints—historians.

But beyond simple division of labor, there has been a built-in bias in this field against the study of those who do not seem to directly influence events. In the fairly recent past, people who fell into that category were thought to be best studied as "potential interest groups" whose influence and therefore relevance to political science was that they might create "severe disturbances" if they were to organize.[79] Twice within a twelve-year period, presidents of the American Political Science Association felt it necessary to point out that the agenda of questions studied by political scientists was artificially narrow.[80] They both suggested that the problem lay in an inclination to see societal consensus as a virtue rather than as a matter for study or as a possible problem. When the downtrodden have arisen, it has been a matter for discussion. There has always been at least a peripheral place reserved for the study of protest movements, revolt, and revolution.[81] But when the downtrodden do not arise, they retreat from the pages of the journals—some trade-off presumably having made their conditions bearable or even satisfying.

But cutting somewhat against this grain is a small body of literature that centers on both the activity and the passivity of the nonpowerful:

> Here is evidence of an undiscovered planet whose mass disturbs the orbit of that which belongs to the powerful.[82]

The genesis of these investigations lies in the "power" debates of the 1960s. Not every aspect of those debates is relevant here and I will therefore not summarize them. Both (all) sides placed great importance on determining how much influence in the political process those from the lower classes had and therefore how much each person's life chances were subject to forces beyond his or her control.[83] As the debates proceeded, it became necessary for the various writers to specify what constituted activity around any issue and what avenues existed within which that activity could take place. This latter point took on special importance when the claim was made that some issues were simply removed from the public agenda.[84] Both sides had to give ground on this issue. Some questions are clearly resolved outside public decision-making bodies. On the other hand, many broad and highly salient issues of public policy *were* decided on various levels and those most affected sometimes seemed rather sanguine.

At that point the nature of the debates changed somewhat.[85] The previous arguments all revolved around situations of conflict and the relative input from different socioeconomic strata. Steven Lukes proposed a facet of power (the "third face") in which conflict was prevented by a dominant class which influenced and molded the preferences of the lower classes.[86] This was the "most effective and insidious" exercise of power. This formulation has turned the thrust of the "power question" writings from detailed community research to epistemological debate. The best example of this transition is the second edition of Nelson Polsby's *Community Power and Political Theory,* which started on the former task and ended on the latter.

Once raised, the spectre of manipulated preferences proved difficult to exorcise. A few absolutists denied that any such category could exist.[87] Others demanded reasonably that claims that preferences can be shaped decisively by others be made testable. That is the territory on which a number of political scientists have been gathering. Some are conscious participants in the power debates, others are implicitly so. This is the "non-barking dog" literature, some examples of which are Jennifer Hochschild, John Gaventa, and Kay Schlozman and Sidney Verba.[88] Each looked at a group on the lower rungs of the socioeconomic spectrum: Schlozman and Verba, the unemployed; Gaventa, coal miners, many of whom are unemployed or incapacitated; Hochschild, low-income whites.[89] Each gave arguments as to why one should expect visible signs of disaffection—usually variants of the commonsense argument offered in the first paragraphs of this chapter. Then, using a variety of interview techniques and historical research, each arrived at a set of answers as to why more political activity was not forthcoming. Schlozman and Verba framed the question as dramatically as possible: they suggested that the unemployed could profitably engage in low-cost activity, around needs that they themselves expressed and which had the possibility of being effective,[90] yet for the most part, they have not done so.

Gaventa went somewhat beyond the claim that a subordinate class facing power may acquiesce even to its own apparent disadvantage. In several places, he suggested that it was the exercise of power, not the absence of a clear understanding of it, that created compliance. The lower classes were vulnerable to various forms or pressure—some close to subtle blackmail.[91] Lindblom expanded on the "vulnerability" theme. The more a working class becomes an objective entity—that is, the greater its distance from its old roots—the more susceptible it is to various pressures from business and government. Thus, these writers stood Marx on his head. Lindblom completed this thought when he claimed counterintuitively that the United States is the *most* class-ridden of the polyarchies *because* its lower classes are less aware of their class standing.[92] The principal effect of class here is to limit or constrain the vision of those who suffer the greatest inequities.

The "power" argument has thus traversed a remarkable distance. The relative passivity that at one point was interpreted as lack of concern or contentment with the political process is now considered one product of a class-divided inegalitarian socioeconomic structure. The potential revolted are now a respectable subject for study, even if the studies seek mainly to explain why power often goes unchallenged.

Hierarchy and its close relative, inequality, are very nearly as unnoticeable as air and as much taken for granted. Writers such as Landtmann, Rustow, and Spence have called attention to the fact that inequality is a product of human decision.[93] But the very pervasiveness of inequality can lead to the tendency to treat it less as part of the political world than as part of the physical world.

We have danced quickly through four loosely defined "schools" in which the response called forth by the existence of inequality has become a subject for debate and analysis. In two of these "schools"—American political science and Marxism—it would be fair to say that this question emerged only after a period of time in which it was thought to be relatively unproblematical. In the other two areas, stability in the face of grossly unequal distribution of resources has been a central concern. Data sets have been offered and positions staked out, some sharply at odds with others.

My own investigation begins in the next chapter. What can be concluded so far is that the connection between inequality and perceived injustice on the one hand, and noncompliant or rebellious thinking and activity on the other is not straightforward. There are many stones left standing. I now move on to consider one very large one.

Notes

1. The last line of a speech given by Carl Oglesby at Antioch College in 1966. The speech was a reading of "The Revolted," a chapter of *Containment and Change*. The quoted lines do not appear in the book. I include the word "men" because that is how I remember the speech; I assume he would have rephrased that in later years.

2. Lawrence Stone, "Theories of Revolution."

3. Nelson Polsby's *Community Power and Political Theory: A Further Look at Problems of Evidence and Inference* is the best example, and one I will use throughout.

4. As for instance in Polsby's argument that the grievances leading to the black riots in the 1960s must not have been strongly felt in the 1950s. Fogel and Engerman make essentially the same argument the basis of their controversial *Time on the Cross*. Both are discussed further in the body of this book.

5. W. G. Runciman, *Relative Deprivation and Social Justice*, p. 3.

6. *Politics*, particularly chapter 5.

7. "For the aim of the people is more honest than that of the nobility, the latter desiring to oppress, and the former merely to avoid oppression" (*The Prince*, p. 36).

8. Ibid., p. 49. I do not think "good laws" are unimportant to Machiavelli, even in *The Prince*. His statements about laws and arms do not suggest that they are one and the same, but that the latter are prior to and necessary for the former.

9. Karl Marx, *Poverty of Philosophy*, in *The Marx-Engels Reader*, R. C. Tucker, ed., p. 218.

10. Robert Dahl, *Dilemmas of Pluralist Democracy*, p. 155; Barrington Moore, *Injustice: The Social Bases of Obedience and Revolt*, p. 474. Neither author suggests that Marx himself said this, but that it is immediately deducible from his vision of the unfolding of working-class consciousness.

11. See, for example, Bob Avakian, *For a Harvest of Dragons*, pp. 41–44.

12. *Economic and Philosophic Manuscripts*, in Tucker, p. 73.

13. Marx, *Capital*, vol. I, p. 154.

14. Ibid., p. 218.

15. Ibid., p. 260.

16. Ibid., vol. III, p. 88.

17. Some readings of Marx would not include altruism in this description. The interests of the working class at the point it is ready to assume power are: first, shared; second, equal to the interests of all the nonexploiting classes. Therefore, in fighting strictly for its own interests, it takes on the interests of all, with no altruism involved. But any common

usage of the term "altruism" would include acts involved in the above process. See Dahl, *Dilemmas*, pp. 157–58. Anyway, we do not have to speculate. Marx many times called on workers to make short-term sacrifices, such as when he argued that British workers should support the North in the U.S. Civil War, despite British economic ties to the South.

18. Michael Burawoy, *Politics of Production*, p. 86.

19. Kenneth Roberts, F. G. Cook, S. C. Clark, and Elizabeth Semeonoff, *The Fragmentary Class Structure*, p. 87.

20. Victoria Bonnell, *Roots of Rebellion;* Steven A. Smith, *Red Petrograd: Revolution in the Factories 1917–18;* Carmen Sirianni, *Workers Control and Socialist Democracy: The Soviet Experience.* On Gramsci's "revolution against Capital" (*Selections from Prison Notebooks*, pp. 34–37) formulation, see Teodor Shanin, *Late Marx and the Russian Road*, for an argument that late in his life, Marx expected Russia to be the country in which a successful revolution was most likely.

21. With apologies to Jessica Mitford.

22. This insightful phrase was created by Teodor Shanin, "Class, State and Revolution: Substitutes and Realities."

23. Andre Gorz, *Farewell to the Working Class: An Essay on Post-industrial Socialism.* He gives Marx one device for linking the socialist future to the actual working class—the "polytechnical worker" which Marx introduced in the *Grundrisse.* Marx mentioned the possibility that capitalist development would in the future force at least some of the working class to reverse the path from multiskilled to detail work. Why Gorz thinks that this aside is the main argument Marx advances about the revolutionary potential of the actually existing working class is unclear.

24. I do not mean to be glib here. Any great social or ethical philosopher such as Hegel can be read to help human beings better understand their condition even if the philosophical project is flawed. What makes the Hegel-in-Marx problem particularly difficult in discussing agency is sweeping and essentially airtight claims are being made about real people and actual historical processes.

25. Eric Hobsbawm, *Pre-Capitalist Economic Formations.*

26. Richard Hyman, "Andre Gorz and His Disappearing Proletariat," p. 283.

27. Karl Marx, *The German Ideology*, in *The Marx-Engels Reader*, p. 193.

28. "The native cures himself of colonial neuroses by thrusting out the settler through force of arms. When his rage boils over, he rediscovers his lost innocence and he comes to know himself in that he himself creates himself" (p. 18). "[T]o shoot down a European is to kill two birds with one stone, to destroy an oppressor and the man he oppresses at the same time. . . " (p. 18). "We were men at his expense, he makes himself man at ours: a different man; of higher quality" (p. 20). Jean-Paul Sartre, preface to Frantz Fanon, *Wretched of the Earth.* You sorta had to have been there.

29. Considering the importance of this argument and the extent to which it has been discussed by activists and academics, it is worth noting that Marx did not spell it out at great length. I was able to find three important instances of Marx's handling the idea: *The Poverty of Philosophy, Selected Writings*, p. 214; *Capital*, vol. I, p. 487; and the *Communist Manifesto*, in *The Marx-Engels Reader*, p. 480.

30. Craig Calhoun, *The Question of Class Struggle: Social Foundations of Popular Radicalism during the Industrial Revolution;* and Said Arjomand, "Iran's Islamic Revolution in Comparative Perspective."

31. Bonnell argued in favor of the urbanized workers in *Roots of Rebellion*; Leopold Haimson ("The Problem of Social Stability in Urban Russia, 1905–1917") and Smith (in *Red Petrograd*) argued in favor of the artisans.

32. Burawoy (*Politics*). In the chapter "Karl Marx and the Satanic Mills," he argues that Marx wrongly took the "market despotism" form of factory organization to be

typical and is quite emphatic in describing these "factory regime" differences as *sufficient* to explain the different outcomes of the English and Russian working-class movements.

33. See, for instance, Nicholas Abercrombie, Steven Hill, and Bryan Turner, *The Dominant Ideology Thesis,* and Frank Parkin, *Marxism and Class Theory: A Bourgeois Critique.*

34. Steven Hill, *Competition and Control at Work,* p. vii.

35. David Lockwood, "Sources of Variation in Working Class Images of Society."

36. In Martin Bulmer, *Working Class Images of Society,* p. 98. These authors studied laid-off workers and found a series of questions based on Lockwood's categories worked consistently for over a third of these obviously nonprivileged workers.

37. Robert McKenzie and Allan Silver, *Angels in Marble: Working Class Conservatives in Urban England,* p. 164.

38. Robert Jessop, *Traditionalism, Conservatism and the British Political Culture.*

39. Newby, "The Deferential Dialectic."

40. At least in his Lockwood-described habitat of small towns and farms (Roberts et al., *Fragmentary Class Structure,* pp. 4, 5).

41. J. H. Goldthorpe and David Lockwood, *The Affluent Worker: Industrial Attitudes and Behaviour,* p. 49.

42. Alisdair Clayre, *Work and Play: Ideas and Experience of Work and Leisure.* Clayre's evidence is sketchy and somewhat weird, consisting of the examination of folk songs and popular poems, but it does have the weight of common sense on its side. Hard work is hard and not always pleasurable. "Pastoral poetry seems to have been invented in the cities" (p. 91).

43. John Westergaard and Henrietta Resler, *Class in a Capitalist Society,* p. 49.

44. Robin Blackburn, "The Unequal Society," pp. 48–51.

45. I am even leaving aside the obvious point that Lockwood and *The Affluent Worker* authors all include a traditional proletarian category.

46. This runs counter to the image of *The Affluent Worker,* which is thought of as an answer to Marx. In fact, it is more clearly directed toward Marcuse and other "incorporationists."

47. Goldthorpe and Lockwood, *The Affluent Worker: Industrial Attitudes and Behaviour,* p. 163.

48. James Davies, "Toward a Theory of Revolution"; Ted Gurr, *Why Men Rebel.*

49. Runciman, *Relative Deprivation,* especially pp. 195–96. Duncan Gallie *(Social Inequality and Class Radicalism in France and Britain)* conducted a study to see if those findings were still valid in the early 1980s and found that they generally were.

50. Richard Hyman and Ian Brough, *Social Values and Industrial Relations: A Study of Fairness and Equality,* pp. 47–51.

51. Ibid., p. 62.

52. Michael Mann, "The Social Cohesion of Liberal Democracy." Mann himself does not pay much attention to this category.

53. Abercrombie et al., *Dominant Ideology,* p. 159.

54. H. F. Moorehouse and C. Chamberlain, "Lower Class Attitudes to Property," p. 22.

55. Hill, *Competition and Control,* particularly pp. 222–30.

56. Robert Blauner *(Alienation and Freedom)* found a similar process among American workers. He called it "dissatisfaction as dignity"(p. 21).

57. Richard Hoggart, *The Uses of Literacy.*

58. Paul Willis, *Learning to Labour.*

59. Ibid., p. 103. MacLeod *(Ain't No Makin' It)* has conducted a similar ethnographic study of the creation of "leveled aspirations" among working-class youth in this country.

60. Frank Parkin, *Class Inequality and Political Order*, pp. 95–101.

61. By radicalization, he seems to mean a concerted movement toward redistribution of resources.

62. Gallie, *Social Inequality*.

63. Michael Mann, *Consciousness and Action in the Western Working Class*. This is especially so since the two countries he mentions as examples of those traditions are France and Italy.

64. Jessop, *Traditionalism*, p. 56.

65. It is not the whole of each writer's work that is most relevant. I am specifically dealing here with Alvin Gouldner's *Wildcat Strike: A Study in Worker-Management Relationships, Patterns of Industrial Bureaucracy*, and "The Norm of Reciprocity: A Preliminary Statement"; Barrington Moore's *Injustice: The Social Bases of Obedience and Revolt* and *Reflections on the Causes of Human Misery and on Certain Proposals to Eliminate Them;* Eugene Genovese's *Roll, Jordan, Roll;* and James Scott's *The Moral Economy of the Peasantry* and *Weapons of the Weak: Everyday Forms of Peasant Resistance.*

66. Moore is in some ways an exception here. His monumental study *Injustice* is directly comparative. His specific case of the German working class is only one of many subordinate groups that appear. One of the few that does not is women, a testament, perhaps, to the fact that questions come or are brought to the fore at different times and that even this most sympathetic of observers has no better luck than the Owl of Minerva.

67. I broach this term cautiously, even though it seems highly appropriate for my purposes. *The Rational Peasant*, a book-length polemic by Samuel Popkin on the moral economy concept as applied to the peasantry, forever linked it to the claim that the subsistence ethic forms the substantial basis for all obligations. The two claims are separable, as they must be for this study, since I will be looking at a group for whom subsistence is clearly not the central issue. Popkin's approach, once the attack on risk aversion and subsistence is ferreted out, seems broadly similar to the use of "moral economy" by E. P. Thompson in "The Moral Economy of the English Crowd in the Eighteenth Century." However, because of the meanings attached to the term, I will only use it when the author involved has done so.

68. This draws from C. B. MacPherson's *The Political Theory of Possessive Individualism*, particularly his description of the existence of well-developed property and market relations in Locke's state of nature.

69. Locke took care to defend his "right-to-revolution" formulation against the charge that it was anarchic by pointing to the willingness of people to tolerate all but the most sustained forms of injustice: "[T]ill the mischief be grown general, and the ill designs of the Rulers become visible, or their attempts sensible to the greater part, the People, who are more disposed to suffer than right themselves by Resistance, are not apt to stir. The examples of particular Injustice or oppression of here and there an unfortunate Man moves them not." (John Locke, *Two Treatises of Government*, p. 466; see also similar comments on p. 463.)

70. Gouldner, *Wildcat Strike*, p. 78.

71. Particularly in *Wildcat Strike*, there is a noticeable disjuncture between the excellent thick description of the work relationships and the strike, and the thin "group theory" that formed the theoretical scaffolding.

72. Gouldner, "The Norm of Reciprocity," p. 175.

73. Stanley Elkins, *Slavery: A Problem in American Institutional and Intellectual Life.* Elkins in some ways launched this recent spate of studies of "comparative inequality" with his controversial use of the concentration camps as a way to understand slavery.

74. His explanation is worth hearing out: "A people at bay or in a prolonged period of defeat in which the initiative belongs to the enemy can transform fatalism into a tremen-

dous moral power. During those times fatalism becomes a way of final victory. It negates the idea of submission at the precise moment and in the precise ways that it seems to surrender to it" (Eugene Genovese, *Roll, Jordon, Roll*, p. 648).

75. This is more pronounced in *Weapons of the Weak* than in *Moral Economy*. In the latter, Scott did not seem to find a great deal to criticize in precapitalist patron-client relations i. untryside.

76. Scott, *Moral Economy*, p. 240.

77. A frequent criticism of Scott's description of "everyday resistance" is that it forecasts a perpetual cycle of damage limitation (Christine White, "Everyday Resistance, Socialist Revolution and Rural Development: The Vietnamese Case," p. 50). White's critique of Scott on this point is interesting, but her description of the case of Vietnam as an example of a country where the peasant "is an active citizen, not a protesting victim" (p. 50) is not very convincing.

78. These are ideal-typical types, of course. James Scott made an appearance in the previous section as a comparative anthropologist, whereas in the occupational structure he is a political scientist; in this section British sociologist Steven Lukes appears as an American political scientist.

79. David Truman, *The Governmental Process: Political Interests and Public Opinion*, p. 511.

80. Easton, "The New Revolution in Political Science"; and Lindblom, "The Market as Prison."

81. The latter more than the two former. Nothing breeds study like success.

82. Elizabeth Janeway, *Powers of the Weak*, p. 6. One objection sure to arise is that if there are perturbations in the orbit of the powerful, this would fall within the domain of normal political science study. My point—and that of the speeches I noted—is that activities of the powerless were treated as secondary matters (Easton) and that nonactivity was ruled out of bounds by definition (Lindblom).

83. The exception to this generalization is that in the early unfolding of this debate, the pluralists sharply separated the economic sphere (see Dahl, *Who Governs?*, p. 294) from the political sphere, a practice that was representative of most mainstream political science at the time. Dahl (various) no longer holds this position.

84. Most famously, Peter Bachrach and Morton Baratz, "The Two Faces of Power."

85. I do not mean to impute cynical motives to the opponents of the early pluralists, portraying them as constantly shifting arguments until they found one that looked good. There was a broadening understanding on all sides and in fact it became hard to distinguish the teams, let alone determine the score.

86. Steven Lukes, *Power: A Radical View*.

87. Robert Nozick, *Anarchy, State and Utopia*, and his predecessor Vilfredo Pareto. In chapter 7, I add others to a modified version of this category.

88. Jennifer Hochschild, *What's Fair?*; John Gaventa, *Power and Powerlessness: Quiescence and Rebellion in an Appalachian Valley;* Kay Schlozman and Sidney Verba, *Injury to Insult: Unemployment, Class and Political Response*. Hochschild also created the name for this category. She asks readers to consider the following salvo from Arthur Conan Doyle on the power debates (*What's Fair?*, p. 1):

"Is there any point to which you would draw my attention?
To the curious incident of the dog in the night-time.
The dog did nothing in the night-time.
That was the curious incident," remarked Sherlock Holmes.

89. Hochschild's interviews included a group of relatively wealthy whites. The comparison between groups is not relevant to my purposes.

90. Schlozman and Verba, *Injury to Insult*, p. 346.

91. Gaventa, *Power and Powerlessness*, pp. 143–45. While "vulnerability" is not his central point, it is one of mine.

92. Charles Lindblom, *Politics and Markets: The World's Political-Economic Systems,* p. 229.

93. Gunnar Landtman, *The Origin of Inequality of Social Classes;* Alexander Rustow, *Freedom and Domination: A Historical Critique of Civilization;* Larry Spence, *The Politics of Social Knowledge.*

2

"Not a Debating Society"

Through the mansions of fear, through the mansions of pain
I see my daddy walking through them factory gates in the rain
Factory takes his hearing, factory gives him life,
It's the working, it's the working, just the working life.

—Bruce Springsteen[1]

I intend to study the problems raised in the first chapter through interviews conducted with hourly factory employees. There are several reasons for making this choice.

The lines of power and authority in a factory are for the most part clear and unmistakable. Some give orders, others follow them. The structure is hierarchical, the decision-making process authoritarian. Further, the inequalities are palpably to the advantage of those in the higher echelons of the hierarchy. Neither juridically nor in custom do many of the formal rights of larger society apply. It is not easy to comprehend from the outside, not even with the help of sociological profiles, the extent to which the working lives of factory employees are lives of subordination. In the early 1970s a great deal of time was spent in academics and popularly on the "blue-collar blues." One worker at the Lordstown, Ohio, General Motors Assembly Division—the supposed standard-bearer of youthful working-class revolt against dehumanizing work—told a Senate investigation committee:

> Every time I passed through these plant gates to go to work, I left America and my rights as a free man. I spent nine hours in there, in prison, and then came out into my country again.[2]

Much of the ink spilled in the power debates has gone toward reaching a mutually agreed upon definition of when an act of power has occurred. Looking at the power relationships in a factory provides a way to make an end run around that part of the debates. It is the *obviousness* of the hierarchical structures that makes interviewing factory workers attractive as a way to gather information on reactions to powerlessness. "A class society is a society of scarce resources unfairly distributed because some have arbitrary power."[3]

There have been unending arguments over whether the United States belongs in this category; there cannot be any over whether this provides an accurate description of factory life.

The subordination of hourly employees during their time at work is not just a custom, it is enforced and reinforced by law. This is another obvious statement, but a matter to which attention must be drawn from time to time. While a great deal has been written about the separation of ownership and control, it has less often been said that the imperatives facing *any* decision-making individual or group have not permitted much change in internal hierarchical organization.[4] It is not necessary to argue strictly from a profit-maximization perspective to see that this is true, although such an orientation would be sufficient to make it so. Any of a variety of goals that a company could set as a temporary bottom line would not likely have an elective affinity to democratizing the chain of command.[5]

Companies do have certain legal obligations vis-à-vis their employees and more defined ones in relation to unions. But among those obligations does not lie the need to organize its affairs at all democratically or to obtain advice from its employees on plant (let alone company) decisions. Virtually every union contract begins with a "management's rights" clause. In the plant I have studied, this clause—a standard one—reads:

> The Union recognizes that, subject to the provisions of this Agreement, the Company has and will retain the sole right and responsibility to direct the operations of the Company and in this connection to determine the number and location of its plants, to direct the working force, to schedule the hours of work (which schedule may include a staggered work week), to establish the schedules of production, the methods, processes and means of manufacturing, and to select and hire new employees including a right to make rules and regulations for purposes of discipline and safety. It shall also have the right and responsibility to suspend or discharge any employee fired for cause and to transfer or lay off because of lack of work, except as provided herein.[6]

The more important the decision, the more legal standing the company has to make it unilaterally. In the most important case of all—whether or not a plant will close—its power is virtually unlimited. When a steel plant in Youngstown, Ohio, closed, a large group of employees fought the shutdown in a number of ways ranging from picketing and occupying corporate headquarters to negotiating to buy the plant. They filed suit against the company, charging that shutdowns were a "condition of employment" and therefore a subject for negotiation. Categories of labor-management relations are divided by legislation and judicial interpretation into "mandatory" and "permissive" subjects for negotiation.

"Mandatory" subjects (wages, hours, working conditions) must be dealt with in collective bargaining. "Permissive" subjects, including areas such as size of the work force and investment decisions, may be negotiated if the parties agree, but may not be made the subject of mandatory negotiations. It is an unfair labor practice for a union to insist that a company negotiate on a "permissible" subject. These are commonplace terms to anyone concerned with labor relations, but to someone looking in from the outside, the scope of unilateral management authority they real may have shock value. The importance of maintaining the division between mandatory and permissive became the crux of the Supreme Court ruling on the Youngstown case as indicated by Harry Blackmun:

> Congress had no expectation [when it passed the National Labor Relations Act] that elected union representatives would become an equal partner in the running of the business enterprise in which the union's members are involved.[7]

Because the unequal, hierarchical, and authoritarian relations and atmosphere which exist in most American factories are so pervasive and yet so hidden from outside and academic view, I cannot resist including the following description from a twenty-five-year steel worker:

> It's always risky to say "no" to a supervisor in a plant. Somehow, it's never completely forgotten. It is commonly suspected that all such refusals are written down and entered into the worker's personal file. In most modern institutions today, in the family, the school, the government, the church, the courts, there has developed a tolerance for dissent, but least so in the workplace. Neither Dr. Spock nor the ACLU has any standing in a steel mill. "Insubordination" is a term heard more frequently at Republic Steel than at the Fifth Army headquarters. The union tells its members to obey all orders given by their superiors, even if they violate the union contract—and a grievance may be filed later. "A steel mill is not a debating society," an arbitrator ruled in a landmark decision.[8]

If the clear status of factory employees as a subordinate group is one reason this study might be worthwhile, then the nonappearance of this fact as a public issue is another. Consider the following assessment of the egalitarian movements of the 1960s by Samuel Huntington:

> Politics focused on the evils of hierarchy and officialdom; arbitrary power, unresponsiveness, secrecy, deception. As a result, people no longer felt obligated to obey those whom they had previously considered superior to themselves in age, rank, status, expertise, character or talents. Within most organizations, discipline eased and differences in status became blurred. Each group claimed its right to participate equally—and perhaps more than equally—in the decisions that affected it. Authority based on hierarchy, exper-

tise and wealth all obviously ran counter to the democratic and egalitarian temper of the times and during the 1960's all three came under heavy attack.[9]

"Authority based on hierarchy and expertise" is probably exercised more forcefully in factories than in any institution other than the military. When "wealth" is added, no institution should have been higher on the 1960s hit list. Some writers[10] thought they saw such a movement under way with the Lordstown workers as the beginning of a "youth rebellion" spread to the factories. But this proved misleading.[11] For the most part, the antiauthoritarian movements of the 1960s did not become significant in the country's factories. There was some increased militancy, as in the summers of 1973 and 1974 in Detroit,[12] and in the wildcat strike movement in the coal fields. But there was no major or lasting movement calling into question industrial authority "based on hierarchy and expertise. This does not mean that there was no "everyday resistance" in factories in that period, of the kind that James Scott described among peasantry. There certainly was and there continues to be. But some groups at that time were righting wrongs with guns in hand, crowds of thousands, and programs of sweeping change, and it is worth noting that nothing of such scope occurred in factories.

Factory authoritarianism can be an invisible subject even to those who look directly at it. T. H. Marshall, to whom the gradual extension of rights into formerly foreclosed areas was the hallmark of human progress, could not find anything to criticize in the underlying undemocratic hierarchy of factory life. According to Marshall, "citizenship in the microcosm of the factory" meant that employees "must have confidence in the efficiency and distinterestedness of management," must not feel "his *incentive to serve* [emphasis added] is frustrated." In Marshall's version of industrial democracy, there should be consultation but "there is no transfer of authority."[13] In a book covering various historical aspects of work relations, Reinhard Bendix told readers three times before the table of contents that "subordination and discipline are indispensable in economic enterprises."[14] That is virtually the definition of a nonbarking issue—one that is settled before the table of contents.

A third reason for studying factory workers is idiosyncratic. During a lengthy period away from school, I did factory work for about seven years. At the time I was a political activist and had no intention of returning to academics and therefore kept no records or accounts. But the situations I entered into and discussions I had taught me a great deal about factory life, giving me a perspective that was different from, although not necessarily better than, the approaches of those who study it from the outside. I will make reference throughout to discussions and anecdotes from those years, purely for illustrative purposes. To emphasize the difference between this and other quoted material, I use italics, quoted and descriptive parts included, enclosed within the > < symbols. Some of the discussions I will refer to took place as any might, between two employees or between management and employee. I was not a "participant observer," since at the time

I held the jobs I did not intend to leave or to use the information. Thus there is not the bias unavoidably present in communication between informant and researcher. Nonetheless, I have labeled these "PO" for lack of something more explanatory. Some other discussions took place with the principals well aware that I was a political activist. These incidents are especially informative when that is kept in mind. I have labeled discussions of this kind "PA."

I worked in three factories between 1975 and 1981, all in or near Cincinnati. The Cincinnati work force is largely comprised of three ethnic groups: those of German descent, blacks, and people recently removed from eastern Kentucky or West Virginia. Diamond International (DI) is a paper and paper products manufacturing division with a work force (at that time) of about 500. I worked there for about three years. My work involved "grabbing" soap boxes and French fry containers and loading them on skids. I never held a union position, although I was active in union affairs. The job was about average in pay scale and benefits.

>Employee to me, repeating what a supervisor had told him: "This ain't no opportunity, this is just a job."< DI, PO

Cambridge Tile (CT), where I worked for nine months while on layoff from Diamond, made tiles and some gluing compounds. In the 1960s, it was a thriving business employing over 500 people. By the time I worked there, it had declined to about 125, with wages only slightly above minimum and hot, hard working conditions.

>"We can't worry about wages anymore. Anymore, we're lucky just to have a job."< CT, PO

In the course of writing this book, I learned that Cambridge Tile has closed for good.

Procter and Gamble (PG) of course makes consumer products. I worked there for almost three years in a variety of jobs, usually as a material handler. They employed about 2,200 hourly employees and paid wages slightly less than the highest hourly wages in the city. Their union was "independent," essentially a company union. During the time I was there, management was experimenting with participatory processes, involving (in my department, for example) a committee composed of employees to make suggestions about features of new equipment which the company had decided to install.

>Written on a plant bathroom wall: "P and G is the best job in the city. Just ask anybody who doesn't work here."< PG, PO

When I worked, I used to think about explaining to outsiders the experience of Friday at the time clock. At the end of Friday's shift, everyone stood anxiously in line with his or her time card, ready to punch out and run nearly at full speed to the parking lot. There is a certain amount of equality at the clock.[15] There were people with sharply different attitudes toward their jobs, but there was a general sense that we were all getting out of jail for the weekend. Part of the process I went through to get approval to do the research for this study involved speaking to a union meeting. When I mentioned that memory of Friday night and that part of what I wanted to do was to describe that sense, there were nods and murmurs of "amen."

✦ ✦ ✦

These are some of my reasons for making factory employees the basis of my investigation of the understanding of inequality and powerlessness. There is one reason I do *not* have for looking at factory workers which must be mentioned. That reason is the argument that the working class by virtue of its relation to the most modern means of production will come to occupy a special role in transforming society. This is the "sociological argument" of Marx mentioned in chapter 1, which, as described there, is linked with assertions of historical agency. Even when the mission of the working class is not put in its strongest form, it can still be imbued with a *telos* that works in and around empirical analysis.

Burawoy, who did extensive and intensive research on the effects of different forms of production regimes, maintains that "the industrial working class still represents the most fundamental point of critique" of the capitalist system, as well as, in his case, of state socialist systems.[16] This book is methodologically agnostic on such claims, although at relevant times I will take note of them. It does not matter greatly for my project whether the working class becomes the gravedigger of capitalism or is automated out of existence in the industrial West. The irreducible fact that both historically and currently this is a grouping of people who spend the majority or nearly the majority of their waking adult hours following orders forms the basis for this study. A few lines after the above quote, Burawoy has this to say:

> However, any failure of the working class to realize this principle [producers collectively controlling their product] in no way invalidates its suffering, nor does it free us of the responsibility of examining the forms of its oppression.[17]

This is unquestionably true, and remains so whether or not the previous claim has any validity.[18] I am exploring the political impact of powerlessness among factory workers, as others have for peasants, women, slaves, and concentration camp inmates. These last two paragraphs have been necessary because among all those groups, the study of the working class has been most haunted by ghosts. For better or worse, I intend to whistle past the graveyard.

The Research

I conducted interviews at a chemical factory in a small northeastern city which I will call Lockland. The plant will go by the name of Northeastern Chemical (NEC).[19] It employs approximately 380 hourly employees as well as another 100 laboratory workers. All the employees belong to the United Chemical Workers (UCW). NEC makes a variety of processed chemicals, primarily for other industries. Only a few consumer goods are manufactured. Partly for this reason, the plant does not swing sharply with the economic cycles. There have been several small layoffs over the last fifteen years, particularly since the 1974 recession when sales declined with the overall economic slump. On the other hand, automation has steadily reduced the size of the work force from a high of about 1,000 in the 1960s.

This plant is neither a hotbed of union militancy nor a sweatshop. The wages are the highest in town for hourly workers and among the highest in the region. There have been only two contract strikes since the plant was built following World War II, the last one in 1964. This is in contrast to the chemical plant David Halle studied in *America's Working Man*, where there were seven strikes in fifteen contract negotiations.[20] The interviews show that this does not indicate thoroughgoing satisfaction but rather that striking has not been seen as a way to resolve important grievances.[21] Since this is a chemical plant, a number of deep employee concerns involve health and safety, a subject about which the company has also had a great deal to say. About twenty years ago, two workers were killed in an industrial accident, described by one employee as "just a fiasco, a real bad fiasco." Memories of that accident are still strong. More recent incidents, within the last year or two, came across garbled and vague in the retelling. Not so this one. People's accounts were remarkably similar to each other, down to small details. Even employees who did not work at NEC at the time know a great deal about the accident. Later, I will introduce someone who came within seconds of dying that night.

The NEC work force has changed over the years, as has the whole American factory working population. At one time virtually all white male, the work force is now about 20 percent nonwhite and 15 percent female. When the plant began operations, a strong component of the work force was ex–coal miners from West Virginia. The first union that successfully organized was the Union of Mine, Mill and Smelter Workers. NEC gradually began to draw in more local employees and transplants from other areas of the Northeast, making the UMMSW an inappropriate vehicle to represent chemical workers. In 1955, it was decertified and the UCW was voted in as bargaining agent.[22]

The work is subdivided into smaller departments in different buildings, which have acquired different institutional characteristics. These separate buildings are also becoming separate accounting units and vary in product, customers, technology, and size of work force. Building A is the newest and has the smallest work force, but is experimenting with relatively new products for which NEC has only one major competitor and is seen by both company and employees as a possible source for expansion. Building D is at the opposite extreme. It is the oldest building, and has the least modern equipment and the most manual labor. I was told by company officials that it also has the highest rate of grievance activity. There have been rumors that the company would like to shut this building down. Buildings B and C are not seen by employees as being in jeopardy, but have incurred the largest losses in work force size as a result of automation. There are several smaller buildings; the other ones where I obtained interviews were maintenance and shipping.

The extent of the division of work areas poses certain potential problems for the research. If each building has its own work environment, there might not be a sufficient sense of "common-ness" among the employees to render information provided by the interviews useful. I do not think this has proved true. Even in auto plants, workers have different foremen, and work in different trades in different departments. The common, linking elements at NEC are these: same union, same contract, same company; frequent transferring between buildings; one industrial relations department; and—not to be underestimated—one set of factory gates which everyone walks through. I think the interviews will show that the commonalities outweigh the division into buildings. The workers do not see themselves primarily as "Building A employees" but as NEC employees. Above all, this plant, as with nearly all American plants, has essentially a pyramidal distribution of power and rewards in which all NEC hourly employees are located in the fat lower part. The Labor Relations Supervisor (LRS) told me twice in a half-hour interview that "We have a traditional hierarchical authority structure."

The following comments from an employee I will introduce later as "John" (who transferred from building D to the newer building A) illustrate the common features:

My impression when I went over there [building A] was that it was going to be more of a challenge and that was one of my reasons for going there. Gee, it's a brand new operation, it's a ground floor opportunity to learn something and get myself into something different than building D. And I thought it would be more appealing to me. I'm finding out now that it really isn't. It's still Northeast Chemical and they still have the same rules and standards.

Lockland is a small city (or big town) of about 25,000. The population is almost completely white and it has had successive immigration waves of Irish,

Italians, and eastern Europeans. In the recent past, its economy has been largely industry-based, but many of those jobs were in crafted consumer goods which are now mass produced elsewhere. The failure of some of these industries in the early 1970s resulted in temporary hard times, but the diversity of the town's industry and the growth of service jobs have brought about a resurgence. NEC occupies an important position in Lockland. It is a steady employer, the largest employer of factory workers and second largest overall. It has also been the town's leading taxpayer. That image of steadiness is important—many of the people I interviewed had parents or relatives living there. Lockland is neither a company town nor a town that has fallen to great depths when its main industry sank.

As with many chemical plants, NEC has been the target of some attacks by those concerned with the possibilities of pollution. Lockland is not a university or college town and the environmentalist groups have generally been grass-roots citizens' organizations motivated by understandable questions and suspicions. The literature of the largest group called for "peaceful coexistence with local industry." The plant has been cited for some violations of environmental standards, but has also been exonerated of specific charges of air pollution raised by the group. NEC has sent mailings to Lockland residents defending its emissions record and is not averse to using its position in the town as an argument in the public debates. In a press release announcing that its tests had shown no dangerous levels of air pollution, the first two sentences asked that people pay attention to its contributions:

> NEC's Lockland plant is a vital element of the local economy. Employing more than 600 people, it is the Town of Lockland's single largest employer, and, for eight straight years, the town's largest single taxpayer.[23]

The Lockland newspaper printed this part of the press release in its story. The conflict between NEC and the environmentalists was quite public and was the subject of a number of volunteered comments during the interviews.[24]

My choice of NEC as a subject was not based on any special features of the plant itself. Researchers in this field know the difficulties of gaining entry to an industrial setting—the ease with which any of the organizations can veto the project, the researcher's lack of a tangible product to offer, and, most important, the risk-averse mentality that pervades industrial relations. I failed to gain entry to two other plants for this study before I came to NEC. Those two factories were quite different from NEC, different from each other, and in a different part of the country. Further, there are individual employees who are cautious about an academic project such as this. With nothing tangible to gain and with at least the suspicion that there might be something to lose, employees are understandably not always predisposed to cooperate.[25]

Given these obstacles, the fact that I had some resources to draw on to help gain entry was the deciding factor in doing the study here. Nonetheless, the final decision is not purposeless opportunism. Since NEC is a large and fairly steady employer, the employees have some history on their jobs. As a chemical plant, it has the virtues of allowing me to make useful comparisons with David Halle's book, as well as being in the industry Robert Blauner foresaw in 1964 as offering an alternative to alienated work.[26]

NEC has a certain average-ness about it (albeit for a high-wage industry). One union official paraphrased what local NEC management has told him on more than one occasion in negotiations:

You have to realize we're not trailblazers. We don't believe in starting something and having other people follow. We let other people come up with their innovative ideas, watch what happens and see if we should follow suit.

Goldthorpe et al. prefaced *The Affluent Worker* study by explaining their failure to find an appropriate "critical case." The difficulty arose from the different sources of workplace hardship: low wages, danger, heavy work, fast work, seasonal work. These hardships were usually cross-cutting rather than reinforcing. The authors claimed that cognitive dissonance led employees to discuss the area of hardship that was *not* present in his or her job, in order not to appear foolish to the researcher.[27] Working at NEC involves one of these hardship areas, dangerous work. In other ways, it is just a factory, no more, no less. I asked the LRS what the company expected of its employees and his reply emphasized the ordinariness of the expectations and the lack of anything "unusual":

We expect that they should report to work on a daily basis, to be as productive as possible when they're here, to do what they're told and to work as hard as possible. But I don't think we expect them to do anything unusual. The average employee costs us about $30,000 a year. Based on what we require these employees to do and based on the skills we expect them to have, I think that's a very generous arrangement. We've had applicants tell us, "I hear NEC is a good place to work. They've got good pay and you don't have to work very hard." That's not something I would brag about, but that's the popular conception.[28]

I gained entry primarily through the union leadership. After I outlined my project, the officers were interested but explained that they could not allow their membership list to be used by outsiders. They offered to help me find volunteers. I hesitated at first, because I was concerned that if these officials played too active a role my study might be too closely identified with them and therefore the interviews would be biased.[29] When I decided to proceed, I stressed the importance of getting a representative cross-section of the work force. The company was advised of the study and had no objections. They gave me a tour of the facilities and the LRS sat with me for the interview quoted above.

The union officials gave me an initial list of names. I added more from a variety of sources—primarily from suggestions elicited from each person I interviewed. I conducted a total of thirty-three tape-recorded interviews, not including those with the LRS and the union president. Of the thirty-three, five were with union officials above the rank of stewards. I covered most of the same ground with them, but added a few questions related to their union experience. It had been my original intention to put these in a separate category, but the interviews convinced me that such a separation would have been artificial.

The interviews were open-ended. An approximate questionnaire appears as Appendix A, but the actual questions varied considerably from person to person. The interviews were conducted in a number of locations, including the plant itself (after working hours), people's homes, and restaurants. One was conducted at a bar with two people at the same time; this was the only time at which more than one person was present (a husband and wife were interviewed, but at separate times). Interviews varied from a half-hour to two hours, with the average being about an hour. I gave each person a short synopsis of my project, but I tried to tread lightly on the content so as not to cue the discussion. Although most of the questions were not asked verbatim as they appear in the appendices, there were three which I tried to ask each person in the same form. Those are the questions labeled "Expect," "Absolutely Wrong," and "One Thing." There was no forethought in duplicating these questions; they simply emerged during the early interviews as the basis for thoughtful reflection. I also conducted four re-interviews in which I took more biographical information and asked both some broader questions and some follow-up questions from the first interview. The re-interviewees will be introduced by name as relevant. Appendix B is the core of the re-interview, although it too varied widely.

I should say a word about the presentation of quoted material. Obviously, it is important to report what I heard accurately, but there are problems in doing so. The questions and answers were oral and people added a huge amount of "nonsubstantive" words—fillers, false starts, rambling before returning to a point. Substantive information is also lost in the transition from oral response—with the subtlety of voice inflections—to printed quotation. I have taken some liberty in reducing the former, while attempting to preserve the latter through italics or underlining or in rare cases exclamation points. Any emphases in quoted material represent my attempt to reproduce voice inflection. None are my own attempts to call attention to a point. This is crucial because there are times when I want to indicate not just what a speaker said, but what he or she emphasized. Even with this device, a great deal is lost in translation.

The people I interviewed were friendly, sometimes animated, and in a few cases willing to help in any way they could. I was, however, turned down personally by thirteen people, and while I do not have an accurate count of how many people turned down the union officials' requests, my sense is that it may have been about twice that.[30] This introduces the possibility of bias in the sample on several counts. If so many people turned down the request for an interview, could there not be a possible overrepresentation of articulate, perhaps better-educated employees? Might not those characteristics be correlated with some particular set of answers to my questions? Of the possible biasing elements, this one is the hardest to answer. Most people who turned down the interviews did so with a curt "not interested." Nonvoters can be interviewed; those who refuse to be interviewed cannot be. In every plant in which I worked, there were always some people who were opposed to the union leadership because it was too militant, and some because it was not militant enough. Would the *type* of person—exogenous characteristics—be biased toward the traditional power base of a union leadership: white, male, over thirty, perhaps skilled? Would the *range* of opinion I heard be narrower than the range in the plant?

My answers are "yes" and "but not fatally." These problems are so obvious a possibility that I was able to convince the union officials to be careful of them. I also did some compensatory searching when I looked for people outside the names I was given (twelve of the thirty-three I found on my own). As a result, the sample is fairly representative of the work force in external characteristics, with one exception to be noted. Eighteen of the thirty-three were production workers, eleven were in maintenance, four in security. Five were women. Production workers came predominantly from buildings A and D, although at least one each came from buildings B and C and shipping. Eleven people had five years or less, thirteen had between five and twenty-five, and nine had over twenty-five.

Late in my investigation, well after the interviews were completed, NEC contracted with an organization for a national study of its employees, which of course included Lockland NEC. The research team conducted workday interviews and reported a participation rate of 80 percent. I was given a copy of the results by an interviewee. Since I do not have official access to the document, I can neither cite it nor study it in depth, but I can make this important generalization: although the results were not available until I was virtually done writing, on every major contention I will make but one, the survey data agreed at least roughly with my estimations. That one area of disagreement was that these researchers found somewhat more support for NEC's health and safety programs than I will indicate in chapter 3.[31] This indicates that the care I took to try to find people from various subgroups helped create a sample that was not far out of line with what a truly randomized sample would have produced.[32]

The one irremediable problem is that there were only four nonwhite interviewees. This underrepresentation flattens out the responses. Observation, literature, and common sense combine to indicate that nonwhite workers are less convinced of the justice of economic institutions than their white counterparts, and therefore are less inclined toward compliance or acquiescent attitudes, by whatever yardstick they are measured. Schlozman and Verba, for example, found black workers a great deal more "class conscious" than whites and even slightly more "class conscious" than "race conscious."[33] Similar conclusions are drawn by Leggett,[34] but these should not be startling findings. There is no remedy proposed here, other than to keep this fact in mind.

The principal reason why the interview data are not fatally biased is their intended use. I convert the data to numbers very infrequently. The sample was not large enough nor the method of selection random enough to achieve much precision in the results. Information about the working class has come from a wide variety of research formats, in a spectrum ranging from the national surveys of the Michigan Survey Research Center, with job categories selected out, to the qualitative interviewing of Robert Lane and Jennifer Hochschild.[35] Each has value and the fact that such a diversity of approaches exists can only enrich the overall understanding of working-class attitudes. None would be sufficient by itself.[36] My study falls closer to the "qualitative" end of the spectrum. The respondents brought up a number of points they wanted to discuss and I was able to vary the questions somewhat to fit the person's experience (and degree of talkativeness). For example, my questions do not immediately call for normative evaluations. I was interested to see whether these would be volunteered; if so, it might provide some evidence to support the notion of an ordering "moral economy." When terms such as "fair" or "right" did come up, I followed by asking people what the term encompassed. In the following pages, I look at the internal consistency of answers, the awareness of trade-offs of different values, the degree of consciousness of hierarchy and inequalities, the extent of the translation of that awareness into perceptions of injustice, and impairment of vision that could be rooted in the structure of the employment relation. On such matters, even with a slightly unrepresentative sample, open-ended questions can yield useful results.

Because I wanted to look at people's own understanding of causal relations, a few of my questions, particularly in the re-interviews, may look antagonistic. It is not a comfortable matter for an interviewer to demand that a person explain how he or she can possibly hold contradictory positions A and B at the same time. But the nature of the problems being discussed makes that necessary, and I wish I had been even more forceful at times in trying to get interviewees' explanations for seeming inconsistencies.

Generalizing from a case to a population (here, a population of factory workers) is always a risky business. I have used several resources to help check my conclusions. My own experience is a "deep background" guide. That is, it has alerted me to the presence (or absence) of outlier opinions, and to the existence of wide areas of factory life not usually discussed outside work. I have used and referred to several different types of case studies or local interview sets when appropriate. Broader public opinion data that include but are not limited to blue-collar workers can be used as a broadbrush basis for comparison. Given that this research is not intended as a sociological profile of the American working class, but rather as a case study of the question of subordination and compliance, I continue to draw comparisons with studies of the British working class and of other subordinate groups.

All this research is itself subject to the limitations pointed out by Scott in his discussions of everyday resistance among peasants:

> History and social science, written by an intelligentsia using written records which are also created largely by literate officials, is simply not well equipped to uncover the silent and anonymous forms of class struggle which typify the peasantry.[37]

"Silent and anonymous" forms of struggle are not just typical of the peasantry. They may be even more silent, for the purpose of remaining anonymous, in a factory setting where dossiers are kept and there is a much higher degree of integration.[38] Nor does open-ended interviewing provide a magical alternative to official records or surveys, not even when the interviewer has worked in a factory. I worked in low-, middle-, and high-wage plants and in each case, there were a host of "silent and anonymous" acts, ranging from "throwing a wrench in the line"—

> *"Every once in a while, someone will toss a screwdriver in the belt to give everybody a rest. You can't do it too often because they [the company] usually knows what's going on."*< PG, PO

—to calling in sick, faking injuries, taking advantage of technicalities in order to stall, and simple goofing off.[39] At times even small-scale collective action is just as hard to see and as hard to find out about.

>*My line leader, during a changeover ("make-ready") after a particularly hard run, called the crew together and told us to "Jump in there with both feet and f— around."* < DI, PA

>*Another older worker in the same crew told me proudly about the company's attempt to take one person off a five man production unit. "They couldn't get nothing done. He [the supervisor] would come out and talk to us and while he was talking—bloop!—here*

comes the tail [the end of a roll, something which costs the com-
pany hundreds of dollars of down time]." The person who told me
this may have been the least militant person I met while I was there.
< DI, PA

This is not the kind of information that is passed on freely to someone with a tape recorder. I did succeed in soliciting some of these stories from people in the re-interviews by turning off the tape recorder, but even then I noticed that their stories usually involved other people, not themselves. Perhaps the best way to uncover some of this activity would have been to get a job at NEC myself; unfortunately my request to do so was turned down by management. There is no simple solution to the problem, only a grim satisfaction that everyone else faces the same problem.[40]

Even with all these limitations, the interviews provide an important source of information for evaluating my central questions. NEC employees expressed a wide range of reactions to their working life—trust and skepticism, fear and complacency, resignation and quiet hostility. One man followed me out of his house and halfway down the driveway, angrily shouting about NEC's safety practices; another told me three times after I had already turned the tape recorder off what a great place NEC was to work. Sometimes these conflicting thoughts are expressed by the same person in the same sentence. This was not at all unexpected and simply points out that the ''answers'' to my questions do not provide one smooth picture of an undifferentiated class. Charles Sabel looked at the working class movement in some countries and situations where it was very militant and some where it was not, and warned the readers in advance:

> No single theory of blue-collar behavior accounts for this variety of opposi-
> tion; and no theory that predicts the militancy of any one of these groups
> accounts for its acquiescence in authority as well as its revolts against that
> authority.[41]

Behind all the interview material loom the massive facts of hierarchy and grossly unequal rewards. The degree to which the employees I talked with expressed a wide variety of views toward those facts is the clearest indication that these thirty-three people do represent a reasonably fair sample of opinions and are therefore worth listening to and discussing.

Notes

1. "Factory," copyright 1978 by Bruce Springsteen, reprinted by permission.
2. Quoted in David Ewing, *Freedom Inside the Organization*, p. 19. Some in the power debates would dispute the contention that he was a "free man" outside the plant. Gerald Hunnius, in "On the Nature of Capitalist-initiated Innovations in the Workplace,"

attacks this formulation explicitly (p. 287). The point here is that he felt strongly he was not free while at work.

3. Richard Sennett and Jonathan Cobb, *The Hidden Injuries of Class*, p. 159

4. Actually, it has been said, twice at least—Edward Herman, *Corporate Control, Corporate Power*, and Nina Glick Schiller, "Management by Participation: The Division of Labor, Ideology and Contradiction." Also, I am aware that the argument about separation of ownership from control usually is made to suggest the *possibility* of different forms of internal organization, not the likelihood of it.

5. Eric Batstone, in "Systems of Domination, Accommodation, and Industrial Democracy," p. 259. Batstone says that any normal list of immediate management goals— elimination of scrap, of breakdowns, of labor disputes, of accident reduction—makes participation look counterproductive to those whose future depends on meeting the goals.

6. Contract of NEC and the CWU.

7. Staughton Lynd, *The Fight against Shutdowns*, p. 223.

8. Charles Spencer, *Blue Collar*, p. 83.

9. Samuel Huntington, *American Politics: The Promise of Disharmony*, p. 179.

10. Stanley Aronowitz, *False Promises: The Shaping of the American Working Class;* Barbara Garson, *All the Livelong Day*.

11. Although the youthfulness of the work force and the number of workers who had served in Vietnam was an important fact in the Lordstown strike, the target of the wildcats was the speedup program of the newly formed General Motors Assembly Division (GMAD), which the workers called "Go MAD." At almost the same time as the Lordstown strike, General Motors workers at the Fisher Body plant in Norwood, Ohio, were staging the longest strike in GM history against the same program. At the heart of this strike were ex-Appalachians and blacks. Age was not an important factor.

12. The famous incident in 1973 in which two black Detroit autoworkers locked themselves in a power cage and shut the plant down to demand the firing of a racist foreman was just one of several militant rank-and-file protests in those two years.

13. T. H. Marshall, *Class, Citizenship and Social Development*, pp. 221–27.

14. Richard Bendix, *Work and Authority in Industry: Ideologies of Management in the Course of Industrialization*, p. ix.

15. To be specific, it is "segmental equality" as used by Douglas Rae (*Equalities*, p. 30). I never understood the value of describing hierarchical segmentation as a form of equality, but perhaps it has some purpose as applied to a situation like this one.

16. Michael Burawoy, *Politics of Production*, p. 2.

17. Ibid.

18. This will explain why I have been using vocabularies interchangeably which are not normally used that way. "Dominant-subordinate" and "capitalist class–working class" are pairs that, used to describe roughly the same sets of people, have taken on contrasting meanings derived from the Weberian and Marxist traditions. Fortunately, but not fortuitously, my purposes do not require any lengthy discussion of the possible unity or disunity of these two schools. When employees are at work, the two traditions overlap in describing their situation. See Frank Parkin, *Marxism and Class: A Bourgeois Critique*, pp. 52 and 69, where he argues in the Weberian tradition. The Weber-Marx debate is not moot; it simply is not the issue here.

19. As is standard practice, and by agreement with the company and union, I am using fictitious names for the company, union, town and individuals. In order to make this more than a formality, I have altered some facts that could be used to identify any of the above. Since at times the identifying potential and the relevance of factual material are highly correlated, there are conflicts. I have tried to make the altered facts fit the real facts as closely as possible, but if there was an error to be made, it has been on the side of

preventing disclosure of identities. One exception: I have been extremely circumspect in altering any quoted material from the interviews.

20. David Halle, *America's Working Man*, p. 158.

21. I am using the word "grievances" here in its everyday and social-science usage rather than in its technical meaning in industrial relations.

22. This material and some other information in this section did not come primarily from the formal interviews but from off-the-record conversations with retired members of the company and work force.

23. All this information is taken from documents in my possession. Because of their clear identifying nature, they cannot be cited.

24. The thrust of this paragraph comes from and should help demonstrate the concept of the "privileged position of business" described by Charles Lindblom in *Politics and Markets: The World's Political-Economic Systems*. Later I torture that concept somewhat in showing how business can be "privileged" in the way Lindblom meant in relation to its own employees.

25. There is another reason for people to be reluctant to participate, grounded in a well quoted line from Studs Terkel's *Working:* "The American working man isn't dumb. He's just tired, that's all" (p. xxxiv).

26. Halle, *America's Working Man;* Robert Blauner, *Alienation and Freedom,* chapters 6 and 7.

27. J. H. Goldthorpe and David Lockwood, *The Affluent Worker: Industrial Attitudes and Behaviour.* Actually it would be more accurate to say that it is difficult to find a case in which all the hardship areas are *absent,* which was the case the authors were looking for. It is not hard to find one in which they are all present. I worked in one.

28. Two points need to be made here: the $30,000 figure is hourly wages plus average overtime. The most an employee can make working forty hours is $25,000 in the highest grade. Second, the context makes clear that what the LRS meant when he said that he "would not be proud about" this particular reputation was that he was trying to change it—that is, the fact of easy work, not the reputation.

29. See, for example, David Berg, "Failure at Entry," p. 34, for the effects of the method of entry on the study.

30. It would be difficult to obtain that figure. The union president assigned members of the union's Plant Committee to solicit people. They in turn often assigned the requests to department stewards. I do know from discussions with stewards that a diligent effort was made to find volunteers.

31. One possible explanation is that in the copy of the results made available to employees (the one I obtained), results from white- and blue-collar workers were not disaggregated.

32. Since I cannot use the figures or cite the study, the best I can do is make it available with some conditions to anyone who wants to evaluate the accuracy of this claim.

33. Kay Scholzman and Sidney Verba, *Injury to Insult: Unemployment, Class and Political Response,* p. 176. The reason for the quotation marks is that I have been very carefully avoiding the term "class consciousness" so far. Scholzman and Verba give it an operational definition.

34. John Leggett, *Class, Race and Labor: Working Class Consciousness in Detroit.*

35. Robert Lane, *Political Ideology;* Jennifer Hochschild, *What's Fair?;* this is a spectrum of surveys. There also is an assortment of on-the-spot or picaresque studies (Richard Hoggart, *The Use of Literacy,* is an example of the latter) which have their value.

36. Richard Hamilton and James Wright in *The State of the Masses* (particularly pp. 91–94) make a strong case for the superiority of survey data in workplace research. They

claim that "field studies" are susceptible to bias based on nonrandom selection of site, respondents, and material quoted, as well as being inaccessible for secondary analysis. "Field studies" actually come in three forms: participant observation, ethnographic study, and qualitative interviewing. While nonrandomness is a problem, it is mainly a bar to generalizability. That is a risk worth running for the contributions these methods can make in presenting people's ideas in their idiosyncratic complexity. I would also argue against opponents of survey research if they were to make a case that only field work yields worthwhile results. Survey research permits more precise statements because it allows a better estimation of the size of various strands of opinion than other methods can. On the matter of secondary analysis, I, like most other people doing field studies, have kept my tapes.

37. James Scott, "Everyday Forms of Peasant Resistance," p. 9.

38. See Michael Adas on "avoidance protest," ("'From Avoidance to Confrontation: Peasant Protest in Precolonial and Colonial Southeast Asia," and "From Footdragging to Flight: The Evasive History of Peasant Avoidance Protest in South and Southeast Asia"). The latter article argues that the more integrated the system, the less possible avoidance protest.

39. These do not appear on the surface to be commendable activities, let alone "class struggle." They may not be. But within the context of the factory, they all fall within the definition of resistance offered by Scott in "Everyday Forms of Peasant Resistance": "Only those survival strategies which deny or mitigate claims from appropriating classes can be called resistance" (p. 9). The one constant claim on each factory worker is for his or her time.

40. Halle (*America's Working Man*, p. 76) points out the same problem, and he was given resources far in excess of mine. He spent two years on the research, was free to walk around the plant, was allowed to use company time for interviews, and was given company grievance and absentee records.

41. Charles Sabel, *Work and Politics*, p. 2.

3

Daily Life

[B]ehavioral science studies of workplaces tend to be tales of horror. When people who work there read the studies, they might respond with "Oh hell. It ain't that bad."
—Robert Schrank[1]

I have no complaints, other than—you know—everyday normal complaints.
—NEC employee

This chapter describes and begins to explain a paradox. Viewed from the outside, factory work seems hard, dirty, boring, and dangerous—in short, oppressive. NEC is no exception. Such objective standards as one can bring to bear seem to confirm the sense of the adjectives. Testimony from NEC employees is littered with negative comments about many areas of work. But the broadest, virtually unchallenged consensus around any particular description of NEC in the interviews was that NEC was "a good place to work." How can this be? What can we learn from it?

One common reaction of the academic researcher in his or her first confrontation with factory life is surprise that people can put up with jobs that seem to be so demanding and unfulfilling. The sense of shock is magnified by the fact that most employees stay on these jobs their whole working lives. Richard Balzer and Richard Pfeffer,[2] both of whom spent time in a factory, made special note of their own strong negative first reaction to the industrial environment. A female assembler asked Balzer whether he could do this kind of work permanently. When he answered no, the woman told him that everyone thinks that at first, but that everyone adjusts.[3] Pfeffer, who worked for almost a year, found himself enjoying the challenge for the first few days,

> but to do this [dump hoppers] for a lifetime, to know that one's life would be measured out in trash hoppers seemed inconceivable to me in those first few days on the job.[4]

These reactions—similar to some of my own as I entered factory life—are in

43

part culture shock, in part, indignation at what appear to be harsh conditions, and in largest part a discovery of the very broad range of human adaptability to demands. Culture shock is an almost inevitable by-product of an intellectual's immersion in the world of industrial work. I mention this not to rehash truisms about class bias but to point to the value of looking at observations not yet colored by adaptation. (I return at the end of this chapter to a brief consideration of the possible value of this "shock" for the hands-on factory study genre.)

Outside observers perceive and describe hardships in factory work because they are there, by any measure one can define. When the "blue-collar blues" were a hot item in the early 1970s, the U.S. Department of Health, Education, and Welfare (HEW) compiled a report that cited studies showing the huge array of job-related problems. The more repetitive, unskilled, and tedious a job, the greater the risk of heart disease, ulcers, and arthritis.[5] Blue-collar jobs were related to various types of mental-health maladies including "psychosomatic illnesses, low self-esteem, anxiety, worry, tension and impaired interpersonal relationships." The authors added that "failure to adjust" to a work pattern need not be the sole definition of mental-health problems: "A person who becomes an automaton in an automated factory may have adjusted perfectly, but he hardly enjoys good mental health."[6]

Another study of factory work established that difficulties caused by the work experience do not disappear with the Friday night race to the parking lot; work isolation and alienation act as an independent variable in constricting choice of leisure time activities. "The job has a long arm indeed."[7]

Job Tasks

Previous studies have suggested that any satisfaction related to hourly jobs came from factors extrinsic to the job itself. Eli Chinoy and Charles Walker made detailed case studies of assembly-line workers and found that satisfaction in production was defined negatively, as "avoidance of strain, discomfort and inconvenience."[8] The most compelling attribute of a job off the line was that it *was* off the line. This portrait coincided with the British "instrumentalist" (or "privatization") theory described in chapter 1. While an instrumentalist orientation does not inherently preclude an interest in the work tasks, it does contain a large streak of "putting up with it."

>*After I spent some time talking with a thirtyish employee (who had been at P and G about twelve years) about some of the conditions of work I thought were unfair: "Why do you care about that anyway? I just put in my eight and go home. Then I put my feet up and listen to Trumpy [a popular local sports talk show host]."< PG, PA*

NEC employees describe their work in ways not greatly different from the descriptions of autoworkers studied by Chinoy and Walker. There are dissimilarities, of course, that should be kept in mind when reading their comments. The work at NEC is not assembly in any respect and requires much less interaction among employees than does auto work, or even than the small assembly jobs I had.[9] Also, a great deal of the heavy manual work, called "bull-work" at NEC, has been eliminated. Heavy work is confined to some nonautomated areas of building D as well as to certain categories of mechanics. Some of these conditions led Robert Blauner to suggest in 1964 that technology of chemical production might offer a nonalienating alternative to the assembly line.[10] It has become commonplace to disprove Blauner. But perhaps more interesting than the continued existence of alienation is the fact that he did correctly point out some important differences in technology. The following general assessments of work cannot, then, be laid at the feet of a technology that by its physical existence turns people into robots.

Since the production and maintenance categories are divided by clear contractual boundaries, I will let them speak separately, followed by the observations of maintenance workers on production jobs.

Production Workers

Speaker A: The jobs are silly. I mean, most of the jobs you could train an ape to do. It's boring, people compete to see who can do least. I just go there for eight hours a day and try to forget it.

Speaker B: Let's face it, factory life stymies anybody with any kind of intellect, 'cause you're not allowed to use it, correct?

The first of these speakers also said that her own job was "ridiculously easy" and that NEC was "the country club of factories." The second has one of the more demanding and physical jobs in building D and took strong exception to the "country club" characterization when I asked him about it. Nevertheless, their view of the work itself was similar. "Boring" is not necessarily the worst of all epithets, but the use of that term in describing production jobs is so pervasive that it takes an act of will on the part of the listener to separate it from the term "working."

Q. How about the job itself?
Speaker C: It's all right. After a while it gets a little boring, monotonous. When you're low on seniority, the foreman will have you doing all these other things. That's what I was doing, running around.

> *Speaker D:* There really isn't a lot of satisfaction in the job. It's boring. You're always fighting the machines.
> *Q.* Could it be any different?
> *Speaker D:* No. I've only worked in one factory but I tend to think they're all basically the same.

This last point—that "they're all basically the same"—came up in several discussions, usually with an inflection that indicated that the comment was too obvious to be worth making. The fact that the respondents knew I had worked in a factory may have been a contributing factor, but the almost condescending tone of the several people who mentioned this suggested that they put this fact on a par with telling me that the sun rose in the morning. "They're all basically the same" was a distillation of the essence of the HEW findings—particulars vary, but working in a factory means doing factory work, nothing more. The following employee had transferred into the newer building A after many years in building B.

> *Q.* Some of the reason I'm interested in the differences you can feel in the two departments is that I wondered—the company starts this new product, it's more up-to-date technology—if they'd also try to create a different kind of working environment too at the same time?
> *A.* Well, I don't think you can really, I mean when you work in a factory, working in building A and building B, there's not really much they could do in a different working environment—you're working in a factory, you know?

> *>A story told by the person training me to shake out baked tiles about his friend George, fired before I arrived: "The foreman came back to warn us about the tiles breaking on the floor. He said he didn't know if it was horseplay or carelessness but it had to stop right away. As soon as he turned around, George hit him right square in the ass with a piece of tile. You got to keep something going, you know, or the job will get to you."< CT, PO*

Maintenance Workers

Some of the proponents of the "deskilling" argument—that all forms of work have become degraded with the separation of conception and execution—would not see much difference between production work and the skilled trades.[11] Craft work in a factory ("maintenance" at NEC) is certainly different from nineteenth-century craft work in which skill was put to use in the creation of the final consumer good. It is also different from production in many ways, including method of appointment (qualifications weighted more strongly than seniority), object of work (keeping the plant itself in order), pay (although this difference is not huge), and plant status (more time with management, varied work, sometimes night classes and, at NEC, state certification in some categories). Craft is always among the most desirable jobs in any factory and concomitantly carries with it a higher degree of satisfaction with work tasks.

Speaker A: I love to do things with my hands, accomplish things. I like to weld in tight spots. It makes the day go fast. They sent me to school, it was hard but I got it done. Now I get into different things everyday.

Speaker B: I've worked at NEC for thirty years. I didn't know I would be here thirty years. It satisfied some needs I had at the time I needed them. [The context makes it clear this does not simply refer to pay.] I have been able to express myself and have had upward mobility.

Speaker C: I started working these big giant units and I liked that. I liked it a lot. I was in complete control of the whole machine. I was a one-man army. You may take four or five machines that are built by the same company, the same blueprint, and ain't one of 'em gonna operate alike. Every one of them's got their own personality. They've all got their little idiosyncrasies.

These sentiments were by no means unanimous or unmixed. The last contract contained language that sharply restricted the number of moves the employees could make, locking them into a job after one transfer between buildings or trades. While this applied equally to maintenance and production workers, it was aimed primarily at restricting the movement of maintenance people. The fact that movement had to be limited contractually suggests that even these more flexible job tasks got old after a few years. One maintenance employee in his young thirties, who generally enjoyed what he was doing, felt that he did not *want* to become too attached to a job:

I don't know about the rest of the population, but I don't believe it's right to just veg out on a certain job and be content with it. I think you should always strive for more.

My point here is not to estimate the depth of satisfaction among maintenance people but simply to note that there were some in this category who found some opportunity for creativity in their work tasks. It would not be accurate to say of this group, as a pair of English sociologists said about workers in a plant they studied: "87% of the workers exercise less skill at work than they could if they drove to work."[12]

The most emphatic and unambiguous critique of daily job tasks was that made by maintenance workers of production work. Every maintenance worker I interviewed had started at NEC in a production job. The length of time they stayed in that capacity varied from six months to nine years. Some mentioned dislike of production work as the principal reason they had moved to maintenance. Some of the flavor of the differences between maintenance and production workers can be seen by the name for an additional contractual increment to maintenance—"inequity pay." This was a nickel raise in each contract above the percentage raise for the whole bargaining unit. (Percentage raises already favor those in higher classifications.) The "inequity" also appears in the evaluation of work. The words as they appear below seem critical enough; they cannot, however, convey the decisiveness with which people announced their position on this point.

[A thirty-year veteran, five in production]: I can tell you right now if I'd been in production I wouldn't be here talking to you. I would have left a long time ago. Boring. The jobs there are like peeling a carrot. There are five or six different ways to do it, but you're still peeling a carrot.

The worker quoted above ("Speaker C") who liked being a "one-man army," eleven years in the plant, five in production:

I had a clock number instead of a name. It was, you know, robotics. "You will come here at such and such time of the day, punch this card, work this machine, this job."

A highly trained, licensed welder, ten years in the plant, two in production:

I didn't enjoy coming to work at all. You didn't go home feeling like you've done nothing. Do this, do that—you don't work that hard, but after a while your brain turns into a vegetable.

A twenty-year employee, nine in production, responding to a question about why some people seemed to dislike production jobs:

> I think it's different [maintenance work], I really do. People in pro-duction—once you've done it for a number of years, what can be positive about it? It's not enjoyable no more, you just go in, do the thing and come out.

A machine maintenance man, eight years, two in production, volunteering a comparison between the two categories:

> I worked in building C as a material handler. Basically, the reason I didn't like it—now I'm doing a little bit more with my hands and I like that a little more. Just driving a fork truck, it's repetitious—just, pick up this box, bring it here, fill up this crate with so many pounds—it's just like being a janitor, you're doing absolutely nothing. I may get a little more dirtier now, but I like working with the wrenches, putting things together, you feel like you're *doing* a little something, it's more constructive.

Finally, a bitter and disillusioned eight-year maintenance worker, who spent two years in production (he also was not very enthusiastic about the maintenance work either):

> Q. Why did you move [to maintenance]?
> A. I was bored with it, bored with production. Couldn't handle the moving a couple of valves and waiting for the process to continue. Too much of watching the clock. Maintenance I figured would keep me busy. Time goes by faster.
> Q. Do you think most people who work in production get bored?
> A. I'd say. Some people are happy being bored, though.

The perspective that maintenance workers bring to bear on production jobs is a special and revealing one. Some writers on periods of popular turbulence or revolution emphasize lateral mobility, separation from ingrained routines, and physical surroundings, resulting in a broader basis for comparative evaluations of the fairness of social structures.[13] As mentioned in chapter 1, W. G. Runciman established that blue collar workers evaluate their life possibilities with reference to other blue-collar working groups.[14] The relatively slight upward movement from production to maintenance (slight in relation to the overall societal reward distribution) provided for these employees a comparative perspective from which many of the negative aspects of production work stood out clearly. The negative comments above are a small selection. Some of the comments include the notion that production workers were "doing nothing," not the same as "boring." (One maintenance man said that he wondered why people got paid for some of the jobs.) This could not mean simply that there was little work. The jobs these former production workers held covered the whole range of buildings and within-building classifications. Some of those jobs keep people quite busy. But from the vantage point of someone fixing a machine, watching dials and packing or moving material is "doing nothing." Maintenance employees by definition do not work directly on the company's marketed product, and the fact that when in the past they had, some thought of it as "doing nothing," suggests that the concept of workers being "alienated from the product of their labor" is more than poetry.

The testimony above is intended to show that NEC employees with the partial but not unambiguous exception of maintenance workers agree with the HEW report, Pfeffer, Balzer, and the others who do not find much inspiration in job tasks. These comments should not be confused with, or taken as the equivalent of, "job satisfaction." Job tasks are only one aspect of "everyday life" in the plant, and are therefore only one part of any individual's overall assessment of his or her job, which would include (at least) pay, relations with other employees, and an implied comparative analysis of other opportunities. The employee who said that when you are working in a factory, you are working in a factory was making a similar point to the one made by Charles Dickens, who wrote: "I went, some weeks ago to Manchester, and saw the *worst* cotton mill. And then I saw the *best*. There was no great difference between them."[15]

As opposed to these relatively unvarying "job tasks," there were a variety of hardship areas that differed from plant to plant, as chapter 2 indicated. In the chemical industry generally, including NEC, there are at least two such areas: shift rotation, and health and safety. Halle also took special note of these;[16] in fact, it would be impossible to write about the chemical industry and not do so.

Shift Rotation

Many chemical employees rotate through all three shifts. This is partly due to the continuous-processing nature of the technology. Since some of the buildings run all day and all week, four full crews are required to staff three shifts. But it is also partly due to tradition. Two of the jobs I worked also rotated and there was no other explanation for either (as far as the employees were told) than custom.[17] About half the hourly jobs at NEC rotate. Since most of those that do not rotate are divided into shifts, only about eighty jobs at NEC are straight days. It has already been noted that the contract includes standard language permitting the company to assign rotating shifts if it wishes. The schedule for the majority who do rotate is called "seven and two"—seven days on, two days off, then moving on to the next shift. Those on this schedule thus have only one weekend off a month. One thirty-five-year veteran who had rotated "seven and two" almost his whole life pointed to his camper during the interview and commented that one weekend a month had not given him much time to use it.

The harmful physiological effects of rotating shifts have been well documented. Some established correlates include poor sleep, fatigue, loss of appetite, and social dislocations.[18] Other problem areas that have been studied include increased safety risks, stress, and loss of social prestige. These have not been established conclusively, but every researcher who talks to shift workers—and this researcher who worked swing shift for six years—hears enough negative comments about rotating that it is impossible to assume these problems are artifactual. The tendency has been to find more rather than fewer problem areas as research on shift rotation progresses. In a finding particularly relevant to NEC, one research team wrote that the practice of week-by-week rotating is "the least satisfactory of any [arrangement] devised."[19]

Ten of the people I interviewed are currently rotating, while nine more did so for substantial periods in the recent past. No one gave "rotating shifts" as the reason for *wanting* to hold a particular job. Several had bid onto the job they held, which could only be obtained at the cost of rotating shifts, but no one singled out the "rotation" factor itself as positive. Some said they did not object to rotating, others simply hated it and some gave it as the reason for bidding off a particular job. As chapter 2 explained, the numbers are not as important as the category of responses they describe. In the case of shift rotation, there is something like a Pareto-minimum—a situation that affects no one positively and some negatively. Since the objective evidence is so strong,[20] and since my respondents are so similar in their comments to Halle's, I will simply give a few illustrative and heartfelt examples:

Speaker A [the older worker who regretted the nonuse of his camper]: I think rotating shifts—you never get used to it, you never seem to—you always want to—. Before, I used to like bouncing around and the different shifts. Now, I don't know, at my age or whatnot, I'm getting a little tired of it.

Speaker B: I finally had enough of shift work. It really plays havoc with the home life. The kids were missing me. I could see it in them, it was causing problems. They said, "Are you going to be home?" I said *[to himself]*, enough is enough.

Speaker C: You can't do that shift work forever even if you have nerves of steel.

Speaker D: Nobody should have to work shifts. Shifts is—some people say they like it, but it's something you never get used to, because your system just about gets adjusted to one shift, you're on another one. It did a job on me.

Q. It doesn't do much for your family life, I guess.

A. No. No. *Definitely* not.

Someone might want to argue that my own aggregate figures show that rotation is a limited problem, even if a real one. Only about half of the hourly employees currently rotate, even fewer on the demanding "seven and two" schedule. But this seriously understates the severity of the problem. If the evidence regarding adverse health and social effects of rotation is valid, then there is no reason to disregard the past or even lagged effects on those who rotated for years. Further, the disagreeable aspects of rotation constrict the job choices of those who do not work it. Most maintenance workers began in a job I will call "production repair" (PR) when they first moved out of production. PR workers work as "jacks of all trades"; they are troubleshooters for any repair work. They also rotate. This is the highest-status job in the plant and offers the most varied work, but the company has had a difficult time keeping it filled because of the schedule. Three people even gave rotation as the reason for turning down an offer to move to supervision. These were high-seniority employees who had worked their way up to day jobs and were not willing to subject themselves to an unspecified number of years of rotating as shift foremen. The arguably coercive aspects of choice limitation are discussed in a later chapter.

Health and Safety

If some limitations can be put on the set of those affected by shift rotation, none can be on those subject to the health hazards of working in a chemical plant. The texture of discussion about health and safety is very different from that of shift rotation. It is at once less impressionistic—people have accumulated pieces of scientific arguments and some facts and figures—and less consensual. People stake out widely different personal positions that are not a product of different exposure. Further, the vocabulary is strongly cued by several sources, notably the union and the company. Health and safety is such a pervasive concern for chemical workers that it cannot be usefully discussed in one subsection. It came up in various ways during different parts of the interviews, sometimes as the lead-in to the whole discussion. "Everything here is pretty much health and safety," one employee told me in response to my usual opening question about what kind of job he did. My limited discussion of the question here is intended to give health and safety its proper place in the daily routines of NEC employees.

Evidence from research is not as helpful in pinpointing the nature of this hardship area as it was where shift rotation was concerned. Industrial accidents, one indicator of health and safety problems, have a variety of causes, some of which are overrepresented in chemical plants, some of which are not.[21] In overall performance, the chemical industry does not do badly in comparisons. According to an index prepared by the National Safety Council on the number of deaths and lost working days per million man hours, the chemical industry falls well below the national average.[22] But because the products have very different and potentially highly toxic components, generalizations do not mean a great deal in this industry. Both short- and long-term effects vary by the nature of the product. Some of the negative consequences of work with chemicals in particular locations go well beyond what anyone could argue would be accepted by a rational employee as an acceptable risk, assuming the availability of information. Employees at the Rohm and Haas plant in Philadelphia, for instance, were exposed to high levels of bischlormethyl ether (BCME) for years before it was classified as a carcinogen. The result was at least twenty-five cases of lung cancer in one department.[23]

The knowledge of catastrophic possibilities, not the frequency or likelihood of their occurrence, is what underlies the special concern chemical workers have toward industrial health and safety. Even the knowledge itself might have harmful effects: "Emotional stress is exacerbated by the lack of power to prevent further exposure, and the need to confront agonizing choices between personal safety or family health and earning a living."[24] The fear is of what *might someday* happen (the Bhopal scenario), or what might someday be found *to have already* happened. The first is similar to the fear of flying; most likely the trip will be uneventful, but the consequences of an event make even the slim possibility worthy of some thought. The second can take two forms. There is the Love Canal scenario—the possibility that a company may be knowingly committing unsafe acts because the likelihood of detection is small. There is also the laboratory rat scenario—the possibility of exposure to a chemical whose dangerous properties only come to light in the future.[25] In either situation, the employee at some point comes to realize that he or she has been exposed to toxic substances in the past, perhaps for a long period.

Tests at NEC have not indicated any major violations of safety standards. A dumping violation citation several years ago was a spur to tighter safety regulation. The tests following the environmental charges mentioned in chapter 2 did not show excesses in emissions. The union has waged a vigorous campaign around health and safety and has been responsible for many changes such as the installation of bifurcators. The fatal accident mentioned earlier and described later had only peripherally to do with the fact that NEC is a chemical plant.

Yet a chemical plant it remains. One new employee, who had worked for many years in another industry (and was thus no overly nervous neophyte), related one of his first experiences at NEC:

When I used to work in building B, the first day I worked with this one chemical, it was filtered and what they called the heavy part gets settled so the liquid passes through. So it's our job to take this filter apart. The first time I did that, I took in my first breath of fumes from this chemical, I thought I was going to die right then and there. I lost all my breath. My eyes closed on me. I watered, I couldn't do nothing at all. All I could think of was I ran as fast as I could to a window, get some oxygen. I wish somebody had told me to wear a gas mask.

NEC uses several chemicals and solvents that have known toxic effects, including one OSHA-labeled carcinogen and eight others in which preliminary test results have shown cancer in laboratory rats.[26] In addition, combinations of chemicals in use at NEC can form BCME and cyanide. Many employees seem convinced that the heart attack rate is abnormally high. While a study done by the company disputed this, a more recent study done on behalf of the union suggested that the original study underrepresented the number of heart attacks.[27]

The respondents tended to be either highly supportive or highly critical of the company's health and safety program. When I asked the ending question about what the employee would change if he or she were given the power, health and safety was mentioned more than any other subject (eight times). The following characterizations, given by employees in the same building, define the widely held polar positions:

Q. What do you think of the health and safety program?
Speaker A: Oh, they're good, strict. I can turn *[a problem]* in and get it fixed right away. If you turn it in as a safety problem, it'll get done.

Speaker B: They pound you with safety, safety, safety, but they want you to do more work and if you do more, you can't do it without—you'll have to break some safety rules. But they don't care if you do that.

Praise and support for the health and safety program went along with defensiveness toward allegations made by other employees, by the environmentalists, or by vague "outsiders."[28]

A recently retired maintenance worker:

They talk about working with chemicals but hell, I was there thirty-six years and I'm as healthy as the day I walked in.

A twenty-nine-year employee, a Lockland resident:

You've heard all the talk from *[names environmental group]*. Regardless of how townspeople feel about cancer, cancer and heart attacks are hereditary. You hear "NEC" everyday and of course you'll think something's wrong. They've put on all the controls they can. Maybe they go overboard.

A thirty-three-year production worker, also recently retired:

You can talk about chemical hazards, but it's a heck of a nice place to work. People who complain don't tell you about their history of allergies. It happened that a lot of people get emphysema, but most of them were heavy smokers.

But even this last respondent, who was unremittingly hostile to any criticism of NEC's health and safety program raised the uncertainty factor immediately after the last quoted statement.

All the chemicals tell you how to use them. But sometimes, you never know, you're sitting on a keg of dynamite. You can see the blueprint, but not the fire.

If this by the very fact of its contradictory tensions illustrates the "Bhopal scenario," the "laboratory rat" scenario was best expressed by a very new (four-month) employee who walked over to his piano during the interview and handed me a label taken from a drum he handled every day at work. It read: "Contains [chemical name]. [Chemical] causes cancer in laboratory animal tests."

I read it for about two weeks in a row and it stared me in the face and stared me in the face and I said, "Well, I want to take that home." We had no masks, no protection. You breathe this stuff all the time and there's no way that you can get around it. Now, they come out with a mask. But what happened to the *years* these people were working around it all the time?

The difference to the employee between the "laboratory rat" and "Love Canal" scenarios is minimal. In both cases, the employee is told at some point that he or she has been working for years with potentially life-threatening substances.[29] The knowledge that this situation has occurred and the fear that it may occur in the future is part of the stock of daily, mundane experience of working in a chemical plant.[30] The following was a matter-of-fact and nonrecriminatory recounting of just such an incident by a fifteen-year maintenance worker ("Chemical X" is the OSHA-listed carcinogen):

I guess I was there a couple of years when they came up with that Chemical X is a known cancerizing agent. I worked around it when I was on production repair. When you break a line on a pump or something, we would go out there with just our regular clothes on. I don't know whether the company was aware it was a dangerous chemical or not; it was up till the past several years now they really tightened down on it. On the same job like I said I did when I first started here, now you suit up for it, rubber boots and all that.

You never suited up—you get it on your hands and—you almost wash your hands in the stuff. Going back to the early part of when I started, they had a plugged condenser, so they asked me to open the feed leg. I pulled the feed leg, I could see inside, I said, "What is this stuff"—no gloves, reaching in to unclog it, right? It could just run all down, I go to wash the stuff off with water, it won't come off. Water just slides across it. So I said, "What is this stuff"? The production supervisor said, "Oh, it's got a little of everything—a couple of solvents and Chemical X." A couple of months later, they had this safety thing about Chemical X. Now your heart jumps. *[laughs]*

Good Place to Work

The laugh at the end of what is not a very funny story can help in sketching a summary of everyday life at NEC. Those writers who described a "blue-collar blues" would find much here to substantiate their case. Job tasks are dull, shift rotation is an aggravation, and health and safety is a constant concern that is manifested in both defensiveness and fear. Long-term exposure to a carcinogen provokes a laugh, and not a dismissive one, since this employee was a thoughtful man who understood he had been put at risk. Another employee described overall orientations to work this way:

There's a few people that like to come to work every day, are really gung ho, really into it. And there's *quite* a few people that just put in their time, do what they have to do not to get noticed by the wrong people and go home.

The negative reactions to daily routines should not be mistaken for employees' complete estimate of life at NEC. Dozens of "job satisfaction" surveys have found that 70 to 80 percent of the work force indicates satisfaction with their job. I do not intend to take issue with that. What has to be done is to reconcile those findings with the kind of coexisting critical comments I present here and in the following chapters.[31] The specific areas discussed above are well within the "informal contract" which Barrington Moore argued is "negotiated" between subordinates and superordinates. The most critical comments people made will be seen in later chapters, centering on *violation* of the "terms" of the contract, not on the terms themselves. My purpose here has been to look at the negative aspects of the terms. This might be thought of as a cost of acquiescence.

That this is so makes the paradox noted in the first paragraph of this chapter even more worthy of examination. NEC is identified by everyone as "a good place to work" as a whole. "Good place to work" is an evaluative category created by the respondents themselves. I did not ask anyone a question using those words. The question that most often drew that phrase as a response was something like: "Tell me what it's like to work there. How does time pass, how do people get along?" One respondent immediately rephrased that, asking me,

---

Do you mean, like, is it a good place to work and all that?

While it was not my intention generally to do so, my questions asked people to think in terms with which they were unfamiliar. The volunteered category of "good place to work," on the other hand, was one with which people felt very comfortable.

Of course, this has not yet said anything of substance. The fact that NEC employees were familiar with this conceptual category did not necessarily imply that their evaluation would be positive. Why, especially, do those who express anger about many aspects of the job regard NEC as a good place to work?

Since this "good job" attitude was nearly consensual,[32] it was associated with the full range of attitudes on other questions. There are three fairly distinct and useful subdivisions among the respondents. There are those people, characterized above by another employee as "gung ho," who like their jobs. They enjoy the work, enjoy the pay, do not mind very much the rotation (or do not rotate), and do not worry a great deal about the dangers. These are people who declined to make any critical comments about their jobs when the questions invited them to do so.

It's a nice place to work. Time goes fast. Place runs pretty smooth.

This same employee would not entertain the possibility that there was any obligation on the part of the company to him, as the following nonresponsive answer indicates:

Q. What do you expect from the company?
A. Well, they've been pretty good. I never got laid off since I got here. It's a good, steady job.

The essence of this category is the expression of preference, a consistent and indisputable assertion that the employee likes spinach.[33] For the rest of the employees, the "good job" formulation is a considered judgment, not a simple preference.[34] What are the elements of a "good job"?

The most common ones are "The pay is good," "The work ain't that hard," and/or "Pretty much, they don't hassle you." This may not strike the reader as revelatory, but this is a group that evaluates some aspects of the job negatively, often including the three areas described above. These comments are comparative. They tell us what rough yardsticks are used for evaluation of what constitutes a good job.

A mechanic in his mid-thirties:

If you want, I'll summarize just about everything that I've been saying to you. I have enjoyed working for NEC. They are a very safety-conscious company. They are interested in the health and welfare of their employees. Granted, there's always room for improvement. That's where I get stonewalled. At this point in my life I've been remarried, I've got six children, I've got a two-family house, but as far as working down there with that company, I've done just about every job they have there in that plant. All right? I've kind of reached the saturation point. Where do I go from here? Where do I go from here?

It would be easy to argue that this worker keeps a clearly defined balance sheet and that "good place to work" is the expression used to capture the most favorable distribution of values he can achieve. That analysis would underestimate the force of the repeated question at the end of this paragraph.[35] The speaker wanted to make sure I knew that this was an important problem for him—he introduced it as a "summary" and repeated it twice after that point in the interview. "Good place to work" involves acceptance of a certain degree of pain—"everyday oppression" in James Scott's phrase.[36]

One employee had been recommended to me because "he's a guy who speaks out." He offered his overall evaluation of NEC five minutes into the interview.

It's not a bad place to work for. You don't work hard, that's for sure.

He even had to fight his wife's overall assessment of NEC:

My wife can't stand the place. She thinks it's a bad place to work for. She thinks someday she'll get a call saying—whatever. She sees things in the paper. A lot of things. But I tell her it's not that bad. The money's not bad. What can you do?

It became clear that he had many specific, strongly stated grievances about particular foremen, safety, the potential closing of building D, and the lack of communication. After each one, he repeated his general evaluation: "pay is good, job's not that hard," or its equivalent, "you can't complain." That phrase might be the best way to capture this category—people who "can't complain," but do.

The argument so far has been that certain aspects of the job that might look distasteful to an outside observer (particularly to an academic researcher) are not viewed as counting toward an overall summation by the employees. They go with the territory. There is one variation on this pattern that merits special attention as the third subcategory. Stephen Marglin argued that one of the original purposes of gathering cottage workers together into a factory was to reduce the amount of employee discretion to one choice—whether or not to work.[37] Several people directly and quickly equated "good place to work" with "it's hard to get fired."

Speaker A: The company to me is lenient on a lot of things. That's why I say it's a good company to work for. I think in order to get fired here, you have to have literally a fork truck carry your records over.

Speaker B: They treat the employees really fair here. It's a really hard place to get fired out of, I'll tell you that much.

Of course, it is reasonable for people to see relative job security as one important way to evaluate their employers. But there is an important and revealing nonsequitur in this equation. None of the people who used this argument to explain "good place to work" offered even the slightest doubt about their own job security. Once industrial employees get past the probationary period, they know that the line between a job in jeopardy and a secure one is not a fine one.

>*When I first started working at Diamond, an older employee took me aside and told me to work hard for forty-five days, the probationary period. "And then you got 'er made. Somebody would have to beg this company to fire him."*< DI, PO

So the fact that NEC does not fire many of its postprobationary employees is given critical evaluative importance. "Hard to get fired" is the outer boundary of the informal contract that which exists at a "good place to work." The immediate use of the first as explanation of the second (particularly when neither phrase was used in any question) is some evidence that satisfaction of this condition is sufficient to make other aspects of daily factory life—even ones specified as unpleasant by these same people—endurable.

There is also some indication that certain exceptions to the "hard-to-get-fired" outer boundary are considered normal. As mentioned in chapter 2, some of the sensitive production jobs in buildings B and C cannot be filled from within the plant because they have the reputation of being "easy to get fired from." The LRS went to some lengths in our interview to affirm that this was more than just a perception:

My feeling is people probably think we are getting a little more strict with the application of discipline. I would have to say that's probably correct. For instance in the *[B and C]* area, we're having a lot of discipline because of operator error.

In addition, NEC has made efforts to be more selective in retaining new hires. According to a union official, almost half the new hires in the past year were fired in their probationary period. While current industrial relations regards probationary employees as having virtually no rights, these are simply transitory legal definitions. There is no reason why any employee cannot make use of this information in evaluating NEC. The questions ask people to think in ethical or moral categories, not juridical ones.[38] The "hard-to-get-fired" explanation for why NEC is a good place to work thus not only grants legitimacy on the single condition of unthreatened employment, but also contains certain blind spots, or areas in which exceptions will not be noted.

A number of authors exploring the nonbarking-dog problem point out that superordinate classes do not need acquiescence from lower classes; they merely need compliance.[39] As long as people do their work, the extent to which they see hierarchy and inequality as legitimate is only of limited significance. This argument has particular force in an industrial setting, where integration is high and the discretion of the employees relatively low.[40] Stephen Hill provided a good short summary of this position:

> Provided that workers in practice do their jobs, system integration is not destroyed by the rejection of dominant values or non-violent social conflict in industry. Pragmatic acceptance, rather than normative consensus or endorsement, is what matters for system integration.[41]

This "pragmatic acceptance," according to Scott, "mimics hegemony" but is not equal to it.[42] What this chapter suggests is not that "pragmatic acceptance" is an incorrect characterization of the response to subordination at work but that it is an incomplete one. People *could* go about their jobs without accepting the burdens as inevitable, but it seems that at NEC, it would not be accurate to say that they do. "Good place to work" is a summary, a higher rank of evaluation than expressed grievances, even strong ones. There were respondents who used that phrase virtually through clenched teeth:

This is a pretty good company. But as far as gratification—what I'm doing with my life—this is nowhere.

We cannot ignore the first sentence simply because the second seems more compelling. This acceptance is more than pragmatic—it implies a degree of legitimacy. If people simply trudged to work at NEC because they had to make a living, and carried with them some critical view of the hierarchical work arrangements, there would have been no reason for the positive overall summary, particularly when such a summary was not solicited.

Another, earlier explanation of why people who say they "can't complain," do and then add that they are not complaining is that of Frederick Herzberg.[43] He divided needs into two disjunct categories: avoidance of pain and striving toward realizing potential. "Job satisfaction," according to Herzberg, is normally positive evaluation of the ability to avoid pain. Then "job dissatisfaction" is not the *opposite* of satisfaction, it is an additional evaluation of the self-fulfillment factor. Herzberg also introduced the possibility of ranking needs by linking his two categories with Maslow's hierarchy of needs; within the context of a workplace, the main thrust of Maslow would be that immediate physical needs must be satisfied first, and once satisfied, would lead to articulation of further needs tending in the direction of self-fulfillment.[44]

I asked the four people I re-interviewed why they thought people who had negative comments about aspects of NEC all agreed that it was a "good place to work." These four were among the most analytical and insightful of NEC employees in describing negative aspects of factory life. But they also all used "good place to work" phraseology in the first interview. When I asked them about the paradox—both in their own views and those of others—they gave the usual answers: good pay, work isn't that bad, not much pressure. These answers are consonant with relying on Herzberg's separation of satisfiers from dissatisfiers to resolve the seeming paradox. My reason for not relying on that formulation comes from these words (in response to an unrelated question) from one of them:

We had a conversation in the lunch room the other day. Here's some people in the production end of it that are pretty talented, hard-working conscientious people. There's not really an opportunity there for anything other than what they're doing. I think people look at the future and say, "Damn, I'm going to be doing the same job twenty years from now." *That's the way it is down there and that's the way it goes.*

If NEC satisfies material needs, the Herzberg-Maslow theory would suggest that self-fulfillment needs would become more prominent as criteria for judging the job. The speaker's last line indicates that they may be more prominent, but *not* as a criterion for judging the job. This speaker, like others, ranked NEC as a "good place to work" based on other criteria. Further, some of the sharpest and most widespread criticisms concern factors that should fall in the hygiene category—the "seven and two" rotation, and health and safety questions. These factors are excluded from an overall evaluation of the job, just as self-fulfillment is.

The reason for discussing Herzberg is that he made an important and perhaps overlooked contribution in separating satisfaction and dissatisfaction into different categories. But "satisfaction" at NEC does not appear be a variable at all. Given the unanimity around the "good place to work" evaluation, there is no way to determine what a bad place to work might be. What constitutes an everyday complaint, the "bitch in every job" which does not go into the moral tally sheet, seems quite elastic. Perceptions of particular injustices abound, but not perceptions that hierarchical workplace structures are unjust.

I began this chapter by noting that the spontaneous response of intellectuals on going into a factory is that such work is generally disagreeable and, if projected over a lifetime, nearly intolerable. The point has not been that outsiders should check their value systems at the timeclock but that continued exposure to factory life would probably cause those systems to change. Mine did, and as the woman suggested to Richard Balzer, everyone's does. The negative reaction to factory life of someone not immersed in it is an important method for retaining critical judgment in the face of the "perilous capacity for getting used to things."[45]

A former concentration camp prisoner, Victor Frankl, wrote of the following episode:

> Long after I had resumed normal life again (that means a long time after my release from camp), somebody showed me an illustrated weekly with photographs of prisoners lying crowded on their bunks, staring dully at a visitor. "Isn't this terrible, the dreadful staring faces—everything about it."
>
> "Why?" I asked, for I genuinely did not understand. For at that moment I saw it all again; at 5:00 A.M. it was still pitch dark outside. I was lying on the hard boards in an earthen hut where about seventy of us were "taken care of."

We were sick and did not have to leave camp for work; we did not have to go on parade. We could lie all day in our little corner in the hut and doze and wait for the daily distribution of bread (which, of course, was reduced for the sick) and for the daily helping of soup (watered down and also decreased in quantity). But how content we were in spite of everything.

All this came to my mind when I saw the photographs in the magazine. When I explained, my listeners understood why I did not find the photograph so terrible: the people in it might not have been so unhappy after all.[46]

It should be unnecessary to say that I am not comparing factory work to life in a concentration camp. I am suggesting, however, that there is a parallel between the relative peace and satisfaction Frankl found in tiny comforts as a prisoner and the acclimatization that takes place at work. Later chapters examine in detail the significance of the argument that relative to other personal possibilities, NEC *is*, for its employees, a good place to work. Frankl's reflections on seeing those photographs should sustain us until we reach that point.

Notes

1. Robert Schrank, *Ten Thousand Working Days*, p. 76
2. Richard Balzer, *Clockwork: Life in and outside an American Factory*; Richard Pfeffer, *Working for Capitalism*. Pfeffer worked; Balzer wandered and interviewed. See also Barbara Garson, *All the Livelong Day*, for another first encounter with factory work that expresses incredulity at what people will put up with.
3. Balzer, *Clockwork*, p. 5.
4. Pfeffer, *Working for Capitalism*, p. 38.
5. U.S Department of Health, Education, and Welfare, *Work in America*, p. 82. These HEW findings are not easy to interpret. The authors do not claim that there is a direct correlation between factory work and these problems, although the evidence leads one toward the conclusion that they think there is. The independent variable they use most often is "job satisfaction," which is strongly inversely correlated with the degree of blueness of the collar. Sometimes they specifically use factory work as the independent variable, and often information about their dependent variables comes from studies of factory work (for instance, the Kornhauser study). At times, however, they use "occupational stress" as the independent variable, a feature more of certain professional categories. Overall, I think the thrust of the study justified the sentence.
6. Ibid., p. 87.
7. Martin Meissner, "The Long Arm of the Job: A Study of Work and Leisure," p. 260.
8. Eli Chinoy, *Automobile Workers and the American Dream*, p. 66; Charles Walker and Robert Guest, *The Man on the Assembly Line*.
9. There is a tendency to underestimate the number of employees working in assembly-line conditions. That number is quite small if the definition revolves around working on a line that begins with a hook and ends with a finished product, snaking all the way through the plant. Each of the three jobs I worked involved small units of people working cooperatively on a product moved on a conveyor, with the speed of movement set by management. None would show up in assembly-line statistics, but each had important similarities to that kind of work.
10. Robert Blauner, *Alienation and Freedom*, chapters 6 and 7.

11. Harry Braverman, *Labor and Monopoly Capital;* David Noble, "Social Choice in Machine Design: The Case of the Automatically Controlled Machine Tools."

12. R. M. Blackburn and Michael Mann, *The Working Class in the Labour Market,* p. 290.

13. Christopher Hill, *The World Turned Upside Down,* pp. 85–86; Eric Hobsbawm and George Rude, *Captain Swing,* chapter 3; Willem F. Wertheim, *Evolution and Revolution*: "Physical mobility may loosen many people from their natural environment and produce a greater awareness of the fact that society as it exists, with its injustices, inequalities and misery, is not unchangeable" (p. 209).

14. W. G. Runciman, *Relative Deprivation and Social Justice,* pp. 145–46.

15. Quoted in Stephen Marcus, *Engels, Manchester and the Working Class,* p. 31.

16. David Halle, *America's Working Man,* pp. 115–19; see similar comments in Duncan Gallie, *In Search of the New Working Class.*

17. The jobs went around the clock, but not through weekends. We rotated through all three shifts, but could just as easily have worked steady shifts. Many plants divided into shifts do so.

18. Peter Finn, "The Effects of Shift Work on the Lives of Employees," pp. 32–33.

19. Charles Winget, Lewis Hughes, and Joseph Ladou, "Physiological Effects of Rotational Work Shifting: A Review," p. 206.

20. I am using "objective evidence" here and elsewhere in the spirit Charles Lindblom does (*Politics and Markets,* p. 208)—studies of various kinds that reveal a condition regardless of the perception of the actors involved.

21. Of course, the famous retort from industry is that you are safer in a factory than in your own home. One well-known way in which the rate of lost-time accidents is made to appear lower than it actually is, is by bringing people to work the day after a serious accident, sometimes to do nothing more than lie in a doctor's office and read. Having seen the issue from both sides, I think I can tell the reader unequivocally that I am safer writing this study than I would be if I were one of my subjects.

22. Charles Perrow, *Normal Accidents: Living with High-Risk Technologies,* p. 104. The figures are: national average, 2.5; chemical industry as a whole, 1.46; chemical processing (the category NEC fits), 1.62.

23. David McCaffrey, *OSHA and the Politics of Health Regulation,* p. 46. McCaffrey reports this discussion of risk assessment in an inquiry following the classification of BCME as a carcinogen:

> Senator Tunney: Ma'am, can I ask you: Did you or your husband, to your knowledge, have any understanding that he was working with a material that would produce cancer?
>
> Mrs. Aummen: No, he didn't. . . . You think that when you see one man die and then another man die, maybe he thought, because I know I thought about it, why are some men dying right after the other? This has to be something, right? But when you work, men together on this one chemical, and they die one after the other . . . I don't think my husband would have stayed if he had known.

24. Dorothy Nelkin and Michael Brown, *Workers at Risk,* p. 38.

25. One example would be the carcinogenic properties of what I will call Chemical X, which OSHA did not regulate until 1979 (McCaffrey, *OSHA*).

26. Unfortunately for the flow of this section, I will not be able to name the specific chemicals and solvents, since that information has the potential to reveal the identity of the plant.

27. This study is another document I cannot cite. Same story as above.

28. Some of the intruding "outsiders" were not very far outside. One man who lived

near NEC and whose wife worked even closer said he heard from her "all the time about NEC," meaning about the potential health problems. He said that she simply did not understand the care the company took.

29. The moral assessment of the company's role is quite different, of course. In the first case, the necessary information may simply not have been available—although even the limits of what information is available are not wholly determined by science. A company can pursue studies more or less vigorously.

30. This borrows from the important distinction Ronald Mason drew between the "mundane" and the "trivial." What happens ordinarily is worth thinking about until proved trivial (*Participatory and Workplace Democracy*, p. 14).

31. Richard Hamilton and James Wright's *The State of the Masses* is a broadscale, even vitriolic attack on "workplace critics" and "advanced intellectuals" who, they claim, come from the "Hieronymus Bosch School of Industrial Relations" and find much more wrong with work than workers do. I suppose I am from that school, and yet I have the same takeoff point as Hamilton and Wright—the consistently high "job satisfaction" evaluations. The NEC-sponsored national survey indicated that this was true here also, just as I estimated from my sample (my work was done and nearly completed before that survey and before I read the Hamilton and Wright book). But here, qualitative interviewing unquestionably helps. I found that many people simply discarded what would seem to be important factors in thinking about job satisfaction. The NEC survey also substantiates the existence—sometimes even the predominance—of many of the critical attitudes I have found.

32. Nobody said it was not a very good job or used any other language that could be construed that way. Two people did not volunteer "good job" phraseology, and, as mentioned above, I did not solicit it. Although I want to stress again that the numbers in each category are not reliable, I provide them here for those interested. Of the thirty-one who used "good place to work" phrases, twenty proceeded to complain loudly, vociferously, about particular aspects of life at NEC. Only three maintained consistently that the job has no important negative features. Five people among those who thought NEC was a "good place to work" were consistently and overwhelmingly negative about virtually every aspect of the job. Five immediately associated "good place" with "hard to get fired." No significance tests are offered, for reasons explained in chapter 2.

33. As described in Vilfredo Pareto, *Manual of Political Economy*, p. 45. But see chapter 7, wherein spinach takes on a class character.

34. I am making provisional use of Lindblom's distinction between simple preference and volition, *Politics and Markets*, pp. 134–37.

35. Certainly, that "stone wall" can exist in any occupation. What then does this have to do with an analysis of factory life? The mechanic himself answered that, pointing out the wearying effects of lifelong physical labor right after the "rut syndrome" lines: "Twenty-five or thirty years of pulling on wrenches, it's physical work. It keeps me in great shape now, but I hate to think what it might do to me thirty years from now."

36. James Scott, "Everyday Forms of Peasant Resistance."

37. Stephen Marglin, "What Do Bosses Do?" p. 93. Even if Marglin's overall argument were rejected, or if one were to maintain that there was no *intention* on the part of the early factory system architects to produce this dichotomized choice range, the effect would be the same.

38. There was one exception that proved the rule was not a rule. In response to the "Absolutely Wrong" question, one (relatively young and new) employee brought up just such a problem: "I saw an employee fired on his probation—a good employee, a good worker—because he was late for a second time. I found that to be unjustified. An employee that had never worked midnights before. That's showing no consideration. He was treated just like a machine and it was just, 'out the door.' "

39. Jennifer Hochschild, *What's Fair?;* Michael Mann, "The Social Cohesion of Liberal Democracy"; James Scott, *Weapons of the Weak: Everyday Forms of Peasant Resistance;* Nicholas Abercrombie, Steven Hill, and Bryan Turner, *The Dominant Ideology Thesis.*

40. But not nonexistent. Not even the most Taylorized work situations have eliminated crucial areas of employee discretion.

41. Stephen Hill, *Competition and Control at Work,* p. 228.

42. Scott, *Weapons of the Weak,* pp. 324–27.

43. Frederick Herzberg, *Work and the Nature of Man,* particularly chapter 4.

44. Ibid., p. 141. Herzberg's terminology is "hygiene" (the first three of Maslow's need hierarchy) and "motivators" (the last three).

45. Barrington Moore, *Injustice: The Social Bases of Obedience and Revolt,* p. 69.

46. Viktor Frankl, *Man's Search for Meaning,* pp. 75–77.

4

Industrial
Non-Democracy

>Director of Personnel to me during my orientation meeting after
being hired: "I tell you what, there's a lot of guys out there *[motions
toward plant]* that ain't worth—two cents. I'll know you're a good
employee if I never hear another thing about you. The best people
are the ones I've forgotten about. Someone might ask me at a
party—'How about Smith, hasn't he been there twenty years?' I'll
say, 'Who? Smith? He must be a hell of a good man. I never heard
of him.' "< PG, PO

The last chapter evolved from the need to explain consensus that emerged
from variation. There was agreement that NEC was "a good place to work"
among those interviewees who had widely different evaluations of specific
aspects of the job. This chapter examines variation that follows consensus.
There is agreement that employees do not participate in workplace decisions,
but there are different evaluations of whether or not this constitutes an indictment.

A great deal has been written in recent years on the subject of democracy
and participation at work. The discussion of forms, purposes, and potential
outcomes and problems of workplace democracy has been so widespread in
some corners of academia that it is regarded as an idea whose time has
already come.[1] But at NEC, as at most other American plants, the time of
democracy certainly has not come to the shop floor. In particular, it has not
emerged as a well-defined demand from hourly employees. In David
Halle's extensive investigation of chemical workers in a similar setting,
virtually nothing is said about participation or the lack of it. While Halle
did not ask specific questions designed to tap people's feelings on this
subject, it would certainly have come up on its own if it had been a raging
(or even smoldering) issue. This chapter addresses the various frameworks

employees use to understand their lack of formal control over decisions that affect them.

In Order to Form a More Perfect Factory

A number of different, although perhaps not competing, claims are made in discussing the exclusion of workers from decision-making authority. More precisely, different virtues are claimed *for* increased participation by employees in "control" issues that are now usually the prerogative of management. The arguments for extension of control are usually based on some variant of "right," "self-fulfillment," or efficiency.[2]

The argument that uses "right" as its cornerstone is logically prior to the other two, since in its strongest form it does not need the support of the others.[3] The right to participate, it is claimed, comes with citizenship in an economic organization, which should not be seen as private but as part of the political sphere. The arguments (and counterarguments) about the right to participate in decisions of economic enterprises are similar to those about participation in state affairs.[4] The presumption of rightful managerial prerogatives based on ownership is seen as no more legitimate than the claims to ownership of town government by nobility in preindustrial England.[5] The "self-fulfillment" argument appears in two forms. One is that increased participation may be an answer to the "blue-collar blues."[6] It is a means, in other words, to create a work situation that is not stultifying. The other is that participation at work is vital training for producing democratic citizens.[7] Decision making on an immediate level has a carry-over effect, which could translate into an increased sense of political efficacy. The efficiency argument, when it is not a subsidiary of the other two, is usually made by management. Quality of Work Life (QWL) advocates trying to transplant "the Japanese model" to U.S. industry, centers on greater employee-management interaction, and sometimes distributes low-level decision-making power to hourly workers.[8] Outmoded Taylorism, according to the QWL supporters, has produced negative work attitudes; contented workers come to work more and produce more. Also, some forms of participation would increase the employees' interest (mental and real) in the company's competitive standing. The bottom line here is the bottom line—no payoff, no participation.

>*During the time I was at Procter and Gamble, the management began talking about "Japan-style" employee involvement. They had employees watch the NBC documentary "If Japan Can, Why Can't We?" even shutting down the production lines for an hour. My Departmental Manager (Roll-On Department) formed a group of employees composed of representatives from each job classifi-*

cation. The official name was the Roll-On Advisory Board, but it was immediately dubbed ROLAID in the department. The initial purpose of ROLAID was to solicit employee participation in the installation of an automated load former. The formation of this group was put explicitly in the context of a new approach to employee-management relationships. Decision making, it was said, would no longer be one-sided. The notes from an early ROLAID meeting established the actual parameters of decision-making powers clearly. Each topic introduced would start with a discussion of "boundary conditions." Those boundary conditions indicated which subjects would be untouchable. The boundary conditions for the introduction of the new load former were no increase in manpower, no increase in pay rates, no increased overtime. Also, there was an operative presumption that ROLAID was not free to decide not to install the load former.< PG, PA

The differences in goals among these various advocates of participation are matched by differences in program. There is an especially pronounced difference between the first two groups and the QWL position, in regard to both how extensive the decision-making powers should be and how binding they would be. Many of the new managerial approaches involve either "work humanization"—rotating or diversifying jobs—which involves no new decision-making authority, or the creation of work teams that either advise management or exercise control in carefully delimited areas.

>In the ROLAID experiment, the same document mentioned above specifically addressed decision making, explaining that final authority still remained with the department manager.

If a decision is made that is contrary to an individual's or the group's opinion, an explanation will be provided that will hopefully provide the basis for the decision.

Naturally, in telling us that ROLAID would mark the end of "one-sided decision making," the department manager did not stress this point heavily.[9]< PG, PA

Stephen Wood called this managerial trend "team Taylorism" and drew the important distinction between problem-solving groups (such as ROLAID) and autonomous work groups with actual decision-making authority.[10] At their worst, such groups can simply be a means for managers to make use of the knowledge workers have developed of the productive process[11] to increase efficiency. This does not mean that changes introduced by such work teams are trivial. In fact, for those who are not yet convinced of the rock-ribbed authoritarian structure prevailing in U.S. industry, it should be eye-opening that such limited and tentative practices as solicitation of employees' opinions on how best to do their job are described as increased participation. Some NEC workers do not feel that the company does even this; it has not even occurred to others that it should. Further, the distance between team Taylorism and the democratically controlled economic organizations envisioned by other participation theorists is so vast that they cannot be considered the same beast. This chapter explores elements common to employees' perceptions of decision making and desire for more participation, as well as the differences that exist among the interviewees on whether there is an issue here at all.

The Ancien Régime

As chapter 1 pointed out, management at NEC has a self-avowedly "traditional hierarchical structure" in which the employees are expected to "do what they are told to do." Industrial hierarchy is precisely traditional; that is, there is nothing particularly onerous about employee-management relationships at NEC. On the one hand there is not even the slightest pretense of democratic decision making; on the other, it would be misleading if this fact conjured up images of Simon Legree–type supervisors roaming the plant with whips. The relationship between "front-line supervision" (the revealing term used by the company) and the hourly employees can contain a certain amount of flexibility and can also vary with the personality of the foreman. In a study of factory organization in five countries, Tannenbaum found an "informal participativeness" in American factories that may have helped soften the impact of hierarchical authority.[12] This "participativeness" should not be confused with any of the forms of participation described above, not even the superficially similar team Taylorism. It refers instead to a consultative *style* of discharging orders, a bedside manner.[13] Style can vary from one foreman to another. I usually started the discussion of decision making by asking, "When there are important decisions to be made, who makes them?" This was often met with bewilderment. "I don't follow you." "What do you mean, decisions?" What I hoped for was an answer covering the whole range of conceivable decisions, from investment to personnel policy to job tasks.[14] But it seemed so foreign to some people that they should even think about these areas that when I attempted to rephrase the question, I usually narrowed the range down to decisions about their immediate job tasks. When I did not narrow down the question myself, sometimes the respondent did by latching on to some specific about his or her daily routine. The more the question became reformulated this way, the more it tapped this "informal participativeness."

Q. When there are decisions that have to be made about your work, decisions along the lines of setting standards for work, quality of work, how a job gets done, working hours, overtime—who makes those decisions?
Speaker A: Any problems, ask your foreman.
Q. You've worked this job for a while—I assume you know it pretty well. Do foremen or other supervisors consult you about work before they make decisions?
A. Yes. Sometimes they'll ask you what you think. I'll give them my opinion. Sometimes listening to more people, you get a better result.

Q. When they—the company—has a decision to make of some kind, whether it's to do with what gets produced, when it gets produced, type of machinery, new machinery installation, any of those range of decisions, how do those decisions get made?
Speaker B: I don't think I follow that now. What do you mean?
Q. Well, as you're working, you face a lot of different situations that require making decisions, what you do, when you do it, how fast you work—
A. *[cuts in]* The company has their choice of that.
Q. Do they ever ask your opinion about questions like that?
A. Sometimes, yes. Sometimes they do, yes. *[Gives example of informal consultation during machine installation.]*

Revealing something of the limited value of this participativeness, the next lines of speaker B were:

I think they more or less did what they were going to do originally anyhow. Until something goes wrong and they say, "Gee, maybe I should have done it that way."

This question about decision making is substantially rhetorical. Having worked at several factories, I knew who made decisions and I was fairly certain that everyone I asked would know also. With the exception of the above-noted daily give and take with foremen, no one mentioned any form of participation. It is no secret "who governs" factories; it is not an arena of much mystification. That may be why people had so much trouble with this question—it must have sounded odd for someone to ask them if they had participated in such areas as investment decisions, personnel policy, or production rates. While the following descriptions of authority at NEC may be unsurprising, their directness (and ingenuousness) does well in capturing factory authoritarianism:

Q. Who makes decisions *[various types]?*

Speaker A: The higher-ups, always. We're the last ones to find out.

Speaker B: It usually comes from this building here. *[We were in the administration building.]*

Speaker C: Well, I guess Mr. *[supervisor]* would be the one to do that. Then whoever's job it is would have to do it.

Speaker D: The officials, the suit and tie fellows make the decisions. Everything's a big secret, everything, until the hammer comes down.

Q. How are decisions communicated?

Speaker E: They pretty much tell us.

Speaker F: The foreman tells you how they want the work done.

Speaker G: They just kind of pop it down through the plant.

These comments are not presented simply as perception, but as description. That is a risky inference to make, since one of the points of this book is that conditions may be misperceived. But the process of participation in a factory is so tangible that it is hard to imagine a situation in which workers were consulted or given a role in decision making and then telling an interviewer that they were not. Of course the principal reason the inference is warranted is that it is not in great dispute: companies are not legally obligated to allow hourly employees direct participation in certain types of decisions, and for the most part, they do not do so.

The purpose of the last paragraph is to introduce the one controversial aspect of industrial relations and exclusion from control. Could not the existence, importance, and legal standing of trade unions cast doubt on the above generalization? Collective bargaining is a process that involves the participation of each (unionized) hourly employee in at least an indirect manner.[15] Certainly, there are areas such as pay, health and safety, and promotions where a unionized company does not make unilateral decisions. Although it is difficult to draw strict lines around "control" issues,[16] it has happened that American unions have traditionally done just that,[17] and as a consequence have left many facets of work life completely to the discretion of management. These are often the most immediate questions of job organization and staffing, as well as broader ones such as marketing and purchasing.

The standard "management's rights" clause at NEC, quoted in chapter 2, delineates which issues fall within the core prerogatives of management as awarded by the legal category "permissive" subjects. But I had no sense from any party that the existence of such "off-limits" issues was itself a question. I asked both the Labor Relations Supervisor and the five union officials I interviewed about the existence of the boundaries. It took considerable prompting on my part to get them to acknowledge that boundaries existed. But when they carefully considered the questions I posed, they generally agreed that on some matters the company had the right to act unilaterally.

From the interview with the LRS:

Q. Are there areas in which the company feels it has the right to make decisions that are not within the boundaries of union discussion?

A. If you take a broad reading of labor law, it tells you that any terms or conditions can be mandatory subjects for discussion with the union. Read with a loose interpretation, that's a fairly broad application. There are very few things you could think of that would be outside that limit. *[Pauses briefly.]* But I think in the area of setting work schedules, of determining work force levels, of deciding which businesses we're going to run here, they are entirely subject to management discretion and management prerogative. The union does not run the business, does not staff the business, does not tell us which businesses we are going to run here.

Q. Have there been disagreements with the union over those boundaries, as opposed to specific disagreements?

A. In those areas, no. I think it's fairly well understood that those are our decisions.

I asked whether the issues inside and outside those boundaries had changed over the years, basing my question on the assumption that the "Japan-style" trend might have made some of the above prerogatives open to question. The LRS told me that in fact in the past he thought union discretion had gone too far, and that he was trying to move some issues, such as training, back into the "entirely subject to company discretion" category.

The union officials were even more reluctant to acknowledge the existence—or importance—of questions that lay legally and practically beyond the reach of collective bargaining. Each of the following respondents either is or was on the Union Leadership Committee:[18]

Q. Are there issues which the company rules out of bounds as far as talking about with the union?

Speaker A: In many cases—the size of the work force, scheduling and those things are covered in the contract. The company does have those rights. Top of my head, I can't remember anything that ever came up where the company would say, "We're not talking about it, period."

Speaker B: We come together with a contract, we agree on a contract. That is an outline of what we are supposed to do. Now the company has to abide by it, we have to abide by it. Whether or not we're going to work on a particular job for a particular length of time, the company decides that. If this clickety-clack is more important than that one, then that's the way it goes. So they make these kinds of decisions. Then when they determine if they want overtime, that's my decision.

Q. Does the company ever consider some areas out of bounds for negotiations?

A. Yah, I would assume so. Sure I can recall a few things happening that they simply didn't want to talk about and they didn't talk about it. They do have the bottom line. The only tool we have, of course, is the strike, but nobody wants that.

The role of the union is limited to incursions on a "bottom line" (authority) which belongs to the upper reaches of a nonelected hierarchy.[19] In an investigation of the assumptions that underlie interpretation of labor law, James Atleson points out that management's rights are not principally derived from the laws regulating labor relations, but have been held to preexist, to allow discretion in most areas not specifically covered by the regulations. He cites a U.S. Supreme Court ruling that pinpoints the relationship between property rights and the standing of unions: "Organization rights are granted to workers by the same authority, the National Government, that preserves property rights."[20] Granting and preserving are not the same thing, nor do they imply equal status. Property rights preexist positive law.

While there are legal barriers to challenging managerial "core prerogatives" (Atleson's term), American unions have probably been particularly reluctant to widen the scope of bargaining. They have largely endorsed the notion of workers' organizations as a countervailing force.[21] Or, as one twenty-year mechanic and ex-union official put it more bluntly,

---

The company makes the program and then both of us, the union and the company, enforce it. They enforce the bullshit and we enforce what we think is important.

Nonparticipation: Fact or Problem?

What we know so far is how people would describe the lines of authority at NEC. But what do they think about them? Is the inability to participate in the making of decisions a problem? If so, which decisions? Or is there a simple trade-off—(relatively) secure employment for acceptance of authoritarian structures? John Witte, who took part in and studied an experiment with democratic workplace procedures, found that preference for increased participation was not overwhelming, but was "far from total apathy."[22] More specifically, the types of decisions in which people wanted more say were those that most shaped their immediate work experience, such as "work procedures" and "work rates." Conversely, people had little desire to say much about more distant questions such as "management salaries" or "selecting management." A troublesome problem was the relatively small number of people who wanted increased participation in personnel questions such as hiring, firing, and promotions, even when Witte directed respondents to think about those practices in their own work groups. His conclusion is that workers created a distinction between those decisions that affected themselves as individuals (how to do their jobs) and those that affected others as well (personnel matters). NEC employees, it will be seen, make roughly similar distinctions. Witte also found a direct relationship between current participation and the expressed desire for more. In those (decision-making) areas where people felt they were not presently involved, there was less desire for an increase in participation than in those where people already had at least some minimal involvement.[23] My interviews suggested that an important tale lies therein, which I will develop later, although I should note that the nature and number of my questions were not such as to allow me to present differentiations as fine as Witte's.

The difficulties of describing variation in qualitative interviewing are greater than those of establishing consensus. Any claim that people are divisible into categories X and Y is open to immediate challenge on the grounds that the responses may not be representative of the population (therefore, it is possible that the "category" might not actually exist), and that the nonstandardized questions might cue different responses (thus making it hard to decide who belongs in which category if it did exist). In fact, the positive aspects of qualitative interviewing—allowing people to explain their answers and provide their own definitions—make coding inherently more difficult and more subjective.

The principal division is that there are those to whom nonparticipation is a fact only, and those to whom it is not only a fact, but also a problem. These categories, while mutually exclusive, are not theoretically exhaustive. There are other alternatives. But the only responses (six) that did not fall in one of these two groups were ones that either were incoherent, or in which I did not ask the question. I justify making this division on two grounds. First, the employees divided nearly equally on this point. I am not saying that the population of NEC does also; I am saying that this makes it unlikely that either category actually does not exist, given an only slightly unrepresentative sample. Second, people placed themselves in the "problem" category. Some workers clearly had some negative evaluation of the decision-making process *prior* to my asking them questions about it.

Fact

The first category is certainly not as interesting or even as definable as the second. It is comprised of people who did not add evaluative comments to questions about decision making.[24] There is more chance of randomness in a nonevaluation and these responses may be particularly sensitive to question wording.[25] This is why most responses in this chapter are in a question-and-answer form, even at the risk of repeating virtually the same question.

I am taking a small liberty here. Some of the comments *were* "evaluative," but were positive. The difference between these and the negative evaluations were a difference of kind, not of category. The "positive" evaluations were usually in the following form: after the question and answer indicated that the company makes decisions:

Q. Can you think of any other way decisions could be made?
A. Seems okay to me.

The reader may want to conclude that in fact there are not two categories but one plus residual answers. The value of focusing momentarily on those who do not give evaluative answers will become apparent when their answers are contrasted with those who do. The fish take no notice of the water, it has been argued,[26] and it appears that some do not. But there are other NEC employees who have a well-developed sense of being wet.

The first group should not be understood as being composed of complacent employees. This chapter examines decision making only, and there are other areas for workplace dissatisfaction. Even in this specific area, what is exhibited in this category is not that the employees express satisfaction with NEC authority structure but that they decline to give decision making any separate existence from job tasks. There is work to be done and the company is organized in such a way as to get it done. There is no process apart from the orders themselves. Decisions may be right or wrong; they may also be benign or distasteful.[27] But their purpose suffices for their legitimacy.

Speaker A: Most of our orders come through writing—black and white, typewritten *[lifts a sheet of paper]*. We—whether we like the orders or not we try to take care of them. If we don't think they're right, we'll do them to the best of our knowledge. You're there for—you're not there to play. You're there to do your job and then go home. A lot of the younger guys—and even some of the older ones, even me as far as that goes—they come out and give me an order, at first you think, "What the heck do they want to do this for?" And you think it's all wrong. But you gotta think, "They're the ones who—they're the boss." And you gotta make an effort and try to do it, whether it's right or wrong.

Speaker B: Actually, we can't have a say too much about—we're given a job to do, regardless. I mean, if it's new or old, our foreman says go and install this piece of equipment, make revisions on it, we have to do it. You get the work done. That's what you're after anyway, to get the job done. A lot of people come in here just to put their time in, but if we don't keep the place running, the company ain't gonna make money. I mean, they're here to make money. Our job is to keep the machines functioning for them to make that money.

It is tempting to read "pragmatic acceptance" into these two comments, since both employees stress the "have-to-get-it-done" aspect. But the only coercion involved in their scenario is the coercion of the bottom line; that is, the acceptance of the company's definition of efficiency. In addition, if acceptance had been predominantly pragmatic rather than normative, one might expect some critical attitude to show up in response to other questions related to decision making. But both employees were asked if there was any better way for decisions to be made and both answered that there was not.

In the participatory project Witte studied, one of the experiments was to eliminate "lead men." The employees had difficulty with that one, first informally reconstituting the functions of a lead and then bringing the role back in full. When Witte asked employees why they had been so resistant to the lack of a lead, one replied, "Authority is the way we are used to working."[28] "Getting used to" is central to acceptance in industrial production.

>I can't remember any job too hard for someone to tell me, "You'll get used to it." At Cambridge Tile, I worked shaking tiles next to a baking furnace. The temperature was over 130 degrees in the winter and we were not permitted to open the nearest window because it would then cost more to keep the furnace at the right temperature. When I trained on the job, my trainer told me that within a week, I would not even notice the heat. He was right.< CT, PO

In the preceding chapter, people got used to boring and onerous job tasks and unhealthy working conditions. Here, these two respondents have gotten used to hierarchy to such a degree that there appears to be no decision-making process at all, simply the flow of orders. Another employee stated the matter even more simply. While the answer appears trivial, it becomes interesting if taken seriously as his best (and complete) effort to respond to the question as posed:

Q. When there is some question about the work you're doing, when there's any decision to be made, how do those things get made? Who makes them?

Speaker C: I go in at night, generally I'm on my machine most of the time. But if they need another machine, they'll change me.

The last three speakers, A, B, and C, totalled more than one hundred years at NEC. But the same nonevaluatory attitude is also demonstrated by much newer employees.[29] Speaker D has been there two years, and Speaker E, six months.

Q. Sometimes a company will introduce a new procedure, a new job, or there will be some situation come up in which a decision will have to be made about how to do something. Have you had any of those kind of experiences and if so, how do they get handled?

Speaker D: I might have. I can't really think of them off hand. But if you have—if you didn't know how to do something, or you would have to ask how to do something, I think you would have to go to the foreman. Check with him and see what's right and what's wrong, because he oversees everything and he has to see that everything's done right.

Q. What sort of decisions are you involved in? Do they ever ask your opinion when they change your job or make new rules?

Speaker E: That's not much of my business. I guess the people in *[the administration building]* do that. I just do my job and go home. A lot of people walk around here with an attitude. I guess it's just human nature that you don't like the company you work for.

I specified earlier that this group was not wholly complacent. Some people in it "walked around with an attitude," but did not include decision making as an object of that attitude. Since any outcome must have been the product of a decision at some point, there are some informative inconsistencies in some respondents' accounts:

Q. When they change a job, when the company decides either to automate or in any other way change somebody's job, how is that decision made?

Speaker F: It usually comes from this building here. They control everything here, scheduling, everything. In 1975 there was a building down here, they used to make *[product name]*. And they found out it was taking more to make it than they could buy it from Japan. So they closed that building down and of course people lost their jobs down there.

Q. Do you know if in that situation the company talks with the people involved about it? Or with the union?

A. It goes right through the union. Everything here goes through the union. If they decide to close a building down, they close it down and lay you off. That's it. There's nothing you can do about it.

Q. Can you imagine any process different from that?

A. I don't think so. What do you mean? What are you trying to get to? *[I basically rephrase same question.]* Well, that's a hard question. Like I said, everything goes through the union.

Q. Do you feel that the way decisions are handled is reasonable?

Speaker G: Yah.

Q. Can you think of any different way it could be done?

A. No. Nobody wants to hang themselves, so if somebody finds something they don't know what's going on, they go up. They put the responsibility on somebody else who knows.

[In a later part of the interview, in response to the "Absolutely Wrong" question.]

A. What the company does sometimes is bring in outside contractors to do the work. According to the contract, all they need to do is, they notify us and say they are going to do it. So we had a meeting over that—they said that's all they're going to do, notify us. It's a big joke. Why even notify us when we have no—when we can't even fight it?

Q. Have there been any grievances filed about it?

A. Can't. Nothing there to file a grievance. According to the contract, all they have to do is notify us.

In the first case, the employee insisted that everything goes through the union while in virtually the same sentence he gave an example of a (very important) decision that he understood did not. In the second, the employee specifically was upset about exclusion from control, but had not thought of that when I asked him about process. These are not nonattitudes, if by that one means random observations that convey confusion more than contradiction. They are nonevaluations.

The resolution of the problem of inconsistency here is the obstacle posed by the presence of the boundaries described above. Both employees brought up problem areas beyond even the limited control of the union, and they noted the unilateral nature of the decision-making process. Both disagreed with the outcome. But neither raised any questions about the legitimacy of the process.

What may characterize the responses of people in this group to questions about decisions and authority is that orders are given and work proceeds. There is little expressed recognition of the existence of some structure of authority in which alternatives are weighed and decisions made. Process and outcome are not separate. The introduction of some formality in process is an important aspect of the program of most of the participation theorists. To those who advocate workplace democracy on the basis of "right," the existence of a process by which a citizenry can make decisions not subject to veto by a higher authority is the essence of legitimacy. To those who emphasize the "carryover effects," it is the act of participation that is most important; and for that, the more formality, the more carryover. Ronald Mason made into a cornerstone of his argument for participation at the workplace the "Proximity Hypothesis"—"the closer two experiences approximate each other, the more likely there will be a transference from one experience to the other."[30] That a section of the work force may not recognize that a decision-making apparatus does currently exist—a "traditional hierarchical" one—may explain, in part, why the demand for workplace democracy is louder in academia right now than it is on the factory floor.

Problem

There are employees whose views on exclusion differ sharply from those just discussed. When I asked the ending question on what people would change if given authority (the question labeled "One Thing" in the appendix), seven answers were some variant of "NEC should listen more to its employees." Only safety was mentioned more and only these two were mentioned more than once. There was also a difference in how some people fielded the question. Some of the other questions did not slide down well. They clashed in either vocabulary or substance with the terms in which people evaluated their own experience (as the "good place to work" section describes). Questions such as those labeled "Expect" brought some puzzlement and usually short, indecisive answers. The "participation" questions themselves drew a number of "What do you mean?" responses, as discussed above. Such was not the case in this group. The answers given by employees were immediate and emphatic, and sometimes had the feel of prepared speeches.

Q. Are employees ever asked their opinion on work situations?
A. Never. Never. Never. You hear a lot of rumors. And then you just

see it posted up. The employees are not consulted at all, or do not have any say or any anything as far as being involved in any change.

The very fact that employees deliver these speeches on the subject indicates its importance to them. In a variation on the theme of those who discuss "agenda setting," it could be as significant to know what people think *about* as what they think.[31] For some workers at NEC, aspects of the nondemocratic authority structure are a problem and a focus of critique.

Q. When there is a decision to be made regarding work *[I name some]*, who makes those decisions and how do you hear about it?
Speaker A: It's made way over our heads and we hear about it at the last—we don't have any say at all, if that's what you're asking me. The hourly people don't count. It's a terrible state of affairs. I see it happening every day and it's getting worse.

Speaker B: Who? Us? Listen to us? They don't know us from the fork trucks. They just want us to do our jobs, not make trouble and go quietly out the door. That's what I do. When I tell them something, they don't listen anyway.

These two employees provide the unifying theme for this group: "They don't listen and we don't count." But the fact that some people identify aspects of a factory authority structure as a problem does not tell us *which* aspects are objectionable. One candidate might be the immediate relationship between employees and supervisors. Could there be a lack of the previously described "informal participativeness?" Since that relationship can vary with the personality of the foreman, this would tend to trivialize the critique. But it does not seem that this is generally so. Most people (not just in this group) found an occasional supervisor to be "too pushy" or "too production-oriented" while others were not. Virtually everyone found their own foreman "someone I can talk to." Charles Walker, in a classic study of assembly-line workers, found that they usually did not think of individuals in supervision as responsible for problems they had with the job as a whole.[32] The employee quoted above who felt that "We don't count" explicitly discounted the specific relationship of foreman to employee as the source of the problem:

Q. Is there a big difference between different people you've worked under—different foremen?

Speaker A: Yes. But not that it matters because they can't do anything about it. Different personalities are easier to get along with, that's all.

Others found blame in vague forces that they did not claim to comprehend, but that sounded suspiciously like market forces:[33]

Q. [name several decisions] Who makes those decisions?
Speaker C: [laughs] The higher ups, always. We're the last ones to find out.
Q. In some situations, you must know more about a particular piece of machinery than somebody higher up. Do they ask you your opinion before they go ahead and do something?
A. They don't ask you outright but—I don't think they ever ask you, 'cause they don't want to admit that a worker is smarter than the engineers.
Q. Can you think of any other way decisions could be made?
A. Hmm. I don't know. That's a business—I don't know too much about business. They do things that maybe don't make sense to us, but it does make sense to them.
Q. Do they involve employees in making decisions?

Speaker D: No. I would have to say that they don't.
Q. [different way]?
A. I'm not sure that's the way it has to be. I don't know the economics of it.

The problem does not seem to be defined as one of supervisor style. But neither is it understood as a lack of formal democracy that should exist by right. No one in this group suggested that denial of the rights of industrial citizenship was the problem (or any other language to that effect). Nor did anyone propose formal control as the solution. While criticism of unresponsive management ran the full gamut of possibilities—from work process to personnel decisions to investment—it did not extend to the structure that underlies all three, which I have been calling factory authoritarianism. There was little discussion of the role private property might play in decision making. In the comments above on ''business,'' the context was markets rather than ownership rights. Property was not seen as a cause of ''They don't listen and we don't count,'' nor were property arguments used to justify the existence of the current structure. The criticism of decision making at NEC was not that hourly employees did not *decide*, but that they were not asked and, when they did voice opinions, were ignored.

Speaker E: I think there's some valid things that people in the building *[his department]* could put into the job and I sometimes feel they don't have the opportunity to. I sometimes feel that valid, legitimate suggestions that are made about what we're doing go in one ear and out the other-type thing and we get a lot of I-told-you-so's afterwards.

Speaker F: Certain mechanics, they don't care any more, because they know how to do their job, but when they come to the boss and say "This is how it should be done," *[they get back]*—"I don't care, do what I tell you." How many times can someone tell you that before *you* don't care, before you don't come and say, "I got an idea"?

The thrust of the criticism in this group about decision making at NEC was that there was poor communication from management, little effort made to solicit employees' suggestions, and a lack of recognition. Most of the examples given centered on the unwillingness of the company to listen to ways of improving specific jobs. I tried to broaden these discussions by asking each person about one or more of three issues that were hot items at the time: the rumored sale of the company, the proposed plan of reorganization for maintenance employees then being carried out, and the possible closing of building D.[34] These were (for the most part) not job-specific concerns. Were people consulted about these decisions? The answer followed the pattern above—criticism of management at NEC for failing to clarify its position or to discuss it honestly with employees.

Q. I've heard from other people about the reorganization plan. Has the company explained what they're doing to people?
Speaker G: No. Not at all. It's all rumors and a lot of them do eventually come out to be true.
Q. Are people concerned about their jobs?
A. Sure. There's a lot of job insecurity. I see it in employees who have been here twenty, thirty years. Our building may sink.

Alternatives

In short, to the extent that decision making was an area of concern to people, the problem was seen as an absence of team Taylorism. The clearest indication that this was so is seen not in the criticisms people had, but in their proposed alternatives and the issues addressed by those alternatives. After the questions about authority and participation, I asked each person (not just those in this group) whether he or she could imagine a factory being run any differently. There has been debate in the literature on subordination on the availability and importance of alternative conceptions among dominated groups. Some recent writings have emphasized the role that alternatives played and play in the experience of lower classes as they undergo industrialization and transition from a traditional to a market economy. Michael Taussig, writing about the Incas, who viewed industrial production as a literal contract with the devil, provided a thematic summary of this research:

> There is a moral holocaust at work in the soul of a society undergoing the transition from a precapitalist to a capitalist order. As the new form of society struggles to emerge from the old, as the ruling classes attempt to work the ruling principles into a new tradition, the pre-existing cosmogony of the workers becomes a critical front of resistance, or mediation, or both.[35]

Francis Hearn and Craig Calhoun have interpreted the resistance of the early English working class as motivated by "a remembered past"[36] in which a vision of what had been recently lost remained as a utopian critique of the present. Early resistance was primarily "a defence of the moral economy."[37] Given this derivation of the resistance to capitalism, it was logical to expect that it would diminish over time. Once the alternative vision disintegrated and the sense of lost rights faded, there was no choice left but adaptive mechanisms—notably reformism and incorporation:

> Without [critical thought], man—as he has proven so often in the past—will either resign himself to, or accept as normal, material deprivation, economic deterioration and the continued denial of self-fulfillment.[38]

Scott disputes the argument that dominated classes cannot conceive of alternatives to their continued subordinate status. Even when the argument is put in its weakest and most defensible form—that it is the "central features of a mode of domination and not just its details" that come to be seen as inevitable—he finds contrary evidence in his study of a village in Malaysia.[39] There is no reason why a subordinate group or individuals in that group cannot at least conceive of a reversal of "the present distribution of status and rewards," and at times the negation of it. The response of people when I invited them to speculate about alternatives does not seem to indicate that such reversals or negations are part of the conventional wisdom of workers at NEC.[40] What did exist were forcefully argued ideas for amelioration of excesses and abuses in the current authority system. Some people in *both* categories simply answered "No," they could not think of any other way of making decisions. This does *not* mean—and I am *not* claiming—that these people are thoroughly acquiescent, particularly since some of them are in the "They don't listen and we don't count" category. Nor am I claiming that they might not come up with alternatives at other times when not faced with a stranger and a tape recorder. What I *am* claiming is that these people do not carry a ready-made alternative with them, some notion of a fair decision-making process against which to measure the current one.

On the other hand, a minority of people in the "problem" category did propose an alternative.

Q. Do they talk with people on the floor about decisions?

Speaker A: That's where you have a real lack of communication. An engineer might come to me and say to me, "Look, I've got twenty-five tons of steel there, I-beams and what not, I've got to make load cells and weigh these things—and I've got to have it by Friday." Look buddy, me and what army? It's totally unreasonable. *[Goes on to say that he did it his own way and forced the engineer to accept it.]*

Q. Let me play the role of the company for a minute. Do you think a company could operate that way? Do you think a company could operate where they tried to make decisions by asking people and tried to get input?

A. I certainly do. I think if the company gives more credit where credit is due and sincerely instills upon the work force that they have confidence in them, that what they expect would be generated. It might be a little slow in coming in the beginning but I think that kind of atmosphere could be generated if NEC was to try to operate more in that manner. People like to generate some kind of enthusiasm about what they're doing for a living.

Q. Can you think of any different way a factory could be run?

Speaker B [the employee who answered with three "nevers" about participation]: I think if there was a better relationship between management and the hourly employees—blue-collar workers—I think it would be a better place to work. I think people would feel more involved in being part of the company, than just considering it an eight-hour job.

When these people specified or when I pressed them to specify how this "better relationship" could be brought about, the principal vehicle turned out to be the departmental meeting:

Q. Do you think there's some better way, or can you imagine a better way that things could be organized?

Speaker C: Personally, I feel that once a month what they should do is get everybody together, shift by shift, sit down and discuss—say, "Is there anything you feel that we can do that would make things easier?" Write them down and do something about it. In the military, we had something called a captain's call where the CO comes down and he asks you your bitches or your qualms. If possible, he gets it changed. Here, there's never a meeting. You never get a chance to tell somebody upstairs, "Look, this should be changed."

Speaker D: People say when some kind of change takes effect, they are not given the opportunity to be made aware of this change. They don't have no say-so in the matter. Whether they would accept that change or not, it's out of their hands. They are so irrelevant to the situation, whether they accept it or not, it's going to happen anyway.

Q. Can you think of any different way a company could be run so that doesn't happen?

A. Yes. I think the same as they utilize the avenue of having safety meetings, I think they should also devise some type of program that would make aware to the employees that, "We're concerned about problems and these are the changes we'll be making. What are your opinions and what are your feelings toward these changes?"

The best overview of team Taylorism comes from one of my re-interviewees whom I will call "Paul." He is forty-six years old, but has only worked at NEC for four years. He previously held jobs ranging from office and sales work to another large factory ("Apex"). Paul has shaped team Taylorism into a coherent critique. These questions and answers are from the first interview:

Q. When a company makes decisions that affect your job, is your experience that they talk to the people involved, or do they just make the decisions on their own?

Paul: That's probably the greatest drawback in a factory. There's no input in these decisions. In most cases, let's face it, they don't even tell the union.

Q. Do you think there is some other way that a factory can conduct its business, other than decisions made in the administration building and then imposed on people?

A. I was hoping you would ask me that tonight. Yes. For example, at Apex we have a situation whereby once a week all the employees in the department meet with management and we discuss the problems that are occurring in that department and the best way to remedy them. I feel they should have that in all plants throughout this country, because obviously this country has a challenge on its hands. I feel the American worker can meet that challenge. However, he cannot meet that challenge if you don't let him become a part of it. They fail to recognize this.

The alternative conception in these responses, which represent the most thought-out in the sample, is that the responsibility of the company is to listen and inform. Neither the ownership of assets nor the location of final decision-making authority is a subject of the critique. In his article on the "Japanization" of the U.S. auto industry, Wood argued that team Taylorism was not even fundamentally opposed to old-fashioned Taylorism, "providing, that is, that it involves [employees] offering rationalization suggestions."[41] Everyone, as indicated in the beginning of this chapter, identified the location of authority ("this building here"). Some simply did not pay much attention to the source of orders—it was as much a part of the working day as clocking in. Others saw it as problem, but those who offered solutions proposed only that the same authority structure be tempered with attentiveness.

The texture of people's sentiments about participation should cast some doubt on the usual "trade-off" argument. In the "trade-off" scenario, workers have simply chosen to maximize other values than workplace democracy, "trading" democracy, in effect, for wages or security. In a world of scarce resources, people cannot maximize all values at the same time and it must not be worth workers' time to demand greater participation. The proof of that pudding is that they have not done so. But for the "trade-off" argument to have any validity, the terms of the trade must be known. People have hypothetically traded a value (democracy) with which they are not familiar in an industrial setting for other values (wages and, less substantially, security) they are trying to maximize. This "trade" does not seem to have been made consciously, and it is not a very compelling theory that tells us that a trade is made objectively, particularly since the "trade-off" theory is the specific archenemy of the theory of "objective interest." This will be the topic of chapter 7.

We have seen that some segment of the work force at NEC does not evaluate the process of decision making as a separate entity. These people were certainly not conscious of "trading" democracy for some other value. Those people who see lack of democracy as a problem might potentially fit the argument. Could the missing pieces of the critique and the alternatives be on some level a trade—the current hierarchical system can stay as long as "they listen and we count?" Obviously, this study cannot answer this question conclusively. But there are aspects of the attitudes on decision making in this second group that make this doubtful also. The accounting of missing questions cannot be taken one-sidedly as legitimating the present industrial order. Those who delivered speeches about the lack of concern by NEC for its employees do so as criticism of the prevailing order. While the range of alternatives that people discussed was limited, the *desire* for alternatives was strong.

Q. Do you think there's a way a company could be changed to make it enjoyable to work for?

Speaker F: There's got to be a way. I watched a program on how the Japanese are doing it. Management and the hourly people got involved with each other. They listen, first off, and they come to agreements. Everybody's got to give a little and I think that would work if the company would come down to our level. These people sit up in *[the administration]* building and they don't know what goes on. They just know what they want to see—*x* amount of production.

The thing I would like to change is the attitude generated by the company as perceived by the people who work for it. The average guy down there, especially the guys that don't have much in the line of education, doing menial labor, their idea of looking at the company is—this company's blood, sweat, and tears. "They just want my labor." I'd like to be able to change that.

✦ ✦ ✦

The arguments in this chapter might seem to imply that employees at NEC are trapped in a perpetual pattern of limited vision and constrained alternatives. This is not necessarily the only possible conclusion. The critique of exclusion as expressed by this group of employees is open-ended. If NEC were to implement several of the alternative suggestions, there is no reason to think new alternatives would not occur to people.[42] There is also no reason why that process could not lead into examination of various aspects of the legitimacy of private ownership and undemocratic control. The sentiments expressed about participation do not warrant pushing the ''missing questions'' formulation to its Marcusian limits. Witte's findings, which suggest that people want more participation in exactly those areas where it is currently permitted, seem to apply also to these NEC employees.[43] If my interpretation of the limited nature of alternatives differs somewhat from that of Scott, it nonetheless does not permanently close the door to the possibility of imagining ''reversals'' or ''negations.'' The search for the cause of the problems discussed by workers in this section has already led several people to question conventional managerial prerogatives. The search for a remedy, on the other hand, may be particularly conditioned by the use of familiar ideas and language. But even the alternatives already held should be understood more as a product of dissatisfaction with the present distribution of authority than as satisfaction with some other. Team Taylorism, while in the stable of contemporary industrial relations, does not yet exist at NEC.

Notes

1. For example, Robert Lane, "From Political to Industrial Democracy."
2. The categories are given different names by different authors, but the names usually describe largely overlapping sets of meanings.
3. It usually solicits their help, though. See Paul Blumberg, *Industrial Democracy*; Robert Dahl, *Preface to Economic Democracy*. The usual conclusion about productivity is that the evidence is inconclusive, but that it is certainly not damaging to the case based on right.
4. Dahl, *Preface*, chapter 4.
5. David Ellerman, "The Employment Relation, Property Rights and Organizational Democracy," p. 269.
6. U.S. Department of Health, Education, and Welfare, *Work in America*, chapters 4 and 5.
7. Carol Pateman, *Participation and Democratic Theory;* Ronald Mason, *Participatory and Workplace Democracy;* Christopher Gunn, *Workers' Self-Management in the United States.*
8. Stephen Wood, "The Cooperative Labour Strategy in the U.S. Auto Industry," p. 417. Sometimes this argument is also made by some on the left who see democratic workplace organization as the key to restoring productivity to U.S. industry (Samuel Bowles, David Gordon, and Thomas Weisskopf, *Beyond the Waste Land*, p. 168; Barry Bluestone and Bennett Harrison, *The Deindustrialization of America*, p. 260).
9. "Summary ROAB Planning Meeting," 1/12/81 (document in my possession).
10. Wood, "The Cooperative Labour Strategy," p. 428.
11. There is considerable discretion involved in every job, including the simplest and most repetitive (such work is called "bullwork" at NEC). See Ken Kusteror, *Know-how on the Job: The Important Working Knowledge of "Unskilled Workers,"* for an account of the skills involved in doing unskilled work.
12. Arnold Tannenbaum, *Hierarchy in Organizations*, p. 216. Tannenbaum contrasted this practice—along with upward mobility and greater pay—with the altered forms of organization in Yugoslavian factories and Israeli kibbutzim.
13. My own experience is that this variation in personal foreman style can be used at its most cynical in the "good-cop, bad-cop" routine. Of course, I cannot provide any data to substantiate this, and it certainly is true that some foremen try harder than others to get along with hourly workers.
14. This is a paraphrase and summary of the arenas of "exclusion from control" taken from Eric Olin Wright, *Class, Crisis and the State*, p. 73; and Stephen Hill, *Competition and Control at Work*, p. 11.
15. The extent of internal union democracy is beyond the scope of this study. The ability of individuals who are not union officials to participate in any aspect of union decision making is often highly vitiated (see for instance chapter 7 of John Gaventa, *Power and Powerlessness: Quiescence and Rebellion in an Appalachian Valley*). This must then be multiplied by the limited ability of the union to influence company practice in order to find the minuscule "participation" that collective bargaining offers to individuals.
16. David Montgomery, for instance, lists the following in an index of "control" strikes in the early twentieth century: "enforcement of work rules, union recognition, discharge of unpopular foremen or retention of popular ones, regulation of layoffs or dismissals, and actions of sympathy with other groups of workers" (*Workers' Control in*

America, p. 98). In the usage of control in this chapter, none of these would fit, since they are not demands for the right to decide. But they are different from wage demands and in Montgomery's context of the changing history of labor goals, they do seem to be "control"-related. The reason for the ambiguity is that when one has no power at all, virtually any demand is an infringement on the prerogatives of the superordinates.

17. For example, Samuel Gompers's rejection of control as a labor demand: "Collective bargaining in industry does not imply that wage earners shall assume responsibility for financial management. There is no belief held in the trade unions that its members shall control the plant or usurp the rights of owners" (quoted in John Simmons and William Mares, *Working Together*, p. 31). Labor had "help" from the capitalist class in making this decision; that is, the imposed cost of fighting for control was higher than that of gaining recognition and incremental wage increases within a stable framework of industrial subordination. See Robert Cole, *Work, Mobility, and Participation*, p. 104; Alan Fox, *Beyond Contract: Work, Power and Trust Relations*, p. 204.

18. One committeeman refused to admit any out-of-bounds areas, no matter how hard I prodded him and provided him with examples.

19. I should point out that this is the *best* case that can be made for unions as a vehicle for participation. Others (Stanley Aronowitz, *False Promises: The Shaping of the American Working Class;* Jeremy Brecher, *Strike!*) argue that one of the main functions of unions has become disciplining the work force for management.

20. James Atleson, *Values and Assumptions in American Labor Law*, p. 61; the case cited was *NLRB* v. *Babcock and Wilcox* (1956).

21. Keith Bradley and Alan Gelb, *Worker Capitalism: The New Industrial Relations*, p. 93; Simmons and Mares, *Working Together*, chapter 3.

22. John Witte, *Democracy, Authority, and Alienation in Work*, p. 27.

23. Ibid. Witte did not draw this conclusion, but it can be extrapolated from the tables on pp. 27 and 28.

24. To complete all the logical possibilities, there was no one who advocated less participation than they currently have.

25. For example, I asked one production worker about a variety of areas of potential decision making. Her reply was a somewhat puzzled, "Oh, we don't have anything to do with that." Initially, I had her penciled in for this first category. On closer listening, I realized that she had latched onto the word "shipping" in my question and thought I was asking her if part of her job was to arrange shipping schedules. It may still be worth noting in passing how foreign decision making is to employees, but this woman's specific response was not a nonevaluation.

26. James Scott, *Weapons of the Weak: Everyday Forms of Peasant Resistance*, chapter 7.

27. These are separable perceptions. Some extremely demanding tasks people are given may not be viewed as "wrong"—if that is given the interpretation of "counterproductive."

28. Witte, *Democracy, Authority, and Alienation in Work*, p. 124.

29. Charles Sabel *(Work and Politics)* emphasizes the importance of "careers at work" in attitude formation (chapter 3). My groupings tended to place the very old and the very young in the first category and those with three to twenty years in the second. There is no basis for inferring that this is a representative finding (for reasons of sample size already mentioned). But there is every reason for future investigation to see if this inverted U-shaped relationship to interest in participation is valid.

30. The "carryover" theorists draw heavily on Jean Jacques Rousseau, particularly his emphasis in the *Social Contract* on the transformative possibilities of hands-on participation: "In a well-run City, everyone rushes to assemblies. . . . As soon as someone says 'What do I care?' about the affairs of state, the state should be considered lost" *(On the Social Contract*, p. 102).

31. Bernard Cohen, *The Press and Foreign Policy.*

32. Charles Walker and Robert Guest, *The Man on the Assembly Line,* p. 140.

33. There is a well-documented tendency for Americans to use market norms to evaluate economic interactions. (Jennifer Hochschild, *What's Fair?;* Robert Lane, "Market Justice, Political Justice"; Herbert McClosky and John Zaller, *The American Ethos: Public Attitudes toward Capitalism and Democracy.* This neither contradicts, nor is it contradicted by, my reading of these employees' comments. In this case, the market ("economics," "business") is responsible for a condition to which they respond negatively (exclusion), but is in itself impervious to criticism.

34. The last two are closely related. NEC was (at the time of the interviews) moving toward making each building accountable for its own maintenance costs and for its own profits and losses. Everyone understood that building D, the oldest building and the most labor-intensive, would be the most vulnerable under such a plan.

35. Michael Taussig, *The Devil and Commodity Fetishism in South America,* p. 271.

36. Francis Hearn, *Domination, Legitimation and Resistance,* p. 107; Craig Calhoun, *The Question of Class Struggle: Social Foundations of Popular Radicalism during the Industrial Revolution.* The two are not entirely in agreement. Calhoun denies that it is an alternative that impels people to resist: "Their way of life is simply being obliterated" (p. 233), and they lash out; hence, his formulation that the resistance to early capitalism was led by "reactionary rebels." The agreement between the two on which the paragraph rests is that it was "a vision of lost rights which moved English people to protest or rebel" (Calhoun, p. 102).

37. Calhoun, *The Question of Class Struggle,* p. 60.

38. Hearn, *Domination,* p. 267. See also Carmen Sirianni:

> A critical theory of society requires reference to utopian possibilities. A purely negative critique is ultimately groundless; a critical theory must justify its normative basis and attempt to elaborate the social possibilities of the human species if it is to have either explanatory or emancipatory power. ["Production and Power in a Classless Society: A Critical Analysis of the Utopian Dimensions of Marxist Theory," p. 35]

39. James Scott, *Weapons of the Weak,* chapter 8.

40. A roughly similar finding for the general population about the nature of alternative conceptions may be found in Paul Sniderman, *A Question of Loyalty,* pp. 168–70. Sniderman also discusses the way in which those alternatives and evaluations of the present interact, as does Mann, *Consciousness and Action among the Western Working Class,* p. 60.

41. Wood, "The Cooperative Labour Strategy," p. 428.

42. This is precisely what happened in Witte's experience, as described in chapter 6. Bottom-line decision-making power was left ambiguous by the democratic procedures that were initiated, and some of the discussions by employees pushed and probed the limits of the company's surrender of authority. See Sabel, *Work and Politics,* pp. 129–30: "[S]uccessful incremental extensions of a group's original claims can, if successful, lead to a shift in the balance of power between contestants, and ultimately to a reformulation of the original claim itself."

43. John Witte, *Democracy, Authority, and Alienation in Work,* chapter 3. In a variation of that finding, workers in two democratically controlled enterprises—the American plywood coops in the Northwest and the Mondragon cooperatives in the Basque region of Spain—have evolved a much wider sphere of questions in which they feel participation is a matter of right (Edward Greenberg, *Workplace Democracy,* p. 52, for the plywood coops; Henk Thomas and Chris Logan, *Mondragon: An Economic Analysis,* p. 191 on the latter cooperatives).

5

Expectations and
Frustrations

Workers are *as a matter of fact units of manpower but must not be* treated *as if they are. This of course is sound policy because workers do not generally like to think of themselves as commodities even though the accountant doing his sums on the computer prices labor in exactly the same way as he prices new materials and depreciation of plant, etc. Translated a bit further: treat your workers as if they are people and then perhaps they will not notice they are commodities.*

—Anthony Lane and Kenneth Roberts[1]

This chapter explores the strategies employees use to try to resolve the tensions inherent in commodification of labor—the principal one being to find and define moral worth in their workday contributions. While these definitions lead employees to make demands on the behavior and attitudes of NEC management, they also help create employee motivation in an area where management goals are vulnerable—the sphere of employee discretion. Sociologists have asked why employees work as hard as they do; this chapter will provide at least part of the answer by examining the self-generated work norms of NEC employees, and suggest ways in which those norms condition important strands of oppositional thinking.

Labor, Labor Power, and Laborer

One of the unavoidable problems of writing about industrial relations is that no language is readily available for making the necessary distinctions between labor and capital. It is not hard to find or create a convincing argument that these two entities approach any contractual arrangement with vastly unequal resources. But this description still leaves the impression of two similarly constituted interest groups with unequal strength working toward mutual adjustment. Part of my project so far has been to examine the informal contract that employees create and use to evaluate their circumstances. There is certainly a process of mutual adjustment in the creation and fulfillment of this contract. But it is not one between similarly constituted, though unequal entities.[2]

One of the building blocks of Marx's political economy was the distinction between labor power and labor. The former was the ability to work, the latter, the process of working. Labor power was a commodity, the only commodity the worker had to sell. The worker was not a commodity, nor was the work performed. The worker *owned* a commodity—essentially putting his or her two hands on the market (although the value of the hands could be increased by previously acquired skills).[3] The capitalist purchased the hands and the worker proceeded to labor. The living person, the work produced, and the commodity "labor power" were analytically distinct. Marx went on to add two other elements with different derivations—the labor theory of value and the determination of the price of labor power[4]—and concluded that in the difference between labor and labor power lay the hidden mechanism of the accumulation of profit. The validity of the latter two elements is not crucial to the argument in this chapter. The picture of a mass of hands on the labor market is, however; it gives us one way to understand why the difference between labor and capital is more than one of unequal resources.[5]

The relationship between the living capitalist and capital itself is a contingent one. "Common sense" may fail here, since that relationship has been so well defined for so long that it may appear natural. The two are theoretically separable. There are laws governing ownership of productive property that have changed in important ways even when the essentials of ownership have not (owners of chemical plants, for instance, are no longer completely free to pollute), and which, being socially produced, are capable of further change should the outcome of the current relationship come to be seen as socially unacceptable. Those who argue that management is more important than ownership in guiding the affairs of corporations are describing an even more historically time-bound relationship.[6] While the capitalists may be "capital personified," the personae and their physical counterparts retain their separate existence.

On the other hand, the process of labor involves both labor power and the laborer combined into one rather inseparable person. The marketed hands only come attached to a sentient human being, no matter how much either their owners or purchasers would like that not to be so. This fact has two consequences, stemming from the two perspectives of the relationship, the perspectives of employer-laborer and laborer–labor power. In the first case, the employer is faced with the problem of a commodity with a mind; that is, the exact feature that distinguishes hands from other tools carries a problem with it. Even the most subdivided tasks can be carried out with varying speed and quality. Managers *must* therefore pay attention to the discretion employees have in carrying out their jobs. In the second case, there is no "instrumental" attitude on the part of employees, no matter how consciously or cynically constructed, which can be completely successful in allowing the employee to divorce him- or herself from that person who goes to work for forty to fifty hours a week. I look here at each of these in turn, although the interview material gives information mainly on the second, since my study as a whole concentrates on attitudes among subordinates. Toward this end, I begin to make more use of the re-interview material and will introduce some additional characters. The re-interviews were even less structured than the first ones, and in some cases, I have not reproduced the question to which a comment was made because the interviewee took off on an informative tangent. Most of the information from the original interviews was taken from answers to the "Expect" question: "What do you expect from the company? What do you think they expect from you?"

Discretion

>A ten-year employee was discussing good and bad supervisors with me shortly after I started. "Most of the time, it doesn't make any difference. The job is there, you do it. But there's always going to be a time when they want a little extra out of you, something that isn't required. That's when you can get them. If a guy [supervisor] gives you a fair shake, you do it. If someone's been a pain in the ass, that's when you stick it to him."< PG, PO

Claus Offe pointed out that any employer "has, for better or worse, to rely on the willingness of the worker to 'give away' his/her physical and intellectual capacities by applying them to concrete labor tasks."[7] If at one moment a job seems defined by management, the next moment it will change, as my former co-worker indicated above. The degree of discretion is certainly not high in most jobs at NEC, not even in the "new working class" chemical operator jobs,[8] which are the very jobs about which a maintenance employee said in chapter 3, "You just go in, do the thing and go home." But management understands that the "willingness" in Offe's description can make a dollars-and-cents difference. In my interview with the LRS, I told him about the "Expect" question for employees and asked him in reverse form:

Q. What do you think employees expect from the company?
A. Newer employees are expecting more and willing to contribute less than, say, the older part of the population—I think we're finding somewhat less of a willingness to work hard, less commitment, to put in time and waiting for good things to happen down the road. [Other answers indicate that he did not mean people were leaving; rather, that they worked with less effort.]

Q. [I asked about the anticipation of upward mobility. At first, he took it to mean only promotion to foreman. I clarified that I meant "within the bargaining unit."]
A. That's our objective—not only to get people here but to get them to do as much as they're capable of doing and as much as we're prepared to pay them to do.

The fact that the company wants to get people "to do as much as they're capable of doing" may not seem noteworthy,[9] but his contrast of that goal with "getting people here" and his echoing of Offe's "willingness" variable indicate that discretion is a source of concern to management. When another member of NEC management gave me a tour of the plant, I asked him (in a discussion I did not tape) how they evaluated new hires. He told me there were three criteria: the record of the new hire in coming to work on time and every day; job performance; and whether or not the employee kept a "positive attitude." He said that if only the first two criteria were met, they would still attempt to terminate the worker at the end of the probationary period, although not always successfully. This policy on new hires suggests that NEC is not satisfied with the simple purchase of hands, knowing that they come attached to a person who may misuse them. It also demonstrates the problem that demanding a "positive attitude" poses for a hiring and promoting process based ostensibly on bureaucratic rationality.[10] Industry does not leave obedience to chance. If people do not come equipped with a positive attitude, NEC takes some steps to insure that they will learn it. This is Paul's description of the socialization of new hires:

I'm working with a new employee. This new employee has sixty days' probation. This new employee, whenever the foreman says something, she has to jump. Okay? That person to me is being overabused as far as work goes. That person doesn't have a chance to rest. Foremen take advantage of new hires in all factories. The company says, now's our chance, we can do anything we want with them.
Q. All new hires might be a little scared.
A. That's what they do, they throw that into them. The foreman jumps on you—"I want this done *[snaps fingers]*, I want this done. And when you're finished, do that." In all the jobs I had, the same tactic is used. What they do is, they jump on that person the first day and they instill fear in them. "I'm God Almighty and what I say goes." They got you in a kind of stage of turmoil. And then when an older person tells you based on his experience, you're not going to believe him, because you're new, you're scared. Even if what the person is telling me is true, I cannot

> afford to listen to him. That's the key word. I cannot afford to listen
> to him. Case closed.

This coercive orientation is intended to give the employee some indication of what the company regards as a positive attitude. One common mechanism for using compulsion to inculcate obedience is "busy work"—the practice of assigning employees (particularly new hires) a whole range of nearly useless tasks when a machine is down.[11] The reason a company takes extra measures with new hires—"overabusing" them in the probably unintentional but highly apt phrase Paul used above—is that there is also a countersocialization process taking place. I have already pointed out the discretion involved in even the most standardized production jobs. This gives employees the opportunity to assert certain (limited) prerogatives about the time and pace of work.[12] Management knows that at some point, every new hire will learn the employee-influenced work norms, but wants them to hear supervisory expectations first. Another new employee explained the role that other employees played during the breaking-in period:

> They'll tell you what to do, how to do it, how fast to do it—break you
> in to the whole atmosphere of the plant and tell you—"if you do this,
> you'll be fine."

A second speaker, now with ten years in, reflecting on her first weeks:

> When I first came to work here in building D, we used to fill the
> hoppers. And I saw that if I worked at about an even pace, on an
> average night I could fill about seven hoppers. The second day I
> was there, they told me, "you are to fill no more than four hoppers
> and that's it, no matter what else happens." And this was the older
> people, the people who had been around there for awhile.
> Q. Well, why did they do that?
> A. That's just the pace they wanted to keep. The company went
> along with it as long as they got their work done.

The probationary period is not the only time when socialization and countersocialization around "willingness" take place, but it is a particularly important one.[13]

It has been argued that the existence of discretion in performing jobs is a source of informal power workers have achieved. Michael Crozier called such power "control over conditions of uncertainty."[14] The countersocialization discussed above does in fact indicate some ability to control work pace, but there are limits. NEC employees seemed to know just how far their discretion extended. The following comments were in answer to the "Expect" question:

Speaker A: I might have a bad day here and there, just like anybody else, but they understand that, as long as they can usually rely on you. If I go in, they give me a job assignment, I know if it's a hot job or not. If it's a hot job, they expect me to produce. If it's not a hot job, they expect me to put eight hours in. That's maintenance. In production, it was whatever routine you were involved in.

Speaker B: As long as you don't give 'em a screwing, they won't come down on you.

Halle documented a similar range of discretion and obligation. He described in detail some of the work secrets that operators accumulate, including shortcuts, knowledge of machine idiosyncrasies, and operation on the borderline of danger. The company was fully aware of the existence of this secret knowledge and was willing to tolerate some variation in production (based what use could be made of the secrets) in exchange for overall regularity and quality.[15] What he was describing was not anything particular to chemical workers or to skilled workers, but a specific example of the push and pull inherent in the "willingness" factor, a concrete instance of the distinction between the purchase of labor power and the process of labor.

Employee discretion, limited but real, is something of a loose cannon for employers. There is potential for loss of substantial control over the work process; at least there is constant vying and bargaining over the use of time. There are four possible resolutions to this problem of control, three of which are the result of the company's strategic choice. They can lose—that is, they can settle for the lowest output commensurate with formal fulfillment of job requirements. This is a rather costly alternative. It would be precisely a surrender to the "systematic soldiering" Frederick Taylor identified as industry's central problem. They can police, the opposite of settling; this would mean constant supervision and surveillance. If a company could gather up all the production secrets, give a constant flow of orders, and apply penalties for failure to carry out those orders, there would be no room for discretion. But this is also a costly alternative as well as being too cumbersome to have any chance of succeeding. The process described above in socializing new employees is an attempted shortcut to achieve those ends, but one the employer knows cannot be completely effective. One of the few advantages for subordinates in any pyramidal system is that there cannot be enough representatives of the ruling authorities to go around. If coercion (in this case, closely supervised movements) has not created an atmosphere that carries over to the lunch table, its effect (on new employees, for example) will be transitory. Another alternative would be to fine-tune the labor process by creating miniature market relations within the factory.[16] Piecework is one form of bribery. Another is merit pay (the few cents an hour difference a company can pay people working in the same job classification). But as Burawoy argued in *Manufacturing Consent*, the bonuses available to workers based on increased output (the situation he was discussing was piecework) did not satisfactorily explain the degree of effort people made beyond what was minimally required to satisfy quotas.[17] While each of these three strategies may be insufficient, and each has a cost (or perhaps more accurately, each is insufficient because the cost would make full implementation of each strategy counterproductive), each also makes an appearance virtually everywhere. Every company will try to bribe and coerce, and every company will also have to settle at times.

But it is also possible that there is some belief system among employees that is not primarily instilled by the company, a system that motivates them to perform their jobs at a level higher than minimum standards. The existence of countersocialization is not evidence of an employee-based work norm of maximum shirking, although it is evidence of a difference between management- and employee-based norms. Juan Martinez Alier found such a belief system among Spanish agricultural workers. The work norm was known as *"cumplir,"* which Alier interpreted as the need to "perform work according to well-established standards of quality and effort, because this is normally felt by laborers as being morally obligatory."[18] Is there some norm similar to *"cumplir"* at NEC? If so, why? To examine this possibility, we leave the discussion of the distinction between labor power and labor and turn to that between labor power and the laborer.

Great Expectations

If management cannot detach the hands it purchases from the person who accompanies them, so too the worker cannot send his or her hands to work alone for eight hours a day. The rest of the body inexorably follows. Unlike the relation of owners to their possession (capital), the inextricable connection between labor power (the workers' possession) and its possessor forces people to try to find some intrinsic worth in their work. Hyman and Brough in *Social Values and Industrial Relations* probe the moral dimensions of what are normally thought of as prosaic workplace relations. Their point is that the exercise of authority at work is both expressed in and reliant on "principles of fairness." An examination of the answers to the "Expect" question reveals expectations shot through with moral terminology. This quality helps explain why people work with more care and speed than is minimally required to retain their jobs.

The "Expect" question did not appear to arouse great excitement. Even among people who had a great deal to say on other topics, the standard reply here was only few lines. But in these brief responses, a large majority gave answers that added some moral category to the simple exchange relation of work for wages and benefits.[19] The categories are described below, but I should point out that I have been fairly generous in assigning a moral dimension; this is both warranted and proper because the nature of the simple exchange relation is so precise. I introduce four approximate subcategories of moral dimensions, which are certainly not mutually exclusive. My concern is less with what divides them than with what they have in common—some expectation about their job that goes beyond the cash nexus.

Conditions

The people who are most problematically part of the "moral" category are those who emphasized some aspects of working conditions. Working conditions are usually included in the holy trinity of orthodox labor relations—the other two being wages and hours. Working conditions can be presented simply as one utility out of many that people might want to maximize. Person X wants more money; person Y prefers that the same investment be made in cleaner floors. I do not think these speakers present their expectations in this light. They convey a sense of injury, even of betrayal.

The following three responses are to the "Expect" question:

Speaker A: They signed a contract with our union to give me work, pay me for it. But there's other things—it's more than just paying a person in a place like this. Better working conditions, cleaner working conditions. In our position *[the speaker is in production repair]*, I think they should give you more help to get these jobs done. At one time, I can remember we had six people, seven people all doing the same jobs that we're doing *[by themselves now]*. And they're getting more work today than they did when they had six or seven people.

Speaker B: Out of the company, I'd like to see more of a work force to be able to get the production out, and the quality, and I think they can both be done. I think they're more concerned about the quantity than the quality. It seems there's always a rush to get the material out to meet deadlines for customers, which maybe there should be a little more flexibility.[20]

Speaker C: Things that I expected from the company that I don't think we get *[I did not ask him simply to tell me what he did not get]*, one is good housekeeping. They say that safety is first and I don't believe that. I believe production is first.

This last speaker continued with what can only be called a tirade about safety that lasted the rest of the interview.[21] All three thought the company had an obligation in the area they described, and felt that they had a right to expect a more hospitable working environment. It is not the nature of the expectation itself that leads me to include them in this category but the formulation of that expectation in terms of right. Each felt affronted at what they saw as management's transgression of decent workplace conduct. Of course, at least hypothetically, each employee could have felt just as strongly about the importance of his particular issue if he felt that NEC's performance were satisfactory. Or the sense of injury could have been similar in the area of wages (although in fact there was no such case here, there certainly would have been at some of the other jobs I have worked). In the first case, it would probably have been harder to discern the response as one separate from a simple exchange demand, but it would have been correct to do so, nonetheless. In the second case—a demand for wages expressing some obligation—it would have been appropriate to place people giving such an answer in this category if the proposed criterion for wages were "fair" rather than "enough." The question asked what people expected and if their answers indicated that an expectation was based on what they considered fair or right, the response can plausibly be said to embody something other than a simple concept of exchange.

Fairness

The next subgroup proposed the term "fairness" as what they expected, although their short answers left it for the most part unexplained.

Speaker A: I expect fair treatment and a safe and healthy work environment.

Speaker B: As long as the company treats me fair, we'll treat them fair. One hand washes the other, right?

Speaker C: I expect to be treated fairly and honestly, which usually does happen.

Speaker D: What do I expect from them? A fair shake. Other than to get a paycheck when its due, no undue pressure put upon me unjustly. I've had bad days where you get very little done and you say—"Look, I didn't get this done." *[They say]* "No problem, we'll pick up on that tomorrow."

Hyman and Brough point out somewhat whimsically that while industrial relations are in reality a "smash and grab" proposition, they are often larded over with talk of "fairness."[22] The above remarks do not define the concept very clearly, nor did a follow-up question asking them what they meant by the term "fair." All the employees who answered with this generality felt that they *had* by and large been treated fairly; perhaps that made it harder for them to single out any of the elements that went into a construction of the category "fairness." It is probably harder to demonstrate dramatically the presence of "one hand washing another" than to demonstrate its absence in a particular case, as the previous group did. But the expectation of fairness—even as an overall gloss—belongs in the "moral" category no less by virtue of its vagueness.

Flexibility

Speaker D in the previous group began to move "fairness" in the specific direction of the next subcategory, which centers on the desire for flexibility. "Flexibility" here is used in a manner similar to Alvin Gouldner's "indulgencies"—areas in which a company permitted its employees to depart from the formal contract. In Gouldner's study of a mine, these included protection in case of injury, leniency in case of absenteeism or work rule violations, and some allowance for personal use of company material (stealing).[23]

Speaker A: I expect to have a job. I expect for the raises to come when they're due, for my pay to at least meet the outside standards. I expect the company to help me in times of need. If I have a problem, I would like the company to help me.

Speaker B: I expect the company to pay me a reasonable wage for doing a good job and to be a little bit flexible with me over and above the contract. If I need an emergency vacation and I've got vacation time coming, maybe they can bend their rules a little bit, which they have for me in the past. They want you to follow their rules—I mean, everybody breaks a little of their rules—little white sins and nobody's perfect in that respect.

Speaker C: I don't expect—just, pay me on Thursday, that's all. *[If this speaker had stopped here, he would clearly have been excluded from the "moral" category. He paused for a second and then went on.]* Don't give me any hassle. Everybody has a good day and a bad day. If I have a bad day, don't bug me, it's just a bad day. Let's say you had a personal problem and needed a day off. You just pick up the phone and call them and say, "Hey, I got a personal problem and I won't be in." There's no hassles. As long as you don't abuse the unwritten privileges, you're fine.

Respect

The purpose of the flexibility people want from NEC is to accommodate personal ups and downs. The insistence on a variable policy of rule enforcement based on personal circumstances clearly cuts against the grain of a workplace relation built solely on the sale of labor power. It is at its core a demand for individualization, a demand made in even broader and more explicit terms by the final subgroup.

Speaker A: All I would ask is that they should be as considerate of me as I have been of them.

Speaker B: I expect from them the interest and concern to be willing to listen and cooperate and show the potential to make things better, to make amends, so to speak.

Speaker C: For me, what I expect out of the company—wow, that's a good one. To be recognized by the company and to be treated as a human being and not just a number. In some cases they do and in some cases you're just a number.

Speaker D: I guess I expect from the company the right to be treated like an individual, to be able to have some input into things, to be recognized for what I do.

Speaker E: I guess I just expect to be treated with respect.

There are, then, in the work force at NEC a substantial number of people who want some other relation to their employer than a simple cash nexus, whether it was "respect," "fairness," "flexibility," or the company's attention to matters on which the employee placed a high value. Some felt the company met its obligation; others, that it did not. Even people who were thoroughly satisfied with NEC's performance in the area they described had to create the category first and then determine how well the company had done. Everyone in this large group shared a desire to find more in factory work than a means of subsistence. The form of the question and the difficulty people had in comprehending it may even have *under*estimated the extent to which expectations could be seen as moral, since it gave rise to quick, word-association–type answers.

Instrumentalism

There are six people who do not belong to the overall category just discussed. In theory, this could cast substantial doubt on what I have just concluded, since I have maintained throughout that the nature and numbers of my sample do not permit me to estimate probabilities. Could it be that there is actually a sizable section of the work force at NEC who expect nothing more for their work than wages? I do not think so, but the reason is not essentially one based on the likelihood that my group above exists in comparable numbers in the population (NEC work force). There is a clear dividing line among the nonmoralists, and those who fall on one side may actually have more moral elements underlying their responses than those we have already met.

As I mentioned briefly in the first chapter, when Goldthorpe and his colleagues discussed the existence of an "instrumental" relation to work, they admitted it was consonant with otherwise competing theses of relative satisfaction and alienation. Their investigation centered on the "satisfaction" possibility, while that of Westergaard centered on alienation.[24] These six people would all fit almost any conceivable definition of an instrumentalist. But only one exhibited any sense of satisfaction. Her answer to "Expect" could serve as a definition of satisfied instrumentalism:

What I expect is a good paying job, security when I get older, good retirement, and medical benefits. I got all that.[25]

The rest of the antimoralist group are card-carrying Westergaardian alienated instrumentalists, so different from this one Goldthorpean that they do not share any common ground on the question of how they perceive the sale and use of labor power. All confine their expectations to the paycheck, but the alienated instrumentalists do so because they do not think there is any reasonable chance of achieving any other value. Work is in the classical sense a disutility—a negative (or at least nonpositive) experience to be gotten over with and not taken very seriously. These people are among the sharpest critics of NEC. Their instrumentalist approach to work reflects what they think the possibilities are for satisfying other needs, not what they would like them to be. As I listened to their answers, I realized that the word "expect" had an empirical ring to them, not a normative one:

Speaker A: What do I expect? Not much. They don't know me. They expect me to do my function and if I don't, they'll get someone else who will.

Speaker B: Nothing, I guess. Just a paycheck. What else could you expect?

One of the interviews was with two women at the same time. "Wendy" started working at NEC after she was divorced. "Thelma," who came in half-way through the interview, was also recently divorced. Both have held previous jobs outside industry, but turned to NEC after their divorces because of its pay. Wendy was specific about staying at NEC for exactly ten years, the length of time it takes to be vested in the pension fund. After she qualifies for the pension (she currently has four years), she plans to leave. She said that in six years, she might be interviewing me on what it was like to write a book. (Of course, there is no presumption here that she will in fact leave at that time.) The discussion became more and more aggressively "instrumental" as the interview went on, the two speakers reinforcing each other. These sections of the interview are not consecutive, but are in order.

Wendy [in answer to the "Expect" question]: I don't expect anything from the company. That's just my type of person. I think the goof-off rate is amazing and I imagine it's that way in all factories. I don't know that you could run it humanistically. What are you going to do? You work within the system and that's about it.

Wendy: You start working when you're ten or twenty, whatever. You go through that stage, it's a paying dues situation. That's the way we're taught, that's how society is.
Thelma: That's what going to work is. It's forty hours of dues I put in a week to do things for me and my kids to make us happy on weekends.
Q. I guess one of the things I've been asking people about is that seems like a high price to pay and I wonder if it is impossible to make work itself more satisfying.
Thelma: I've been trying to answer that question for a lot of years.

Both women were resigned to paying those dues and did not expect to find anything else from the sale of their labor power. Work is unpleasant medicine. It is a precondition for the maximizing of other values. They made no particular demands that work "be organized humanistically" because they did not see such a situation as possible. Is there some level of satisfaction in their comments, some understandable trade-off?

One of the re-interviewees, "John," worked in the same department as Wendy. He is thirty-two years old and had worked in a retail business for a number of years in a different town before returning to Lockland and starting with NEC. He has been there for two years. I asked him, as I asked everyone in the re-interviews, what advice he would give his children (hypothetically in his case—he did not have any) about working "at a place like NEC." His answer helps put Wendy's attitudes about work, exchange, and satisfaction in sharper perspective:

I don't know if I had children if I'd want them to work in that type of setting. I would hope that if I had children they would want more than that. That's an interesting question you just posed. The company offers summer employment for employees' children in college, at the same rates of pay and jobs we all work in the plant—a reasonable wage for someone coming out of high school in summer employment. *[Wendy]* had a son who was going to *[names college]* in the fall. They said, "Why don't you bring him down here and instead of working in Food Bag for three dollars an hour, he can come down here and make nine or ten." And she said, "I wouldn't want him to work in this place even for a couple of months." That might answer the question.

These alienated instrumentalists have uncovered the very situation described by Lane and Roberts at the beginning of this chapter, a situation those authors say that employers try to hide—that workers *are* "as a matter of fact units of labor." They do not try very hard to find or create meaning in their work, but they recognize its absence and resent it in varying degrees. They differ sharply from the satisfied Goldthorpean instrumentalists in being acutely aware of the process of lowering their own expectations. While they also differ from those who want and/or find moral elements in workplace relations, they are unable to detach themselves from their hands sufficiently to overlook the lack of intrinsic satisfaction. In the broadest sense, these people share beliefs about what one should be entitled to expect, but have concluded that factory work cannot be made into anything more than drudgery.

The alienated instrumentalists are a particularly interesting group and crucial to my argument that employee-generated moral elements in workplace relations might help account for uncoerced work performance above minimum requirements. It certainly is counterintuitive to find any support for that argument from this group. To look at the question in more depth, I will introduce "Jill," another re-interviewee. I had the opportunity in the re-interviews to follow up more closely on statements that seemed self-contradictory or had been left undeveloped in the first interview. The heart of each re-interview was a set of questions derived from the tape of the first interview. This enabled me to let the respondent find the consistency and also enabled me to see underlying logic or illogic more systematically than I could have by puzzling over the first.

Jill is a thirty-four-year-old production worker who also began working at NEC after a divorce.[26] She has been there for six years. She had been to business school when she was younger and has been going part time in the last two years. She is a self-defined instrumentalist, as will be quite clear below. As with Wendy, she plans to leave after her tenth year. If anything, she seems even more definite than Wendy about that—she told me the exact day in the future she becomes vested and will resign. She has found herself strongly at odds with the company twice: once over what she felt was exposure to dangerous chemicals, the second time over responsibility for an accident. These incidents are important, because they show the ambiguities attendant on even the most determined attempt to separate labor power from the laborer. In answer to the "Expect" question in the first interview, she said:

I work here for the paycheck. Period. After eight hours, I'm home.

She repeated "It's only for the money" six times in that interview. I decided to make that the focus of the re-interview.

Her self-description never wavered appreciably. (I should point out that she is articulate and ironic, even flippant. Some of her comments do not make much sense if the reader is not alerted to that.)

Q. What motivated you to work there?
A. Greed. Purely greed. I was about to get married and I wanted a house and car.

Q. In terms of what you wanted when you went to NEC, are you satisfied?
A. Yah, I went there for the money and that's what I got out of it. I got out of it exactly what I wanted.

As the interview progressed, she never relented about the purpose of work, but did begin to add a great deal about its content.

Q. You said that you work there for the money, then go home and try to disregard it.
A. Yah, I do.
Q. Isn't that a lot of your life just to put in?
A. Well, yah, you're right. I've been there a long time and it's eight hours a day, but I knew I was getting what I wanted out of it. I could sacrifice those eight hours to the company like I'd give it to anybody else. And when I go in there, I don't *like* it, I'm there for the money,

but—I still do the best job I can. I don't screw off or anything. If they want it done, I do it.

Q. Not many people said they liked production work.

A. No, they're bored.

Q. Still, all in all, generally people will tell me it's a good place to work.

A. You have to keep your attitude straight. My thing is, I'm there for the paycheck, so I go in everyday and say, "Well, next week the paycheck will be there" and I'll get through. But when you can't keep your attitude up, it's tough. Because a lot of times it's very boring. It does get boring. But then that paycheck is there again. It may not be a great place and there's a lot wrong with it, but I'm getting nine dollars an hour.

Q. But on the other hand, you in particular have gone through some difficult circumstances.

A. [Laughs loudly. Does not respond.]

The interview then moved into the more general questions I asked all the re-interviewees. When I was not drawing her attention to the bargain she has just described but to work itself, her tone changed:

Q. You seem like a bright person with a number of skills and interests. You've gone to a few different schools. Do you think—and I won't limit it to NEC—do you think that factory work allows you to make use of your skills and interests?

A. Nah. No. They say they do. They're always encouraging you, if you have any knowledge about this, if you can help us on this project—but when you do, they say, "Oh, terrific" and that's it. That discourages a lot of people. Maybe they just don't want us to have too much of a say, they might lose that upper hand to us, or whatever they have.

Q. Then most people are not too enthusiastic about their jobs?

A. No! [Laughs wildly.] No.

Q. I'm going to characterize the industrial system in the United States, and then I'd like you to comment. It is made up of privately owned corporations which compete with each other in a marketplace and set their own rules for employees, although that is modified some by unions. Does this lead to fulfilling work? Is the paycheck enough compensation?

A. Well, no—but they own the company. They have the right to say how to do things. It's their company. But they could leave a little spot open where people could use their imagination and intelligence. They

like the older guys who walk around like little robots—no problems,
they don't come up with these wild ideas, they like that. It's not
fulfilling, but I think people just get used to it after a while. Just—
"Got to go to work the rest of my life." Is it fulfilling? No, not at all.
You don't feel any involvement in it at all. There's nothing there.

These answers at least raise the possibility that instrumentalism is an attitude
taken from work, rather than brought to it. When her eye is diverted from the
paycheck and extrinsic goals, Jill is no longer so sure her labor is fundamentally
alienable. Finally, in response to the "children" question (she has two young
girls):

I wouldn't stop her *[Jill is specifically referring to equal opportunity
here]*. Who knows, it may turn out she loves doing that kind of stuff.
But I would rather not see her sit around for the rest of her life in a
place like NEC. I'd rather see her use her intelligence.

Instrumentalism of this kind defines the worth of work by its absence. Jill's
comments reveal an alternative to the moral group in coping with the tendency
of workplace authority to reduce them to "units of manpower." Most people
ward off the unflattering implications of this process by creating moral categories as part of the deal; others like Jill try to keep their attitude straight in the face
of evidence that this is a hopeless prospect.

Taking the Dream out of Life

[T]he tendency to slack undermined the worker's self-respect even if it
improved his market position; and self-respect is a much more fundamental
thing than the historically evanescent categories of the free market economy.
—Eric Hobsbawm[27]

What the foregoing has established is that most NEC employees have some
definition of the worth of work that transcends payment for their labor power.
This undergoes a considerable buffeting in the work-a-day existence of the laborer to the extent that some (the alienated instrumentalists) are convinced that
no values can be realized at work other than receiving a paycheck. In other
words, people try to reconstruct the work situation on their own to include values
beyond simple economic exchange, regardless of the degree to which they think
those values can be fulfilled. This reconstruction does not principally come about
because people accept homilies offered by NEC management. While the manager who gave me the tour did talk briefly about the necessity for "positive
attitudes," the LRS was quite forthright in specifying their goal as simply to

"get people to do as much as they're capable of doing" and then wait for something good to happen down the road. But if the company does not directly orchestrate this reconstruction, it does benefit from it. If people are looking for workplace relationships that are fair and flexible, and for the company to accord them respect and individuality, these expectations are likely to temper their attitude toward work; they will tend to feel obliged to make more than a desultory effort in fulfilling their end of the bargain.[28]

I say "tend to" and I mean that quite precisely (if there is such a thing as a precisely qualified statement). Since the distinction between labor power and the laborer is real, people must at various times face the problem of reconciling the moral qualities that they define into the work situation with the reality of work as a disutility; the alienated instrumentalists must face the problem of not just *going* to work, but of *being* there every day. This problem is not hypothetical. It formed the core of several of the original interviews, under the respondent-provided topic of "negative attitudes."

I did not set out to find information from my interviewees about other people's attitudes, positive or negative, but this turned out to be a subject several people wanted to discuss. After some people had spoken passionately and/or indignantly on the subject, I brought it up in a few later interviews. The result is that I have a combination of solicited and unsolicited discussion. The people who addressed this subject seemed to be drawn randomly from the different categories previously discussed, with this one important exception: every alienated instrumentalist felt strongly about the subject. The most striking feature of this set of comments is that the charge of "negativism" applied almost indiscriminately to the company, the union, other employees, and the speakers themselves. People were in varying mixes critical of negative attitudes and themselves negative.

The issue was raised most forcefully by a union committeeman, a twenty-year maintenance employee who told me that he was active in the union principally because he saw it as a vehicle through which he could try to change the "negativism." He saw it mainly as a losing battle:

Q. What does the company expect from you?
A. I would imagine—"dedication" isn't the word I'm looking for. "Patriotism" is the only word which comes to mind, but that's not what I mean, I don't want to associate it with . . .
Q. You mean toward the company.
A. Yah. There's a word for that which escapes me. *[He may have been searching for "loyalty."]*
Q. Do you think they get it from most people?
A. No. No. There's a real and general negative incentive. You get paid whether you do it or don't and I disagree with that and that's one of the things we're working as a union to try to improve that.

> *Q.* So you think that out in the plant there's not a spirit of coopera-
> tive working, or whatever phrase you were trying to find?
> *A.* Family dedication, let's call it. Yes, there is some. However, if
> you were to talk to people one-on-one, they would express a dis-
> like for the company. You hear it constantly—"This g.d. company"
> and so forth, and I disagree with that because none of them would
> leave the company.

Of course, what I was doing was exactly talking with people one-on-one, and
while I heard a lot of negative comments, I heard almost nothing about a "g.d.
company," particularly as an overall evaluation (see chapter 3). This is one
common characteristic of the critique by some employees of the negative attitudes of others: the negativism looks more impressive in the aggregate than it
does up close and personal.

> *Q.* Do you think that's more true among younger employees?
> *A.* I would say it's equal, young and old. In fact, a new person in the
> plant hasn't yet been instilled with this. Once he's been there five
> years, he's working with this negative incentive that's being devel-
> oped, then it's something that's developed. The reason I'm con-
> cerned about it is that it creates an attitude that you can't leave at
> work. When you come out of the place, you're affected by it. You've
> got to have something positive going for yourself and it's not being
> offered at work.
> *Q.* Tell me again where you think this negativism comes from, what
> causes it.
> *A.* It's a reward. You get paid for doing something or not doing it.
> People brag about something they did or something they didn't do.
> You find, "Gee, I got away with this. The only thing I did today was
> scratch my ear." People are proud of what they're *not* doing or what
> they're getting away with. What I would like to see is people being
> proud of something they *did* do.
>
> *[Later in the interview]:* The point I want to make is that you don't leave
> your job here, you take it home with you and that affects your family life
> and your outlook on a lot of things. You get thirty years of that and
> you've got a limit on yourself. That is one part of industry that I don't
> care for. You can see you're limited. It takes the dream out of life.

His description of people proud of what they were getting away with was
echoed by Jill in both her original and second interviews.

[Original]: People compete to do the least. People who have only a little to do try to see if they can do nothing at all.
[Re-interview]: People make a game out of it—seeing how much they can get away with. I think it's silly. You're there for eight hours a day, you might as well do some work. People who don't have anything to do will make a big fuss when the foreman asks them to do something. They'll take the foreman into the office with a union rep, they'll sit there and argue with him for twenty minutes when it could be a five-minute job. People do things like that all the time.

Jill too is critical of negative attitudes, which she sees as pervasive. But to the committeeman who saw the lack of loyalty as the problem, Jill the consummate instrumentalist would be a negativist since she professes no great love for NEC. When people described negative attitudes, or their equivalent, the "I-don't-care" attitude,[29] fingers started pointing in every direction. The most comprehensible form this took was when some employees criticized the work habits of others:

Speaker A: In some respects it was tough dealing with people down there because they were slugs. There were some people that were genuine slugs, man. They were there to collect a paycheck. They felt the company owed them a paycheck. I detested that. Give 'em eight hours work for eight hours pay. What's fair is fair.

Speaker B: Some guys—I don't understand them. They won't do nothing until you tell them and then when you tell them, they argue. I'm not anti-union, don't get me wrong. You need a union. But I wouldn't protect these guys. Make them work.

But sometimes people merged criticism of others or of the company with a description of themselves. People were at times simultaneously intensely critical of negativism and purveyors of it.

Speaker C [a maintenance employee]: They make the big decisions up here *[administration building]* and they just pass it down the line. Nobody cares any more. It's terrible. The I-don't-care attitude is all over. Individuals is what changes it. There's not enough individuals that care. Out of the maintenance department, seventy-five percent of them don't care, because they don't get any credit for what they do. So even those people that used to care, they realize, "What the hell am I working my ass off for nothing." I came off production repair and I gave it my all, worked as hard as I could, hoping I was going to get somewhere. I'm no better off than the next guy. In fact, I'm the sucker, because all the little extra jobs that I did, they expect it of me.

Speaker D [question concerned health and safety]: We *[employees]* have a very bad attitude as far as safety. They do certain things that are safe for us, and other things, they don't want to hear it. So we have a bad attitude around safety, because we feel that they don't care, then we don't care, right?
[Later in response to "Expect" question]: If we do a good job for them, they're satisfied.
Q. How do you think most people do? Do they carry their weight?
A. No. They don't.
Q. Why not?
A. They don't care. Most people come in to pick up a paycheck. They're not conscientious at all. If I owned NEC, I'd fire half of them. Each shift says, "We're number one" and the next group comes in and says they're number one, and nobody's number one. The only thing is, there are some lazy people that just don't care. They just want to come in and pick up a buck the easiest way they can do it. I don't think it's right, but I don't own the company.
Q. Has this changed much in the time you've been there?
A. Attitudes? It goes back to being lazy. When I first went to building B, maybe I never noticed it, but I didn't see people acting the way they are now, not caring.

There is a blind striking out here: it's me, it's the others, it's the company or the union, it's the times. Wendy, who has already told us disparagingly that "the goof-off rate is tremendous" in answering the "Expect" question, finds "don't-caring" everywhere, including in herself.

When you're a hands-on operator and you work with this stuff all the time, you have the practical, they have the theory. A lot of times people who have the theory think that the practical doesn't know anything. So you have a big communication problem. You also develop an attitude when you are doing the practical. You tell them, "This is better" and they ignore you. Then it's very hard to maintain an "up" attitude. You get to an attitude where "I don't care."
[Later]: Our foreman would sit in this office and play with his computer until his job was on the line. Then he would come out and get in the way.
[Later] Q. [After she described an incident in which poor ventilation

sent two people to the hospital]: Why would the company take a new product, a new building *[A],* and not put in the most up-to-date safety equipment?
A. It's money. Money. The safety department in this particular branch is a joke. The new safety person has provided us all the correct safety equipment. You don't do it, it's your problem *[even though this could only be consistent if it were facetious, it is not].* They don't take you by the hand. It's your responsibility.
[In an aside shortly after this]: Why do they pay people who make cars such outrageous prices? From the union, yes, because they have to get rich, the union people.

When the interview was over and my tape recorder off, Wendy asked me whether the women I had interviewed had seemed more dedicated to quality than the men (they had not). I asked her why the question and she explained:

It just seems the men don't care that much. They know nobody's going to do anything to them, since we got that union there, it seems they just don't care. They laugh about it. That makes it frustrating.

Finally, a slip by Speaker C, the maintenance worker quoted above, that illustrates well just how ''blind'' the striking out is:

That's what's wrong with the country—I mean the company—*and the country*—people just don't care.

The speakers are unable to sort out cause and effect; they describe themselves variously as sharing in the climate of negative attitudes and as victims of an ecological negativism created by others. When speaking of themselves, they find negativism to be a rational response to a situation of powerlessness; when speaking of others, they find it ''frustrating.'' In either case it is viewed critically: that is, people seem to be saying that they dislike the extent to which they themselves have stopped caring. No one admits to being part of the problem; it probably would not be logical to do so.

The attribution of I-don't-care attitudes to a large number of individuals at NEC does not seem to be warranted, insofar as my fairly representative sample turned up no one who *justified* negativism. There were no ''negative and proud'' cases. But this does not mean that the perception of negativism is a false one. The work force as a whole, from the perspective of any one of its members standing temporarily outside and observing it, might appear to have a particular climate—in this case, negativism—even when each of its constituents finds it abhorrent. If everyone generally did their jobs, but at particular moments fell into futility or took a what's-the-use attitude, the sum total of negativism would be overwhelming. Another way of saying the same thing is that if the whole work force were made up of people like Wendy and the maintenance worker quoted above, any given Wendy would be just as frustrated as she currently finds herself. More importantly, given the discussion in the previous section, people's attention might be particularly drawn to attitudes they feel reduce the moral value of work. I have argued that people try to create value in their work and that this is undercut by their actual status as units of manpower. "Negative attitudes" would seem a rational response to the discovery of that fact. As Hobsbawm points out above, workers would actually be striking a better deal if they worked only hard enough to get by. But shirking, evading, loafing, or producing low-quality work are not ennobling activities and are not seen as such by the people who occasionally engage in them.[30]

The *critique* of negative attitudes may be a barrier employees build against the realization that they may not be expected to do anything more than send their hands to work. To metaphorize a bit, negativism might be understood as an abyss, with people working close to the edge, observing others falling in every day and knowing that there is no strong reason why they should not fall in also. The quoted responses (to put the matter somewhat less biblically) show people drifting in and out of attitudes that would be called negative by others, all the while retaining a critique of those attitudes as though they were a separate entity.

>*In one department we had to clean up some label plates before we could take our break, meaning each minute spent cleaning was a minute less of a strictly enforced ten-minute break. My partner (working the other side of the label plates) was a young employee who was constantly in trouble, getting reprimanded, for instance, for playing cards while the labels ran out. One day I had done my usual acceptable but basically half-assed job on cleanup and was walking toward the break room. My partner asked me how I could leave with the job only partly done. I said I really didn't care, as long as it would pass. He told me, "I don't see how you can think like that."*< PG, PA

Part of the answer to the question "why do workers work so hard?" seems to come paradoxically from the observations of some that others do not. What I am suggesting here is that people make an attempt to maintain or create a sense of the worth of their work in the face of any good reason to think it has any. This attempt is not the handiwork of the company, but it does help relieve the company of the necessity of widespread policing. It helps explain why people seem to defy market logic; in the exchange of effort for dollars, they (generally) put in more effort than they need to for the same return in dollars.[31]

There are certainly other reasons why people work harder than cold rationality would indicate they should. As was pointed out in chapter 3, some (though not all) people in skilled trades find the work itself varied and interesting. Two women I interviewed described their initial months in production jobs as challenging and even exciting, because they had been told by the company that they were probably too small to do the work. Their description was similar to a description of mountain climbing. Both subsequently left those jobs and told me they hoped they will not have to return to them. Burawoy emphasized the games people devise as the method by which people recast their own workday experience. Since he was working in and studying a factory with payment based on piecework, his discussion focused on the game of quota fulfillment, or "making out."[32] Since quotas are in large part set by the company, and the whole system of piecework payment is initiated by the company, this might seem at odds with my contention that a company need not play much of a role in employees' reformulation of their work experience. But Burawoy's "making out" game is actually a subset of the whole panoply of playful devices that people use to pass the time. His conclusion is similar to mine—people cannot live comfortably with the knowledge that their life's work is that of Sisyphus, even if they are satisfied with the remuneration they receive for it. They see limited opportunities to escape the situation or to change it, so they change the one factor over which they have some control—their interpretation of it.[33]

Class and Populism

Marx assumed that workers' recognition of themselves (or more precisely, of the labor power that they owned) as commodities was an important element in the formation of class consciousness. It is true, as I maintained at the start of this chapter, that labor and capital (and therefore their proximate human embodiment, workers and employers) are unequal in resources and structural position. This is true regardless of the perception of the actors involved. It is also true that there are fairly widespread and shared forms of discourse among hourly workers. Huw Beynon, writing about an English auto factory, used the term "factory consciousness" to capture that language.[34]

But there is an unwarranted leap in inferring from that "factory consciousness" many of the meanings usually associated with "class consciousness." Ira Katznelson, for example, whose purpose is to explore a discontinuity between conflict at work and away from work (in ethnic neighborhoods, for example), says that "the ordinary idiom at work is that of class."[35] But if most things that happen in a factory are "class" happenings simply by virtue of where they occur, there would be no need to describe a category called "class consciousness." Definitions of that concept abound.[36] They have some common features; the one I will make use of is the notion of the irreconcilability of conflict.[37] The purpose of relying on that single definitional aspect is that it contains the idea that interests (of labor and capital) both *do* conflict and *should* conflict.

The "ordinary idiom" at NEC used to describe conflict with management is not that of class but of populism. Halle described populism as the language with which "the American working man" describes the world away from work, but does not pursue the possibility that such language also provides the conceptual framework for understanding conflict within the plant gates. Halle says that populism

> involves the idea of a clear opposition between the power structure, especially big business and politicians, and the rest of the population. According to this view the American people no longer consist of all those defined as citizens by the federal government. Instead, they consist of all those excluded from the heights of political and economic power.[38]

The reader has already seen some common populist imagery: "the suit and tie fellows," "people who have the theory think the practical doesn't know anything." Differences with management were often framed in this language. The company was always looking to promote "the guy with the sheepskin" (meaning, effectively, outside the ranks of production workers), even when, as one worker complained, "The poor guy didn't know the difference between a nut and a bolt." The supervisors and engineers were "book-smart" and "college kids." Those in the upper reaches of the plant hierarchy were identified by cultural differences from those who have to slop around in oil and grime. Differences in power were noted, but the main characteristic people raised of authorities is that they have never gotten their hands dirty, and are *therefore* impractical and arrogant. In his first interview, Paul made this assessment explicitly and incisively:

Q. Do you have any explanation for why *[employee involvement]* doesn't happen as much as it should?

A. I've always had this feeling. People in the office could care less about people in the factory. The factory is out there *[motions away with his hands]* somewhere. "We work in the office, we're different. We dress different, we get paid more, we're better educated." They have that air about them, which unfortunately—there's that air about them. It's as simple as that. To me, the best training in the world would be to take every college graduate, put him in a factory for six months, let him breathe dirty air, powder, chemicals, whatever the case may be. From that day on, he may not respect the factory worker, but he knows his working conditions, he'll respect him in that way.

This populist language is alluringly close to that of class. A finger of accusation is pointed at those sitting in the administration building. Those who do mental work—and are consequently higher up in the pyramidal hierarchy—are said to look down on, ignore, and perhaps "oppress" (in the sense of making life more difficult for) the manual workers. Conversely, manual workers are the producers of value and the possessors of the real, usable knowledge of the productive process. Superordinates play a role in production that seems essentially parasitic. (Remember Wendy's description of her foreman whose contributions ranged from ignoring the actual work—"playing with his computer"—to screwing it up—"getting in the way.")

Paul: I'm the company, right? NEC is not the company. I'm the company.
Q. Well, you're *in* the company.
A. That's true—*but*—if I don't do my job right, you can forget the company. The company is only as good as its workers. When the workers don't work, the guys in administration don't do nothing. They don't make no money. The person down on the shop floor, producing that product—that's the one you have to take care of. Take care of him, all the rest will follow.

But if an important element of class consciousness is the irreconcilability of interests, then the differences between this workplace populism and "class" attitudes are more important than the similarities.[39]

The conflict between labor and the capitalists (not capital, as we shall see shortly) refracted through the populist prism is not inherent, but artificial, not rational, but counterproductive. The hourly employees are prevented by short-sighted and self-serving "suit and tie fellows" from making their full contribution toward what should be shared goals. It is the attitude of the individuals in positions of authority rather than the distribution of power that is responsible for the marginalization of the hourly employees, a marginalization that makes no sense whatsoever from the perspective of those who think that "I'm the company." "Untie our hands, get off our backs, and let us produce and compete" might serve as a summary slogan for workplace populism.

This "workplace populism" may be a specific example of a broader tendency in American society to express disaffection by extolling the underlying virtues of the system. That is one possible interpretation of the massive overview of the surveys on "confidence" done by Lipset and Schneider, who point out that people are often highly supportive of the dominant institutions and the principles of competition and self-interest they foster, at the same time that they criticize self-interested activity when they see it practiced:

Americans certainly value the freedom and competition of both our economic system ("free enterprise") and our political system ("democracy"). But they do not seem to approve of the behavior that is most characteristic of both systems, namely, competition for power and profit motivated primarily by self-interest. . . . [O]ne gets the impression from these data that the public feels negatively about the *normal* [their emphasis] pattern of conduct associated with economic and political competition.[40]

After I listened to Paul's "I-am-the-company" speech in the first interview, I decided to press him on the point in the re-interview. His answer helped me understand where he located the cause of conflict.[41]

Paul: *[Describes a process whereby the company will show interest in and solicit advice from employees.]* Then I am going to be a contented employee and if we're all contented employees, it's going to be a smooth-running operation.

Q. Suppose you were to say this to the guy who runs the local plant, or maybe the president of the company—

A. *[interjects]* I'd love to.

Q. Somebody in some position of authority. And suppose he were to say back to you, "Look. It's a hard world out here. We've got to worry about our bottom line. Don't tell me about contented employees. We're competing with five or six bigger companies and we've got to push people sometimes." What would you say to that?

A. That's an excellent question. I want to commend you on that question and in the whole world if I wanted a question to be asked to me, it would be the one you just addressed. My answer to that question would be, "You're right. We are in a day and age where competitiveness is number one. We no longer can have any laxity in any department in our plant. Every single department's got to be running at one hundred percent plus efficiency. Now, since you want this and need this, then I say this: the two relate, the two go hand in hand." If somebody is contented, that means he's happy. If he's happy, he's going to pay constant attention to his job. He's not going to wander, he's going to make a better product. If he's not contented, you are disappointing him. He'll say this: "If I have to do my job under conditions that are very intolerable, that can be corrected, but yet the company doesn't want to correct them, because they couldn't care less about me, all they're worrying about is the bottom line, they're missing the point. It *will* affect the bottom line, because I am not going to be a happy employee." Okay? I'm going to get to the point that finally that employee says this to himself: "The company doesn't care about me, then I don't care about the

company." Who makes the profits for the company? Is it managers'
decisions or is it employees working down on the floor? I say it's
both. Who is actually physically working this job to put the work out
the door? All these great ideas, blueprints, plans, what have you,
don't mean a thing if you don't have the people down there.

In a study of autoworkers in Michigan, Stanley Greenberg found populist conceptions with many of the same characteristics I have attributed to some of the workers
at NEC. The Michigan workers felt betrayed by companies they felt had not recipro-
cated the loyalty of employees. The corporations were "selfish"—a criticism
clearly distinct from saying that the employees had been hurt when the companies pursued rational self-interest (as "class" terminology would portray). As
with some of the NEC workers, the autoworkers were embittered by what they
considered undeserved marginalization, a denial of their rightful place.
Greenberg summarized their attitude this way: "These workers believe they
care more about the company than the company cares about itself."[42]

Far from conveying any imagery of an industrial structure which promotes
competing sets of interests, the populist conception among the NEC workers and
the Michigan autoworkers is based on a perception of common interests. Those
interests are seen as shared, even when the individual owners do not agree and
wage one-sided class warfare. Workplace populism emerges here from a sense of
injury. It is a characterization of inequality, one that accepts (and is not antithetical to endorsing) some features of the structure of unequal relations while protesting, potentially vociferously, against some of the outcomes of the working of
those structures: powerlessness (the marginalization described by Halle and
Greenberg) and reduction to the state of being "units of manpower" at work.[43]
Nonetheless, workplace populism is far from an opiate. If there were sufficient
numbers in my sample to estimate, it seems likely that populist sentiment would
be found predominantly among those who are most critical of specific practices
of NEC (and American industry broadly). But it does not define its targets very
carefully, tends to celebrate the underpinnings of a system that should at least be
a suspect in the crimes, and at times becomes a smoldering and diffuse resentment of everything and everyone.

Notes

1. Anthony Lane and Kenneth Roberts, *Strike at Pilkington's*, p. 41.
2. Although it is also true, of course, that as unions face owners in bargaining or in
the political process, that aspect of inequality is a fact of considerable importance. Alan
Fox states the impact of unequal interest-group resources well: "Labour often has to
marshal all its resources to fights on marginal adjustments; capital can, as it were, fight
with one hand behind its back and still achieve in most situations a verdict that it finds
tolerable" (*Beyond Contract: Work, Power and Trust Relations*, p. 279).

3. For instance, *Capital*, vol. I, p. 91.

4. The commodity "labor power" is purchased for the equivalent (expressed in wages) of the labor time necessary for the production of the goods and services required to maintain its existence. Sometimes Marx added a social dimension to the price of labor power, "historical tradition and social habitude" (*Value, Price and Profit*, p. 57).

5. Since writing this, I have found a similar use of the concept of labor power essentially as a sociological rather than an economic category in Nancy Schwartz, "The Time of Our Being Together: An Inquiry into the Meaning of Marx's Labor Theory of Value," p. 76.

6. Edward Herman, *Corporate Control, Corporate Power* makes that argument and outlines the webs of law and expectation that bind owner, manager and capital. In addition, managers must forego any help from entitlement theories in justifying control.

7. Claus Offe, "Two Logics of Collective Action: Theoretical Notes on Social Class and Organizational Form," p. 73.

8. Robert Blauner *(Alienation and Freedom)* and Serge Mallet ("The Class Struggle: Death and Transformation at Caltex") both wrote of chemical operators as emblematic of a new working class which more closely resembled professional status—in Mallet's terms, "ducks amidst proletarian chickens" (p. 132).

9. However, in *Bureaucracy and the Labor Process*, Dan Clawson asks why the physical maximum should be regarded as the only fair contribution an employee can make (p. 236).

10. There is a very large unanswered question here. Since a probationary employee has very few rights and can be terminated without cause, how could NEC management be unsuccessful in firing someone they have determined has a "bad attitude?" The informal nature of that tour prevented me from asking that question. My impression—and it is only that—is that NEC management, perhaps in coordination with the union, would like some uniformity in the retention of new hires. The first two criteria are measurable; "attitude" is not, except by Potter Stewart obscenity standards. So the desire to maintain a "willing" work force works at cross-purposes with the establishment of bureaucratic rules.

11. Richard Balzer, *Clockwork: Life in and outside an American Factory*, p. 14; and Richard Pfeffer, *Working for Capitalism*, p. 354. Both wrote about being surprised at how much they resented busy work. I resented it too, although I got over my surprise.

12. It can also lead to exaggerating the shop-floor power of workers. See Bill Watson, "Counter Planning on the Shop Floor."

13. I did not regularly ask questions about the probationary period, so this information is more impressionistic than most.

14. Michael Crozier, *The Bureaucratic Phenomenon*, p. 108. In a related point, Crozier argues that bureaucratic organization made it impossible to coerce workers directly: "they are completely protected as long as they obey the rules" (p. 87). But the rules themselves were not written by a body that was accountable to the concerned population, nor one that was especially benevolent toward them. Rules were written partially to codify the subordinate-superordinate relationship, and as a consequence, have coercion built into them.

15. David Halle, *America's Working Man*, pp. 119–25.

16. Charles Sabel, *Work and Politics*, p. 115: "But in fact the slave owner can never simplify work so completely, nor supervise the workers so carefully, that no exercise of discretion is called for; and still less can the factory owner do so. Nor can the slave or factory owner resist the temptation to increase efficiency by bribing the workers to increase output in return for a (not quite proportional) increase in pay."

17. Michael Burawoy, *Manufacturing Consent*, pp. 83–85. The relation of effort to reward in piecework is usually overstated anyway. On the level of individuals, the exis-

tence of a base rate dilutes the earning contribution of each increment of effort that goes into surpassing the quota. On a plant-wide level, any company that wants to stay competitive (most do) will fix the base rate *and* the rate at which payments are made for average production above base-rate quotas in a manner commensurate with hourly rates in the industry or what hourly rates would be if they predominated. In Burawoy's case, as in many piecework situations, there was a "standard" in addition to the base rate (in his plant, 125 percent). Piecework still retains some particularity. The above logic will not dissuade many people from perceiving themselves as blue-collar entrepreneurs.

18. Juan Martinez Alier, *Labourers and Landowners in Southern Spain*, p. 179. Alier centered his discussion of *"cumplir"* around the same question Burawoy and others posed—why do workers work so hard? "If laborers do not accept the legitimacy of the system; i.e., if it is power and not law which ensures the functioning and continuity of *latifundismo*, how can we explain the positive moral value that laborers give in their everyday life to working with normal care and effort?" (p. 203).

19. Here are the numbers—taken with the usual precautions: twenty-three people were in the "moral" group. Six gave answers revolving around "paychecks and benefits," but of that group, five are in a category of their own not antithetical to the moral people. There were four nonresponsive answers. These comments are not uninteresting, but do not lend themselves well to the point at hand. The LRS also gave a nonresponsive answer to the converse of this question, which has already been quoted.

20. If I could begin the interviews again, I might well formulate a question about quantity and quality. There seems to be a common understanding among factory workers that a company is mainly interested in quantity and a common critique of that fact to the effect that this is often true to the detriment in quality. Actually, the "common understanding" might not be put in the words I have used, so I will let workers themselves say it:

NEC worker: "What you hear from the company is quantity, quantity, quantity. I'm from the old school, quality, quality, quality."

>"What's wrong with the company can be said in two words: quantity and quality. They want the quantity but they don't care about the quality."< PG, PA

To express this in terms of the conceit I have maintained throughout the chapter, "quantity" forces the worker to consider him- or herself as one of many machines—as labor power—while "quality" represents labor, the ability to create.

21. In my notebook next to his words, I have annotations such as "Gets very animated," "Really on a roll, agitated," and "can barely contain himself."

22. Richard Hyman and Ian Brough, *Social Values and Industrial Relations: A Study of Fairness and Equality*, p. 3. They took the original phrasing from Barbara Wooten, *The Social Foundations of Wage Policy*.

23. Alvin Gouldner, *Wildcat Strike: A Study in Worker Management Relationships*, p. 18. Different factory managements have different policies on stealing. At some places, everyone including the supervisors backed their cars up to loading docks and took home tape, wood, and other usables. At Procter and Gamble, the policy was "one bar of soap and you're gone."

24. John Westergaard and Henrietta Resler, *Class in a Capitalist Society*, p. 49.

25. There is a certain randomness to all these answers. On some other day, she might have added some words to the list that would have led me to put her in a different category, and some others might have done the reverse. If I had arranged these answers not into categories but into a spectrum from most instrumental to most "moral," there would certainly have been some difficulties in placing people, but there would also have been people near both ends.

26. Marital status is reported for these women *only* because each stressed that she had turned to NEC after a divorce because she had to reconsider how to maximize her earning potential quickly.

27. Quoted in Hyman and Brough, *Social Values*, p. 27.

28. Bruno Bettelheim wrote of the argument in concentration camps over "building well": "It seems that the majority of the old prisoners had realized that they could not continue to work for the Gestapo unless they could convince themselves that their work made some sense. Thus they had convinced themselves that it did" (*The Informed Heart*, p. 80).

29. There are phrases that float around plants and become common language and metaphors. Whatever the specific context that launched them, they often become plant-wide conventional wisdom.

30. I am speaking of these at this point as methods of performing routine work tasks. When they are used as tactics to obtain specific goals (as in chapter 6), they are not regarded simply as negativism. For a startling example of how the purpose can change the evaluation, see David Moberg, who documented the care that workers at Lordstown put into their work *at the very same time* as they were carrying out a campaign of daylong strikes and sabotage ("No More Junk: Lordstown Workers and the Demand for Quality").

31. This is not an attempt to smuggle a theory of surplus value in by the back door. The theory of surplus value would not require any additional effort by employees beyond what is minimally required.

32. Burawoy, *Manufacturing Consent*, chapter 4.

33. Sabel outlined a series of choices of interpretation open to a young worker once he discovered that the factory was probably his permanent job. One of the choices corresponds to the process I am describing here. "The second choice is to flee, not from the factory, but from all conscious recognition that flight is impossible. That means either a desperate belief in providence or in the possibility of a miraculous escape from a hopeless situation, or an attempt to batter the mind to numbness" (*Work and Politics*, p. 142). The first choice was "integration," which does not seem appreciably different from what he just pictured. The third is resistance, by which Sabel means entrance into union office (I discuss this further in chapter 6).

34. Huw Beynon, *Working for Ford*, p. 98.

35. Ira Katznelson, *City Trenches: Urban Politics and the Patterning of a Class in the United States*, p. 6. The problem is one of omission rather than commission, since Katznelson's purpose was to explain the nature of conflict in communities rather than that at work. I have already tried to indicate how the "ordinary idiom" excludes some questions that most definitions of class consciousness would include—and have done so, I hope, without leaving the reader with the Lukacsian impression that workers "should" be class-conscious.

36. Among others: Michael Mann, *Consciousness and Action in the Western Working Class*, p. 13; Kenneth Roberts, F. G. Cook, S. C. Clark, and Elizabeth Semeonoff, *The Fragmentary Class Structure*, p. 87; Bertell Ollman, "Toward Class Consciousness Next Time: Marx and the Working Class," p. 81; and Halle, *America's Working Man*, p. 205.

37. This is suggested by Victoria Bonnell, *Roots of Rebellion*, p. 7. I am not proposing this formulation as a simple solution to the problem of defining "class conscious-

ness," but rather as a useful tool that will allow me to proceed as it did for her. A recent study by Reeve Vanneman and Lynne Cannon *(The American Perception of Class)* contends that the level of class consciousness of American workers is much higher than ordinarily supposed, a conclusion drawn from the willingness of workers to identify class stratification. But "subjective class"—self-placement and the description of others as members of a working class—does not contain any implications about *conflict*, irreconcilable or otherwise. This leaves out the most controversial and significant of claims made about "class consciousness."

38. Halle, *America's Working Man*, p. 235.

39. This paragraph would have no force if irreconcilability were not crucial to definitions of class consciousness, but then those definitions would not have much force either. I have already pointed out that if class is anything that occurs at work, it conveys no meaning separate from any ad hoc description of workday conflict. That is a methodological problem. More importantly, if any recognition of unequal resources or any conflictual attitudes were tantamount to class consciousness, then Marx and many of his critics and supporters have wasted a lot of words.

40. Seymour Martin Lipset and William Schneider, *The Confidence Gap*, p. 79.

41. Paul is on the one hand intelligent and articulate and on the other a great jumbler of syntax. I have reproduced this verbatim, hoping the reader would be able to follow his intent through the confusing barrage of pronouns. It is not difficult to follow with the help of the inflections in his voice on tape.

42. Stanley Greenberg, "Democratic Defection Revisited," pp. 21–25. While Greenberg's research addressed Reagan Democrats, he has additional information that suggests that the findings are more generally valid.

43. Craig Reinarman, using qualitative interviewing techniques similar to mine, also discusses what he calls "populist delegitimation" *(American States of Mind)*. I would take slight issue with that, since I contend in this section that what are "delegitimated" are the manifestations of authority, not the underlying explanations (legitimations). Lipset and Schneider draw this same conclusion from survey data *(The Confidence Gap,* chapter 12).

6

The Workday
Tug of War

[Slavery] was, after all, a very hard system, and we would do well not to forget it. I would concede that there must have been room in it for the virtuosos, the master opportunists, the ones who "played it cool." But how much room? And how much of the system's infinite variety of coercions could the individual slave absorb without his finally internalizing the very role he was being forced to play?

—Stanley Elkins[1]

Some of the most useful as well as the most heated debates in the literature on American slavery revolve around the relative importance of coercion and resistance. To Elkins, coercion was maximal and resistance minimal, leading to the formation of a slavish personality. This was the acquiescent slave.[2] To Fogel and Engerman, resistance and coercion were *both* minimal, leading them to recast slavery as a system very similar in broad outlines to Northern industry. They came up with a rational slave.[3] To Aptheker, coercion and resistance were both maximal, fitting the "normal" theory of oppression leading to resistance. This was the revolutionary slave.[4] Thorpe and Stuckey wrote rebuttals to Elkins in which they agreed that coercion was high and resistance low, but argued that coercion would not have needed to be as high as it was if the "Sambo" role had been internalized. They proposed the mask-wearing or "master-opportunist" slave.[5] Genovese, finding information that tended to contradict each of the above, created the dialectical slave: "The historical record is full of people who were model slaves right up until the moment they killed their overseer, ran away, burned down the Big House or joined an insurrection."[6]

As I have done with writings on the other nonindustrial authority systems sprinkled throughout the discussion, I introduce this debate not to draw crude analogies or to resolve it, but to establish the centrality of the point at issue. In any superordinate-subordinate relationship, there will be coercive acts of authority and there will be resistance to those acts. When that relationship is magnified by the gross inequalities and hardships of factory work, it is inevitable that there will be plenty of both. So far my study has been of attitudes: negative, compliant, oppositional, instrumental, populist. I have been arguing that there is not a very tight fit between the strands of ideas used to interpret the work experience and such objective evidence as can be mustered about that experience. In chapters 3, 4, and 5, there is evidence of both a lack of recognition of hierarchy and inequality, and an acceptance of it when it is recognized. But this does not tell us much about the possible existence or significance of resistance, since it is perilous to infer behavior from attitudes. The most acquiescent respondent can, with no great loss in consistency, throw the proverbial wrench in the line, while the most determinedly critical can go for long periods without engaging in any oppositional activity at all.

Coercion and resistance, then, are subjects of inquiry independent of those presented in previous chapters. What sort of coercive behavior does this (any) company employ? What kinds of activities do employees at NEC participate in that should be called "resistance," and how should such activities be understood in light of the overall themes I have developed? If I have been emphasizing compliance thus far, it is because compliance is overwhelmingly apparent; many more people follow orders than quarrel with any aspect of them. Routines comfort. But they may also impose burdens, and subordinate groups have always developed means to minimize those burdens (at the same time that they have adjusted to them). For their part, the dominant classes cannot afford to rely completely on voluntary compliance. Employee acceptance of company goals is nice (and as indicated in the last chapter, at times essential), but in a pinch, as Hobbes has told us, clubs are even better. We will examine the clubs first.

By Force and Violence

The overseer's whip was the symbol of coercion in slave society. There is no such image in the industrial system. Coercive mechanisms are broken up into separate parts, each considerably less imposing than the whip. This dispersion makes their collective existence and gravity more difficult to discern. At times, I consider to be instances of coercion what could be interpreted as simply limitation of possibilities. Robert Nozick, in pursuing the character of coercion, distinguished between a threat (coercion) and an offer (which might constrict choices of action available to someone and is therefore an instance of "unfreedom," but not coercion). His discussion indicates above all that there is no place to draw an uncrossable line between the two concepts. He ends by demonstrating that aspects of choice exist for those subject to virtually every act of coercion.[7] This makes the job of ferreting out the coercive aspects of an authority relationship that much more difficult. I should point out that this is a problem not just for the outside observer but for the employees themselves. Some would argue that it is a virtue of capitalism that choice pervades so many individual decisions. It certainly is a convenience for those most privileged that choice is embedded in and at times therefore obscures coercion.

Historically, the owners of private enterprises have been rather successful in soliciting the aid of political authority in efforts to prevent unionization. Where the aid was not direct, there was benign neglect toward violent anti-union activity. This sometimes meant violence or mass arrests through the intercession of private policing agencies (the Pinkertons are the most famous) or state militias. It always meant the legal description of unions as a criminal conspiracy to deny employers the rightful use of their property.[8] This is coercion in its most identifiable and incontrovertible form. It also would appear to be dated information and therefore peripheral to my purposes. But the clarity with which we might view this activity as coercive may be nothing more than the "benefit of hindsight"— which really means our ability to look at events without the distorting prejudices of the time. Are contemporary industrial relations substantially free of coercion of this simple and inarguable kind? To begin to answer this, let us look at how the following statement would have to be qualified:

> Though employers usually foresee serious harm from strikes, they are unable to prevent their organized workers from striking.[9]

The counterexample that comes most immediately to mind is that in 1981, the airline traffic controllers went on strike and were all fired. This might not be a serious problem, however, since the above statement does not preclude anachronistic practices or limiting cases. But there are serious problems for that claim apart from exceptions:

1. Some companies use a variety of strong-arm practices to prevent initial unionization (the necessary preliminary to this claim). Some of these practices are legal, such as transferring people, and threatening to fire or actually firing people who transgress the strict rules governing distribution of union material.[10] Others are not—such as firing people who stay within those rules. The matter of legality may seem crucial when viewed from afar, but very few employees are aware of the laws, and few have any sense at all that a company's rights are bounded. In other words, a company can threaten convincingly and fire quickly without much fear of legal challenge.

>*Soon after I was finished with my probationary period at P and G, there was an attempt by employees to organize an outside union. Cards were handed out surreptitiously at work. I stuck mine in my back pocket at lunch. When I went back to work, an employee who seemed to be a union supporter told me to hide the card. "They'll fire you in a minute if they see that." I thought he might not have known I was past my probationary period and told him I was. He said, "I don't care if you've got six months or thirty years. They'll jump on your ass so hard you won't want to work here." I had no*

knowledge of how accurate his statement was or even what the law was in this circumstance, but to that employee and others like him, it did not matter. I hid the card.< PG, PO

---

2. A company can take measures to limit the effectiveness or prevent the occurrence of strikes by stockpiling or timing contracts to end during slack season. Blatant stockpiling can be intended as deterrence, a show of force.

>*"Make you mad, don't it? But you know there ain't nothing we can do about it." [Said in reference to the huge stock of cartons sitting all around us as a strike vote neared.]*< DI, PA

In the steel industry, the stockpiling-layoff cycle became so regular a company strategy that the leadership of the United Steelworkers signed the Experimental Negotiating Agreement, surrendering the right to strike.[11]

3. Regulations and rulings governing labor-management relations do not make it a fair fight, nor were they intended to do so. The Supreme Court decided in 1938 that striking workers may be permanently replaced by strikebreakers, agreeing with this stipulation of the National Labor Relations Board:

> The Board has never contended in this case or in any other that an employer, who has neither caused nor prolonged a strike through unfair labor practices, cannot take full advantage of economic forces working for his victory in a labor dispute.[12]

After twelve months of a strike, the permanently replaced strikers are no longer eligible to vote in any decertification election. The union is decertified by vote of strikebreakers; the strike ends, all without violating any rules. As one labor lawyer who discussed this imbalance noted, "The 'right to strike' upon risk of permanent job loss is a 'right' the nature of which is only appreciated by lawyers."[13]

4. As argued in chapter 5, labor and capital are different and have different resources. A company might suffer during a strike, but its owners and managers do not suffer appreciably as individuals. Workers must sacrifice even in a short strike. That sacrifice becomes a cost to be calculated in deciding whether to strike. Is there coercion present in the implied statement to employees, "If you want different terms of employment than what we are proposing, you will have to live on $25 a week [strike pay] for x weeks"?

Further, the inequality of resources lessens the likelihood that even the impersonal entity "company" will suffer. NEC, for example, is a multinational company and produces many of the same chemical compounds in other locales. The union leadership emphasized this to me when I asked why there had been relatively little strike activity:

Member of Negotiating Committee: They shipped equipment to our sister plant in *[city]* right after the strike began. They could make as much as we do here. And they produce in places we never even heard of.

These are important objections to the statement that employers are "unable to prevent" workers from striking. Of course, strikes do take place, the above state of affairs notwithstanding. But it might be useful to consider the pressures mobilized against employees considering a strike as coercive.

These past and present examples have involved industrial relations proper— that is, the process of employees choosing representation and engaging in collective bargaining. Since this is the sphere of work that has been most carefully delineated legally, and since recognition that it *must* be defined legally is viewed as one of the major achievements of capitalist democracy,[14] it is instructive to see simple coercion playing such an important role even within that system. There is little definitional problem so far. This simple coercion might be called "power with a twist": companies have the ability to impose some conditions unilaterally without being subject to appeal because of legal structures that favor them. This might be considered an operational, though nonrigorous, definition of coercion.

But I have maintained throughout that "industrial relations" is just one aspect of labor-capital relations, and not the one around which my interviews centered. If coercion were limited to obstacles placed in the way of the realization of collective bargaining goals, the workplace would still be hierarchical, but not authoritarian, as I have been calling it.

"That's Our Money"

It has become conventional wisdom to say that early capitalism replaced the lord's authority with the economic whip of the market. The threat of starvation drives people to work and keeps them there. I will take that one step farther. While at work, the overseer's whip has been replaced by the *dependence* of labor on capital. Richard Emerson (in an article intended as a contribution to the early power debates) posited a situation in which one actor could only achieve his or her own goals by contributing to the goals of another.[15] There is power exercised in this relationship, Emerson argued, even if the superordinate does not order the subordinate to work to achieve those goals. The subordinate must. He or she simply has no choice.

Employees as a whole have no choice in deciding whether the profitability of the company for which they work will affect them. That is not to say that an individual employee cannot ignore the future effects of a particular action on the company. But in the aggregate they cannot, or the fact that they did will be forcefully brought to their attention. The reverse is not true. No owner or manager has to worry about the long-term effects of company policies on the health of its work force, save only that it remain minimally competitive in the labor market. Given unemployment and the difficulties employees face when changing jobs, this is a rather easy criterion to meet. Offe summarized this point:

> [T]he collectivity of all workers must be, paradoxically, more concerned with the well-being and the prosperity of capitalists than, inversely, the latter is concerned with the well-being of the working class.[16]

This confluence of interests (between labor and capital) is exactly a paradox because those who ''must be concerned'' with the well-being of their employer may at the same time have developed strongly felt criticisms of the organization of work life. The following comments are from a mechanic who served briefly as a steward:

It was very interesting to see what the union does have to offer and what it does to its workers down there. I explained to the fellows before I even took the position as a union steward, "Look. I'm not really all that gung ho about being a union man. I want you to understand I know a lot about unions and the history of unions, and I know that a lot of people shed blood to get the working man where he is today, with a bargaining unit. That you cannot allow companies to walk all over you and treat you like slaves." I said, "But on the other side of the coin, you got to be fair about it. You can't just keep demanding and wanting and wanting till you put yourself out of a job because you bankrupted the company. The company's in the business of making money for its stockholders. As long as they show a profit, the stockholders are happy."
Q. When you told that to people, what did they say?
A. Well, you know, you can't help but agree. You can't *help* but agree.

>*We had five people on each printing press. An operator was the director of each press and held the highest-paying and most prestigious job. He also had to deal most closely with the foreman and other supervision. The job of operator was awarded by seniority. A fifty-year-old assistant operator, many years senior to some of the operators, told me that he had decided long ago that he would not move up to operator. "I just don't want the pressure. They take you into that office [he pointed to the administration office] and wind up*

> *giving you a headache. I've seen some of these boys [operators]*
> *take the job home with them. I really don't care enough for this outfit*
> *to do that. Of course, when the press is down, I'll fix it. That's our*
> *money, coming out there [pointed to the finished cartons moving*
> *down conveyor]."< DI, PO*

Lindblom's "privileged position of business" also describes a situation of dependence—in that case, of the citizens of a polyarchy on the health of business. Citizens must take into account when calculating policy preferences that business must be induced to perform. They have no choice in this matter. Business leaders need not even threaten to be awarded their privileged place (although they are perfectly willing to do so at times, as NEC has done in relation to the environmental group). "Creating a favorable business climate" essentially means granting concessions to businessmen. Politicians and citizens both understand that their goals can be furthered by contributing to the goals of business. Employees must similarly "induce" the private officials in charge of their particular enterprise to perform by "offering" (being willing to accept) conditions of employment that are satisfactory to them. A favorable business climate must be created within the workplace. These situations are not similar in that they are analogous; rather, they are two subsets of the broader set of dependent relationships between superordinate and subordinate. In both cases, the obligation to consider the well-being of business exists regardless of the inclinations or attitudes of those affected.

But is this obligation *coercion*? Can impersonal forces coerce? Could it not be better described as a state of affairs? Or, to the extent that some people share a greater cost in a dependent relationship, is it not more simply a burden?

In *Dilemmas of Pluralist Democracy*, Dahl considers the problem of whether "control" is present in this example:

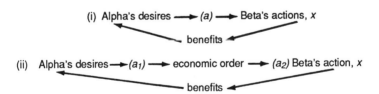

He concludes that while this is not formally an instance of control of Beta by Alpha (because intentionality is lacking), it is "a close neighbor and a mighty potent neighbor at that."[17] I would not object strenuously, nor would this chapter suffer appreciably, if the reader were to conclude that dependence is only a close and potent neighbor of coercion. But there is an important difference between the problem Dahl was examining and the one I am. He was intrinsically interested in defining the relationship between actors, while my study is one of the attitudes and behavior of those in subordinate positions. I am more interested in the effect on Beta of his or her subordinate status. From the perspective of Beta, the impersonal state of affairs described by Dahl looks more like a twin than a close neighbor of coercion.

But even if an impersonal "actor" might be said to coerce, is it proper to say that dependence is one such relationship? Here are three authors touching down on dependence in an industrial setting. None of these three has been discussing coercion in surrounding sentences. The emphases are mine:

> The notion of a fair day's work as equivalent to a wage does not make sense for another reason—namely, the individual laborer's dependence on capital. Proletarian *existence rests* not merely on today's wage, but also on tomorrow's and the next day's.[18]

> System integration is important, in the sense that a complex division of labour establishes interdependencies which *must* be realized and which usually are realized. . . . Workers may perform their roles in the division of labour simply because this is *necessary for the continued survival* of the system on which they themselves depend.[19]

> Immediate producers *cannot survive* on their own. . . . They *must* produce a profit as a condition of their continued employment.[20]

Dependence results in a series of "musts" and "necessaries" on which survival rests.[21] This gives strong credibility to threats coming from a company; more than that, it makes threats unnecessary by sharply constricting choices available to employees. Since one can easily conceive of hierarchical relationships without dependence,[22] it is not tautological to describe dependence as adding coercion to such a relationship. The "musts" for employers do not include this kind of attention to the needs of employees. A company may choose to see its relationship to its employees in this light but it does not have to. An employee may choose not to, but if the collectivity of employees makes that choice, the individual employee will be made to suffer the consequences.

Dependence does not appear at first glance to contain coercion, anymore than the threat of starvation does in the labor market. This makes it especially useful in the exercise of industrial authority, since it is particularly amenable to internalization, which shows up simply as rational calculation. I have already introduced Paul, who we have seen is strongly critical of several aspects of industry. The coercive aspects of dependence stand out more clearly in his words by virtue of its presentation as closely calculated self-interest. The first question and response are from the original interview:

Q. What do you expect from the company? What do they expect from you?

A. We had a saying at Apex—a fair day's work for a fair day's pay.

What I mean by a fair day's work is not just doing a little. I mean producing enough work where it's profitable for the company to employ you as a worker.

Q. But do you ever find there's any conflict between what you think is fair and what the company thinks is fair?

A. You hit on the point that what's fair to you and what's fair to me could be night and day, right? So what I say next is this. I want to know how much you're making in this building. Now when you tell me that you can't afford me asking you for more money, I see it in black and white, then I know that you can't give me. If you can't give it to me and I force you to give it to me, sooner or later I'm going to lose my job, correct? My number one feeling is this—I don't ever want to jeopardize my job.

In the re-interview, I tried to make it as difficult as possible for Paul to maintain this market-based definition of fairness. The outcomes of a dependent relationship can imply painful costs for people at times, even if the alternative—jeopardizing one's job—seems worse. I pointed out some potential negative consequences in order to see how he evaluated them in light of the position described above. Before the next sequence, I reminded Paul of his answer in the first interview.

Q. As I'm sure you know, the company is claiming that building D *[Paul's building]* is not profitable. They're considering plans to close it. The reorganization of the plant involves individual accounting by each building so each one will have to sink or swim on its own. Now let me ask you your opinion on this. In terms of fairness, what would your reaction be if they came to all of you in building D, held a big meeting, and said, "Look guys, this building isn't making it. You're going to take a 20 percent pay cut or you're all out the door." Let's also assume that they were telling the truth, that they opened the books and showed you that. What would your reaction be?

A. Personally, I wish all management would take that approach. Open up the books to employees, make it public. You show me those books, I would take a pay cut gladly because obviously, that's going to save my job and it's the old law of survival. Why would anyone want to give up his job when he can get a cut in pay and still have his job?

His logic would seem to suggest that he might be relatively sanguine about plant closings—if they can't employ you profitably, there's really not much to say about it.[23] But when I presented him with this worst-case scenario, his tone changed dramatically. He became highly emotional (even unable to complete thoughts) and accusatory. What to a company would be a difference of degree (downturn in profits means wage cuts, long-term loss means cessation of operation) forces Paul to shift the norms with which he evaluates events:

Q. Now let's consider the more serious case, and you know this isn't far-fetched. Suppose they come to you and say, "We've got it right down here in black and white that this building loses money. The company as a whole is not losing money and the plant in Lockland is not losing money but this building is losing money"—antiquated machinery, whatever the reason. What would your reaction to that be?

A. Well, unfortunately, like anything else, for everyone in the building, they have no recourse. They can go to the union, but what can the union do if the company isn't making money in the building? *[Long pause.]* See, I've had so many experiences, I can't explain. It's like getting burned. You can't explain to somebody what the feeling is being burned unless you've been burned. To all of a sudden—for management to—and this is probably the worst thing that I feel in this country—let's take an employee who's been there thirty years. He's fifty years old now. All of a sudden he loses his job. What happened to the thirty years when he made money for that company? They didn't say to him, "Hey, you made too much money for me." Correct? Nobody ever says, "What happened to the thirty, twenty-five, twenty years when you're making all that money?" The same thing at Apex. People said the workers at Apex make too much money but they never said it when Apex was making record profits, year after year after year. They never said people were making too much money then. Only when they were having bad years. So the company has to have some kind of responsibility to the people that they hired. When you say "J.J. Smith is going to lose his job"—no. No. J.J. Smith is not going to lose his job. J.J. Smith's *family* is going to lose his job. It's going to affect their standard of living, a whole spectrum. Because if you were to get the statistics on people who have been on layoff, look at the suicidal rate, look at the health factor, look at the children, you would come up with some amazing statistics. They say, "We don't owe you now, 'cause the plant ain't making no money." Well, what happened when the plant was making money? Why weren't you retooling? Why didn't you take this money and buy up-to-date machinery so you could be more competitive? Instead of giving out big bonuses to the vice-president, to the president, to the supervisors?

> Because the employee down on the floor didn't get no bonuses. Now you're crying wolf, you say, "Fine. We don't need you no more." What are you doing to society?

These are angry words, not at all consistent with his previous straightforward cost-benefit analysis. The cost—to Paul and many others—is intolerable, whatever the needs and motivations of those who impose it. The frustration in his voice is a result not only of the nature of the hardship ("getting burned"), but of the inability to do anything about it ("no recourse"). It would be hard to construct any usable definition of coercion that excluded the situation just described. To be clear on this point, I am not suggesting that Paul's use of market norms to define his self-interest is the result of illusion. It is real, given the dependence of the employee on the profitability of his or her company. But it is only as rational as the system as a whole. Why, for instance, should Paul have been so willing to tolerate the demand that pay be determined on the basis of building-by-building accounting?

Both sides of the dependent relationship are present in his answers—that he must take the well-being of the company into account and that the company need not do the same for employees.[24] It is particularly significant that it was Paul who described the workings of dependence in this way. In spite of the views he has expressed about the wrongfulness of the current distribution of power and rewards in industry, and in spite of his populist distrust of those who make decisions, he has no choice but to accede to the demands of profitability. The fact that he did so "gladly" (his word) at first—until the worst consequences were forced to his attention—may indicate internalization, but coercion and acceptance of the choices made under coerced conditions are not opposites. This "privileged position of the company" forces everyone, regardless of attitudes toward authority, private enterprise, or even capitalism as a whole to work and hope for the success of "their" company.

Huw Beynon wrote about a British Ford factory where there had been a bitter strike; his account was filled with continuing employee hostility toward the company expressed on many fronts. Beynon's following anecdote summarizes the nature of dependence-as-coercion:

> When I was discussing possible titles for this book with some of the stewards at Halewood, I tentatively suggested *Never Buy A Ford*. I was told that "the lads in the plant wouldn't thank you for that." Of course they wouldn't. It would have been a bad title. If people stopped buying Fords, they'd be out of a job. Their battle with Ford is tempered by this concern.[25]

Capital and Other Punishment

To this point, the reader might have been temporarily satisfied with my non-rigorous and somewhat playful use of "coercion." But I am heading into some thorny areas, and in order to build toward a clearer notion of that term, I will rely for a short time on its usage in common speech—roughly, the use of force to obtain goals. While economic necessity, as defined by current institutional arrangements, forms one coercive force employees must confront, it is certainly not the only one. Real people invoke real powers conferred on them by those same arrangements. One worker interviewed by Studs Terkel complained of his difficulty in finding "who to sock."[26] He was describing the impersonal coercive force of dependence. On the other hand, Barrington Moore made the German working class the centerpiece of his investigation in *Injustice* exactly because "in the workplace there are visible and concrete human beings who appear responsible for injustice."[27] What he was describing was the exercise of the power of the owners of private enterprise to establish and enforce rules.

Comments at NEC concerning rule enforcement were not voluminous. Several people (not all) felt that safety rules were often enforced in a punitive manner:

They always pick on you for the little stuff and hit you over the head with it, but the big things that we tell them about, they seem a little slow.

There were two other sets of complaints about specific rule enforcement on matters related to safety. Toward the end of my interviewing period, NEC created a "facial hair" policy, which mandated everyone to cut their beards and trim their mustaches. The purpose of the policy was to allow respirators to fit more tightly.[28] The new policy was not discussed with the union. NEC gave advance notice and then sent several people home when they refused to comply. One person had been sent home shortly before I interviewed him. I conducted four interviews after the policy was declared. Three of the four interviewees brought it up as an example of arbitrary and unfair use of power.

The other complaint was that NEC would never take responsibility for accidents, that accidents were always said to be the employee's fault. Why is this coercion and not petty buck-passing? The company controls the official accident reports. The two following comments may give the reader the sense of authority being exercised in deciding the final version of accidents (both people were describing specific accidents, but were especially vexed at the reports).

Speaker A: I have to laugh about when they write out an accident report. It seems like they always blame 90 percent of it—the employees weren't right.

Speaker B: I went down and had the foreman make out a near-miss accident report. He wasn't about to. So I went and saw the grievance man. I had the safety man down and showed him what was going on. The foreman told the grievance man and the steward, "God damn it, if I have to make out a near-miss accident report, I'll make it out, but damn it, he won't like it." And I didn't like it either. He said I went at the work haphazardly. They always turn it.

The "facial hair" issue stood out because it was current. The "safety report" issue may have been particularly bothersome to some people because NEC makes such a public fuss about safety. The crime they were pointing to may actually have been hypocrisy. But the number of people who brought up these matters was slightly less than those who said that NEC was "too lenient." I have previously mentioned that NEC is considered a "hard place to get fired from" (except for probationary employees). One interpretation of these facts would be that looking at the "personal" forms of coercion at NEC is not a pressing task.

I think this would be a mistake—that is, it is looking only at the disaggregated elements of coercion, rather than at its totality. Coercion is more deeply imbedded and more important than can be gathered from the reaction of employees to rule changes or examples of arbitrariness. The company in its conduct of industrial relations certainly believes that its ability to coerce is essential, even if it is used infrequently. In the interview with the LRS, I asked how he would respond to the reverse of the question I call the "Absolutely Wrong" question:

Q. I ask them, "In the time you've been working here, is there anything which has happened to you or which you've seen happen to others around you that you said to yourself when it happened, 'this is wrong, this is absolutely wrong?' " What employee behavior would you put in that category?
A. We have certain offenses, we have a list of posted offenses, unacceptable behavior for which an employee would receive strict discipline. And there are certain types of offenses which we call capital offenses that would be subject to termination. Those are such things as fighting on the job, stealing from the company, tampering with the equipment or willful destruction of company property, serious operator error resulting in huge safety problems or dollar loss to the company. Those are the ones where we would suspend someone immediately pending termination.

This was a formal reply. Every company has such a list—instructive enough as a guide to the policing powers of the private enterprise (note, for instance, the emphasis on the protection of property). But the actual use of discipline usually deviates from written rules. By the time I held that interview, I already knew that some employees considered the company too lenient in dealing with rule violations. Such comments usually arose from the "criticism of negative attitudes" discussed in the last chapter. I asked the LRS about these comments. His response was:

I would tend to agree with those. Everything I'm making comments on is in reference to what we've done in the past. It's not in reference to what I feel is ideal or is even what I feel should be the norm here. I think there are major areas for improvement in running the place. We can be a *lot* more rigorous in the way we apply discipline for attendance and work habits and for things as simple as performance on the job. I would agree with that. I'm pleased to hear that.

The LRS, a relative newcomer to his job, intended that the real disciplinary codes be brought more closely into line with the formal ones. The potential for the use of discipline by management is usually greater than the actual use. But the disciplinary tools were available for his use. Increased discipline could only happen in a quiet tug of war with employees. This conflict is distinctively one between management and employees, not management and union, since the union must adhere to the formal rules. The tugging done by employees is discussed in the next section. But the company can always tug harder.

>*There was an employee at Diamond who was fired for absenteeism after several disciplinary layoffs. The union leadership did not want to arbitrate the case, since the employee did have a horrendous attendance record. There was a vote by the membership to overrule the leadership and send the firing to arbitration. The arbitrator sustained the firing. I read the decision. There was no dispute over the repeated poor attendance or the previous warnings. But the company lawyer also did not dispute the central defense contention that the employee had an advanced case of emphysema (not caused, either party claimed, by work). Nor did the company dispute that there were conditions on the job that made it difficult for someone with emphysema to work. In fact, the company in making its case stipulated that argument as true. They were after a more basic point. They argued, and the arbitrator agreed, that the employee was too sick to work at Diamond*

and may have been too sick to work anywhere. But, the decision read, there was no law that obliged a company to offer such a man employment or to continue to employ him. When this employee showed me the decision, he said, "I guess what this is saying is that if you get sick, the hell with you, go sell pencils."< DI, PA

Force and the procurement of consent—or their Weberian twins, coercion and legitimation—are usually described as two methods of exercising authority. They are understood to be at an equivalent conceptual level, although sometimes it is also argued that the more mature a regime, the more it relies on consent. If NEC does not appear to need to enforce its rules—especially the "capital offenses"—regularly, it could be understood as a "regime" that does not rest on coercion.[29] While most of what I have written so far has argued that workers adapt themselves to the need to follow orders, it is a definitional mistake to see this as a confirmation of the absence of coercion. The *ability* to coerce must be consolidated and maintained, logically prior to and usually physically prior to efforts to elicit support. Legitimation and coercion do not refer to mutually exclusive and competing "regime-tactics." Consider Michael Crozier's brief description of the exercise of authority in a factory:

> The punitive aspect of the conformity achievement process has declined. Direct coercion is still in reserve as a last resort, but it is very rarely used, and people apparently no longer have to see it operate often to retain it in their calculations.[30]

These two sentences cannot possibly both be true. There are two claims here: first, if the number of forcible acts has declined, coercion has declined. But if the "punitive aspect" had actually declined in importance, it would be less a part of people's calculations. If the absolute number of acts of discipline has declined—which must be what he meant—it might be simply because the information about discipline is now more widespread. For people to "retain it in their calculations" coercion simply must be practiced to a degree *sufficient to produce the required end*. If a company finds it can produce those ends with fewer acts of discipline, it does not mean that coercion—"the punitive aspect"—has declined. Regimes may vary in the number of acts of force, but if the reason for that is that people become increasingly aware of what rules they should not transgress—which Crozier seems to imply—the value of coercion remains the same to those who employ it; it may even be said to have increased because they have achieved more bang for the buck. In the slavery debates, Fogel and Engerman attempted to show that whipping did not occur nearly as often as had been previously believed, concluding that coercion was not as important in "persuading" slaves to work as had been thought.[31] In reply, Gutman and Sutch wrote:

The essential statistic is not the average number of whippings per hand per year. Such an "average" does not measure the utility of the whip as an instrument of social and economic discipline. It is much more relevant to know how often the whip and its use were brought to the attention of a plantation labor force.[32]

The second claim is that "direct coercion" is kept as a last resort and can be said therefore to have diminished in importance. *Coercion as a last resort is the cornerstone of any regime and can almost never be said to have diminished.* There is a difference in kind between the use of force to elicit favorable behavior and the ability of a regime to defend its existence through the legal use of force. In the blurring of this distinction lies the key to the misunderstanding that pervades some discussions of coercion. A regime may both employ acts of force and solicit consent; it may even prefer to rely on the second as opposed to the first. But this is an incomplete description of the role of force in regime maintenance. A regime always maintains sufficient force to protect its existence, and more important, creates the *right* to use that force—the legal monopoly on the use of violence in Weber's terms.[33] This should not be confused with the decision actually to exercise that right in any particular instance. Nor should it be confused with the decision *not* to exercise that right, as is usually the case when people write about the decline of coercion in regime maintenance. People normally obey traffic laws. In fact, most people probably feel that traffic laws perform a useful social function. It would not be a happy situation if everyone had to be ticketed frequently in order to induce compliance. But the state retains its ultimate ability to impose sanctions for failure to obey. If you receive a ticket and do not pay, you can go to jail. If you resist going to jail, in the final instance you may be shot and the people shooting you will be protected.[34]

Am I arguing that coercion in any authority system may never vary in magnitude—that is, that it must always have a value of zero or one? The answer depends on which of the two aspects of coercion is intended. The answer to the question, "How many acts of force does a regime use in order to achieve compliance with its rules and orders in the course of daily affairs?" is that not all regimes are equal in this respect. NEC probably uses discipline less than did factories in Manchester in 1780. But if the question is, "Does a regime accord itself the ability and right to use force to maintain itself?" the answer is yes. Except in specific and rare historical moments, that aspect of coercion will always be zero or one. When the army of a regime deserts, as happened in Iran in 1978–79 or in the Philippines in 1985, that form of coercion falls rapidly from one to zero. An even more unusual circumstance occurred in Chile in 1973 when the ability of the Allende regime to coerce was on the verge of moving from zero to one by the creation of militias outside the formal military structure. The generals understood that this was the point of no return and moved quickly to intercept that process.[35]

A dramatic example of the optical illusion created by the difference between tactical and ultimate uses of coercion is contained in the description of attempts by Prison Superintendent Thomas Murton to reform the infamous Arkansas prison system in the 1960s. Virtually all internal disciplinary functions were handled by inmate "trustys" who were flamboyantly vicious and corrupt. The inmates appeared to be in complete control of the prison; trustys carried guns while "free-world" (non-inmate) guards did not. Even the non-trustys seemed to prefer this system of stable brutality to the uncertainties introduced by Murton's reforms.[36] But there is no doubt (Murton expressed none) that the purpose of maintaining a prison system such as this was to enforce the subjugation of the prisoners. State agencies resisted Murton's attempts to modernize the system and eventually fired him. The guns in the hands of the prisoners were real and were used often to shoot other inmates, but the real coercive power lay in the hands of the "state"—specifically, the state of Arkansas and the policing forces at their disposal. They simply found it convenient to have the trustys act as their stand-ins.[37]

A factory authority system does not have recourse to the severity of sanctions available to the political system as a whole. But it can appeal to the nexus of laws surrounding private property and can exercise its ability to banish people from "citizenship" (by firing them) if they challenge the industrial equivalent of traffic laws. The Wagner Act codified for the first time a specific set of activities for which an employee may not be disciplined, such as attempts to raise questions about wages, hours, and working conditions. These are "protected" activities. There are, on the other hand, many unprotected activities that are not illegal. The employer is not prohibited from retaliating in these cases. If employer retaliation (disciplining or firing) seems too "private" to qualify as coercion, there is still the next step: the property belongs to the employer and a fired employee, who has done nothing illegal to that point, may be treated as a trespasser and led away by security guards or police.

>*A young and very well respected employee who had become steward in my department came to me in frustration just a few weeks after he began his duties. He tore a small corner off a cigarette carton. "That's how much rights we've got, and they've got the rest. And then they argue over this* [the corner] *and we can't get nowhere."< DI, PA*

The right to use force stands apart from the daily expression of that authority and is considerably less visible. In his description of the games people participate in at work, Burawoy seemed to imply a great deal of latitude for employees. The games "arise from worker initiatives, from the search for means of enduring subordination to the labor process." But he was also careful to point out that management regulates the game "coercively if necessary": "We do not collectively decide what the rules of making out will be; rather we are compelled to play the game, and we then proceed to defend the rules."[38]

It is useful to know how widely and how prominently acts of force are employed, but that is not the end of the question. If coercion at NEC does not seem to be widely discussed, it may be because only the tip of the iceberg is visible. In the final analysis, "political" power in a factory, as in society generally, does indeed come out of the barrel of a gun.

Resistance—Defense of the Everyday Conception

Workers, we have seen, face a variety of coercive forces, some personal and quite obvious (e.g., a reprimand from a foreman), some impersonal and remote, although no less threatening on that account (dependence). Finally there is the rarely acknowledged but crucial "coercion in reserve"—the rights that a company retains by virtue of laws of private property. The fact that coercion takes these very different forms means that there are different sets of risks involved in opposing any specific policy or, hypothetically, the system of industrial authority as a whole. The risks are also not completely known at any point; any act of opposition takes place with some degree of uncertainty about the consequences. I have maintained throughout that oppressive conditions, including those found in factories, give rise to both passivity and resistance. I have emphasized the former because it is usually argued that passivity is transitory, or from the opposite end of the analytical spectrum, that passivity can only mean that oppression does not exist. The ways in which NEC workers actively oppose aspects of company practices show that there is no challenge to the most important aspects of factory authoritarianism, but this would not be a very successful account if I did not try to take stock of such resistance as does occur.

Dependence, for example, has been used to explain passivity in situations as far-ranging as the quiescence of the Iranian peasantry[39] or that of Arabs living in Israel.[40] It is true that subordinate status implies fewer resources to mobilize in oppositional activity as well as fewer resources with which to enjoy life.[41] Those with fewer resources are then more vulnerable to pressures from those on whom they are dependent. Paul's comments on the need for "one hundred percent plus" efficiency are an illustration of this. "Vulnerability" is not a synonym for dependence but an outcome of it. It is the active ingredient, the way in which a dependent relationship might lead to passivity. Gaventa, for example, argued that the vulnerability of the miners and mine-dependents (different use of the term) led to votes that seemed to register nonopposition to local elites.[42]

"Dependence-vulnerability" is an attractive argument because it locates passivity exactly in the deprivations inherent in subordination, as opposed to the two conventional competing explanations—that people are just dull, on the one hand, or that they do have substantial access to power on the other. Bertell Ollman pointed out quite accurately that "vulnerability" created a problem for Marx, even in the absence of any challenge to his analysis of the hardships of capitalism, past and future:

> Given the conditions which prevailed in Marx's time, many workers must have suffered from this extreme degradation. And, when treated like animals, they reacted like animals, tame ones.[43]

Dependence-vulnerability is a theory of class oppression without class struggle.[44]

But that concept has limited usefulness; since it could apply to all relations between dominant and subordinate groups, it is too broad. It also cannot explain when and why people grant legitimacy to hierarchical, undemocratic, and inegalitarian institutions such as the one I am studying. Of course, vulnerability is *consonant* with such granting of legitimacy, but it neither predicts nor explains it. Abercrombie, Hill, Moorehouse and Chamberlain, and Scott have all appeared in previous pages to argue that compliance on a factual level does not necessarily mean normative acceptance of the goals of a dominant class. My argument has been that while it is true that compliance does not *necessarily* mean normative acceptance, in the case of NEC employees there appear to be many aspects of industrial authority that are in fact seen as legitimate. Vulnerability alone is insufficient to explain why this is so. It tends to make all unearthing of resistance into a refutation of the existence of a dominant ideology and fuel for the "pragmatic acceptance" fire.

As in every factory, there is activity at NEC that is properly termed "resistance." People speak up about particular abuses, decide on certain aspects of their own work routine, and thwart company attempts to change those routines. They define what is a satisfactory relationship with immediate supervision and develop means to "stick the green weenie" to those who violate those standards. There are also ways, including absenteeism, cutting corners, and evading work assignments, in which people try to lessen the overall hardships of worklife. This last set of activities, as I argue later, belongs in a different category. The issues around which resistance takes place represent some fine-tuning of the informal contract that governs expectations of how authority should be exercised. There is a great deal rendered unto Caesar, but there are also important arenas of contention. The form and purpose of resistance at NEC fit well Sabel's description of working-class militancy:

> The worker's militancy is not evidence that he has a second self, more or less rational as the case may be, than his accommodating everyday personality. Rather, his militancy is above all a sign of his determination to defend his everyday conception, which as a whole is comprised of illusions and truth inextricably interwound.[45]

>In my first term at Diamond (I was laid off after four months), I was struck by how seriously everyone took their work, and how they judged other people by the quality of their work. When I went back after layoff and began to know the people in my department and particularly on my press better, I was struck by how much subtle sabotage was taking place that was not visible to the untrained eye. My third impression, though, was the lasting one. Both the first two were accurate and were part of a give and take that operated well within bounds acceptable to the company (although not always maximally pleasing to them). I believe that is similar to Sabel's "militancy in defense of the everyday conception."< DI, PO, and PA

By "resistance" in a factory setting, I generally mean efforts by employees to deny claims that management makes on their time and effort and the attempt to secure as large a return for those two as possible. The last phrase refers principally to collective bargaining and strikes and is often mistaken for the whole category. There have been only two contract strikes and no wildcat strikes in the Lockland plant's entire existence, and the last one was nearly twenty years ago. On the other hand, the battle over time goes on continuously. Resistance exists in both soft- and hard-core forms. In the softer form, employees take advantage of the ambiguities and indeterminacies of production to create their own work norms while minimizing the risks of confrontation; in the harder, they might openly flout some rules or orders in order to communicate a disagreement. There is risk in both situations, but also in both the employees are testing the company in an area where it is least likely to mobilize its coercive apparatus—enforcement of work rules.

>One department I worked in announced that employees were only permitted to use office telephones during breaks. No one paid much attention to that order. (There were some jobs in the department that allowed employees to leave the line for periods of time other than breaks.) I was working cleanup, which meant that I made my own work schedule and break times (one before and one after lunch). I was on the phone shortly after lunch when the foreman walked in and asked me what I was doing. I told him to go ahead and fire me. He told me that was not a satisfactory answer and demanded that I explain what I was doing (even though it was fairly obvious). I reminded him that I determined my own break time and that I had not yet taken my second break (it was just after lunch and it was preposterous to think I was taking a break). He asked me if I had been on break. I told him I would think about it. Later that night, I went back and told him that he could consider that my break. He

knew perfectly well that had never crossed my mind when I was on the phone. Despite the transparency of the whole discussion, he thanked me and was immensely relieved. < PG, PA

Perhaps because resistance of any kind skirts the bounds of plant legality, not a great deal was said about it in the original interviews, and what was said seemed purposely vague. I originally intended that two questions elicit information about activity of this kind. I asked people about conflict at work, including that between employees and management. The answers to that turned out to be uninformative variants of ''No problem, I get along good with everyone.'' People attached negative connotations to the word ''conflict'' and I dropped the question halfway through the interviews. I also expected to find useful information by following up the ''Absolutely Wrong'' question (''In the time you've been here, has anything happened to you or anyone around you where you said to yourself at the time, 'this is wrong, this is absolutely wrong?' '') by asking how the individual or those involved responded. My assumption was that in situations where people told me that the company had crossed some mental line, there might have been some active response. This too was largely unsuccessful, although for different and perhaps informative reasons. The LRS, in his answer given above, clearly linked his answer to the question with action on the company's part—what is absolutely wrong is in violation of the rules, what we do is punish. The structure of the employees' answer was different. Twenty-five of the thirty-three employees responded that there had been some incident that they felt was ''absolutely wrong.''[46] The answers clustered around three areas—health and safety; the incident in which two people had been killed; and the unwillingness of NEC management to take advice from its employees. Only two answered my follow-up question by saying that they did anything about it. One talked to his committeeman; the other was Jill, who went to see a lawyer about what she felt was hazardous exposure to chemicals. The others were either surprised that I expected them to have taken some action, or had concluded themselves that there was nothing anyone could do.

Speaker A [after a disciplinary incident that did not involve him directly, the details of which I cannot repeat]: What can you do? What's done is done.

Speaker B [had been told to perform a maintenance job in a risky area]: There's nothing really to do, that I could see. You go to the union, they say do the work first, then file a grievance. Then the work's done, so what good is that?

These were all incidents that the speakers themselves had specified as being unjust in response to an intentionally moralistic question. Probably the question and intended follow-up reflected a concession on my part to the conventional link between injustice and resistance called into question in chapter 1. I expected at least some employees to have "enforced" the informal contract by individual or even collective retaliation for acts described in answers to this question. If there were *no* situations in which there was retaliation, this would not be noteworthy, but there were. They simply involved situations other than those described as "absolutely wrong."

"His Way—No Way"

The focal point of purposeful and often collective resistance was the "pushy" foreman. Most people described their own foreman as tolerable but had heard of one who was not. The bad supervisor was one who inserted himself into the work routine more than the workers felt was necessary. Their response was to produce *less* for that person. This was partly simple punishment and partly a calculated appeal to higher authority; that is, they hoped the building supervisors would notice and encourage the foreman to change. These first two speakers were responding to questions about whether work varied under different foremen:

Speaker A: The shift I was on—that foreman, I guess he's new, as in a year or more, but he's not really a good foreman because a good foreman, he'll tell you what to do, and then you'll see him maybe twice a night and that's it. This person will bug you and bug you and tell you to do this and that and then the workers will just—instead of giving him the work he wants—will just cut right down and not give him anything.
Q. I suppose that would particularly grate on the guys who've been around for a while.
A. Yah, and then they kind of tell the new people, "If he's like that, just take it easy, take your time, because he's not really going to appreciate what you do for him." If the guy's over there bugging you and bugging you, you'll see a big difference between that and the one that's not. It's really—it's unbelievable the difference.

Speaker B: You have some foremen that just push, push, push and when you find people like that I think you get less work out of the people than if you left them alone and let them do their jobs.
[A few minutes later]: I don't like to try to insult people, but there are some people I will insult because they—they're book smart and that's

about it. They're not commonsense smart. So you get some of these college graduates come in and think that they know everything about a factory. And that's where you get some of them that push, push, push. And you just can't push people to do things. Building C is like—I mean, they got some people there that can make or break you in production. They get a foreman that figures they're going to change the way that building's been running for so many years and those people will break you. Because you can't just change things overnight.

After a few comments such as these alerted me to the existence of this inverse relationship between push and produce, I asked others about it in later interviews:

Q. If there's a foreman in the department that people have trouble with, do you think it's likely that people will not work as hard?
Speaker A: Oh yah.
Q. That they'll hold back somewhat?
A. Definitely. That's one way to—for example, the person that we have in the building that really gets on everyone all over the place—it's like we're back in school, that he's got to babysit for us. Everyone knows their job, but he's still just around pestering, trying to do things his way. No way.
Q. Do you think the other half of that is true, that if there's a foreman that people like, that people will do a little extra for him?
A. It's not the point that—"like." There are foremen that just don't bother you. They know we don't like to be looked over and stuff like that. Like we told this guy, but I don't know what he expected, whether he thinks he's going to get somewhere like that, but he's really killing his own self, because people won't do nothing.

Lest I leave the impression that the decline in productivity for such a foreman is simply the result of some malaise in the work force, I turn to Wendy and Jill who were characteristically blunt:

Wendy: I'm a firm believer that after you get a college degree, if you're going to work in management in a factory, that you should take a course in common sense. Because you cannot go in there and tell some guy who's been there forty years how to do his job. Because he's going to look at you and he's going to sabotage you. And it has happened, more than once.

Jill: It usually happens with a new one. That's the first thing that'll happen. Some kid comes in, he's a foreman, he's going to organize this, he's going to get everything shipshape, he's going to have people doing—Well, the first thing you know is that some of these guys who've been there for a while, all a sudden things won't work any more. Things will break. Production will stop. They'll run him out of material. Can't figure out why, can't prove anything, and they don't know why it's happening. But they can't seem to control it.

The terrain of struggle is the perceived attempt by management to change the status quo—here, a new attempt to rationalize production; there, a "renegade" foreman. The likelihood of the company utilizing its coercive power is small (although not nonexistent). This is true partly because the resistance is carried on quietly. The "guy who's been there forty years" undoubtedly knows the machinery better than the supervisor. But it is also because the company and employees both see the process as one of restoration, an appeal by employees to past norms. This makes the legitimacy of the managerial intervention more questionable.

The re-interviews gave me a chance to find out more about resistance. To put people more at ease, I turned off the tape recorder (although I did tell them their words would be quoted) and asked people if they could provide specific examples of collective activity designed to change company policy. In order to explain what I was looking for, and, not at all secondarily, to make them feel more comfortable in telling me about it, I recounted the following incident:

>*In the job I worked at Diamond, we always relieved each other for ten minutes each hour in addition to the required 10-20-10 break-lunch schedule. This was not a formal arrangement, but it had gone on for years. For reasons they did not explain, the supervisors told us one day that we would have to stop giving and taking breaks. There were three presses, with two grabbers (my job) at each press. The breaks were never given at the same time, since they occurred at the convenience of other people working on the press. The day after we were told to stop the breaks, at a prearranged time (not normal break time, but a time when the higher-level supervision was always around), all six grabbers were relieved simultaneously and in full view of the supervisors. All of us went upstairs to the bathroom, which was our ostensible excuse. There was no problem with breaks after that.< DI, PA*

Although John had been at NEC a relatively short time, he told me of a similar incident:

> Yes, something very similar happened in building X. They get fif-teen-minute breaks every hour there. A new building supervisor decided that he'd put an end to that. So people put in a boycott of overtime, eighty people. People *live* on overtime there, but they turned it all down. It was sort of cutting off the nose to spite the face, but over a few months, the breaks came back. Nobody said any-thing, but little by little you could take more time.

Jill had personally taken part in a similar activity, belying by her enthusiasm in retelling it the "go to work and go home" picture she tried to paint of herself.

> We were working on rotating shifts with continuous machine opera-tion where you couldn't shut down the machine. They wanted us to take an hour after work to learn some new safety procedures. They wouldn't relieve us on the job, they wanted us to do it after work. Well, as it happened, a lot of us didn't want to stay the hour over. I was on first shift and it meant I would have had to stay until four and I was tired and I had responsibilities for my family. One day, I showed up with a doctor's excuse, I had a doctor's appointment for 4:30 in the afternoon and I said I wasn't going to stay. Someone else had an excuse like that and they weren't going to stay. It turned out that all fifteen of us on that shift had doctor's appointments. So the foreman called us into the office and he said, "Well, what can I do? I've got to reprimand you all." But eventually they worked it out so that we got relieved on the job and we didn't have to stay any longer.

Intentional collective resistance at NEC takes the form of duels in the every-day conception. The orientation on the part of the employees is to appeal to old forms of inequality as a norm to rally people to oppose new ones. What is at stake is in no case a major question of how resources or power should be distributed. Break times, minor work procedures, and scheduling blips are not issues for which the company is likely to use severe sanctions. This is not to say that they are unimportant to employees. Even apart from the tangible annoyances of shorter breaks or irregular schedules, there seems to be an element of wounded pride—"You can't tell a guy who's been there forty years how to do his job." In fact, employees may have been able to wage some of this struggle successfully because of the relative importance to employees and relative unim-portance to NEC of the issues involved. It is precisely these areas of relative tactical weakness of the powerful that Scott calls the most significant arenas for the contest of power—class struggle by small-caliber weapons fire.[47] While any single act of denying a prerogative of management may be inconsequential by itself, might the sum of such actions "cumulatively have an appreciable impact on class and authority relations," as Scott has claimed about everyday peasant resistance in the countryside? In his argument, even acts of unalloyed self-interest on the part of the powerless may create a disability for the powerful, with the definitive example being the role played in the Russian Revolution by deserters from the World War I front (peasants moved by instinctual self-preservation).[48]

Of course, what is and is not an "appreciable" impact is not easy to determine, but most conventional usages would probably describe the legalization of industrial unionism as the only appreciable change in industrial authority in this country. That was accomplished only by a many-tiered full-frontal assault. The everyday battles at NEC, as in other factories, occur on a range of questions that are far short of including any of the pillars of factory authoritarianism. What the "guy who had been there forty years" had been doing in those forty years was adapting and coping with a situation of powerlessness—possibly creating small freedoms that seemed worth defending, but always with little cumulative effect on the relation which defines one class as superordinate and the other as subordinate.

Another argument by those who see acceptance of subordinate status only as pragmatic (Abercrombie, Scott, and others) describes coercion as the principal reason for compliance. In some important aspects, this does seem to be true in the tug of war of "everyday resistance" at NEC. These skirmishes are conditioned by the probability of the company responding to specific acts of disobedience with discipline. A common rallying cry for collective activity (not confined to factories) is, "What are they going to do, fire us all?" Of course, NEC could fire them all (for example, in Jill's example above) and it is up to the calculation and above all the instincts of employees never to bring that to a test. Coercion and the threat of its use shape the outlines of what can be opposed and what cannot be. At a minimum, the employees must know which questions they can push and on which they have to give ground. "Everyday resistance" looks quite formidable when pitted against "everyday coercion," but considerably less so when compared to the company's near-monopoly on legal violence and on the coercive force of dependence.

As a result, on some levels, resistance seems to form an important counterweight to managerial prerogatives,[49] and on other levels it seems unthinkable. This can create confusion for both interviewer and respondent. My fourth and final re-interview was conducted with "Tony," who has been at NEC for twenty-seven years. Tony has had a wide range of experiences there. He spent ten years in production, then moved on to maintenance. He worked in several capacities with the union, although he held no union position at the time of the interview. He also worked in several joint committees with management and was asked once to be a foreman. He declined because of the shift rotation. I chose to re-interview Tony because he was highly knowledgeable about many aspects of the company and was given to careful calculation about goals in the workplace and the costs of achieving them. During the re-interview, Tony made what seemed to be hopelessly self-contradictory remarks on the subject of employee resistance and the ability of the company to implement policies. These remarks may be at least partially reconciled by careful consideration of the different levels of power to which he was comparing "everyday resistance."

During the off-tape portion of the re-interview, Tony offered the following story, as graphic a description of employee resistance as I heard in these interviews:

Let's say the department manager of building X goes to one of Mr. [LRS's] meetings and he [the LRS] says, "I want you guys to start cracking the whip. We're going to 10, 30, 10 minute breaks." Those guys are used to more. So the guy says, "Okay." They can do that. But now when they go downstairs to produce product, all of a sudden the chemicals overreact and don't produce as much. The product turns up bad. They don't know why and he cannot find out why. But believe me, it's because of the guys. I'll just give you an example. Let's say your foreman's giving you a hard time. If the press is running good, it takes two minutes to fill an eighty-gallon drum. So they come in and they do this [change the break times]. So the fellow goes downstairs and throws in two bags of the catalyst. If you put in one bag, the press will run fine. But if you put in two bags, it overreacts. So instead of putting out one hundred drums in four hours, now he's going to put out sixty drums. Oh, he's going to be there doing the work. The foreman goes and watches him, he's going to be there filling the drums. So the building supervisor starts asking questions and his people don't have any answers. None. It can go on and on and on. And it's been like that for years and it's not going to change. How do you control that? I have no idea.

This story is very similar to the others solicited in the unrecorded section of the re-interviews (although a little more explicit). But less than ten minutes before that, Tony had offered a strikingly different analysis. We had been discussing the reorganization plan and had been speculating on the possible changes it might produce.

Q. I interviewed [the LRS] after I did all the interviews. I got the very distinct impression from him—this isn't my interpretation, he said it—that he intended to make important changes in the work atmosphere in the place. He talked about tighter discipline, that the place

had become too much of a country club. I've talked to people about it, and they say, "We've heard this kind of thing before. Nothing changes." How seriously do you take it and do you see changes?
Tony: I guess I'm more aware 'cause I work both sides. I don't go and punch my clock and do my job and come home. I'm also involved with *[describes committee with management]* so I work with management very closely. And if they want to change it, they can change it. No doubt about it. They can crack the whip and change it. And there's many people down there who don't believe that that can happen. And they're the people that are in for a rude awakening. Cause it could happen, very easily. It's a whole new regime, a new clique. They're going to make their own policy and that's what's going to happen.

There are three possible explanations for how Tony could have made such contradictory statements so close together. He could simply have been incoherent, saying in each instance the first thing that came into his mind. But the reason I re-interviewed Tony was because he was so lucid about NEC, about the labor movement, and about the nature of industry in the United States. It seems worth considering that there might be something more than randomness here. Second, he could be one of those people who "is in for a rude awakening." That is, contrary to Charles Sabel, above, maybe he does have a "second self" that simply overlooks displeasing information. This actually would fit my overall themes closely. The "everyday conception" would crowd out other information, even when it was Tony himself who collected it. Qualitative interviewing is inherently limited by the lack of a fail-safe method for rejecting explanations, particularly for comments from one individual. But as I puzzled over Tony's statements—probably longer than I did over any other section of interview material—I became aware of another explanation in which the incoherence is reduced (although it cannot be completely eliminated). Tony's remarks can be understood as addressing the different forms of coercion employees face, as we have discussed, and the space each did or did not leave for resistance. When a single foreman tried to change ingrained work habits, he faced the problem of limited and inefficient sanctions. When a "new regime" decided on a new policy, it could not be stopped because that "regime" could be counted on to provide for itself whatever means it needed to enforce its policies (within the limits of the contract, which should have been understood throughout). The daily grind seems almost awe-inspiring in its solidity—"and it's not going to change." But when Tony thought about the forces a "new regime" could mobilize, that solidity evaporated and so did the ability of the employees to enforce old norms. Tony also understood the power of market forces (as interpreted by owners of private enterprise) to turn most "everyday resistance" into sandcastles.[50] We had been discussing the rumored proposed sale of the plant and the declining importance of chemicals in NEC's overall sales:

Q. Are people concerned about job security?
Tony: Oh yes, everyone's concerned. I might be a little more worried because I have relatives who live in Youngstown and they worked in the steel mills. *Fwoosh*—they were gone.

This is just one example, and a very speculative one, of the role of coercion in defining and confining oppositional activity. Another form that activity took could be called "speaking out." People who will vocally and "publicly" (meaning, within the plant) take a company to task for some problem acquire a reputation, almost irrespective of the content of the subject he or she is addressing.

>*Shortly after I became a union member at Diamond, there were negotiations for a new contract. At my first union meeting, I asked a few questions about what the union's negotiating position would be and suggested one issue of concern to newer employees. I probably spoke less than two minutes and was quite matter-of-fact. Later in the week someone from another department who had not been at the meeting said to me—approvingly—"I hear you're one of those guys who talks a lot."* < DI, PA

Several people told me of the possibilities and frustrations of "speaking out" at NEC. The specific backdrop for the following comments is the company-sponsored safety meeting. The remarks do not indicate that anything special about safety molded pressures and counterpressures in the following way; it simply happened that this was the subject of meetings that provided the most appropriate forum for public discussion. Since it was the company that held these meetings, and since people were encouraged to come and talk, there would seem to be no reason for coercive pressure to inhibit people. But such pressure is undeniably there. These quotations are ordered to tell a story. They move from looking at that pressure in aggregate perspective to an individual one, from effect to cause. As in Antonioni's *Blow Up*, successive enlargements finally reveal the gun:

Speaker A: Usually I do a lot of speaking up at the safety meetings and bring up all these things and try to get things done. But you have to speak up and bring them up. You know, there's a lot of people there that just let things go by. For example, with the foreman that we had, everybody would complain, complain. Then hardly no one spoke out but me and *[name]*, maybe one other guy, that's about it. You got to speak up and you know, bring things up.

Speaker B [following discussion of safety problems]: The new safety man came around and asked me my opinions. He was having a safety meeting in one area. The plant manager was supposed to attend it. He said, "If you get a chance, drop by." So the opportunity presented itself and I showed up along with another guy and they were having their discussion and they opened it up for people to say anything, what their complaints were. Nobody would say anything. So I opened up, despite not being in their department and the guy with me opened up. And once *we* did, then the other guys did. But if we had stayed there and kept our mouths shut, nothing would have been said.

Q. to speaker C [after he had lamented the fact that more people did not speak out]: Do most people feel free to speak out, or are most people intimidated?
Speaker C: They feel that they're free to speak out. They're not so much intimidated but they're overlooked or ignored when they do speak out. Like—"What I say don't mean nothing to them. Only what they say is what goes and they don't want to know about how things are as far as we're concerned." It is a great concern of my own because I'm very involved with the labor movement. In most cases people have been contradicted so much that they are more likely to conceal their problems than to speak out. They feel it's a useless deal.

Q. to speaker D [who had mentioned several problems he saw with work procedures]: Have you ever expressed any of these ideas to them or have they asked if there's a more practical way to get things done?
Speaker D: I don't say too much. I just got out of the military and I pay a lot of rent and I get paid pretty good there. I've got bills and stuff and we just had a kid. I just got off probation and there are a lot of things involved there, whether you can get fired that quick or not. We had a meeting one time, it was a safety meeting and I brought up some things that I thought were important to me. And at the end of the meeting, someone came up to me and says, "People who talk too much get sat on."

Everyday Resistance and Negative Attitudes

There is one more form of employee behavior that is sometimes said to belong to the category of "resistance." The first type of resistance, restoration of old work norms, is intentional and almost always collective. "Speaking out" is not always collective (although some of the speakers tried to guide it in that direction), but it is certainly always intentional. But in the discussions of everyday peasant resistance, the following have been discussed as examples (alongside less arguable ones): footdragging, pilfering, evasion, truculence, dissimulation:[51]

> When such acts are rare and isolated, they are of little interest, but when they become a consistent pattern (even though uncoordinated, let alone unorganized) we are dealing with resistance.[52]

What these acts have in common is that they are forms of self-help. What they share with other more commonly accepted forms of resistance is that they "deny or mitigate claims from appropriating classes."[53]

This might sharply expand the scope of inquiry into acts at NEC we could classify as "resistance." In a factory setting, nearly every attempt to decrease workload represents a claim on management, since the principal demand on workers is the unceasing one for time and effort. It was tempting to see the "negative attitudes" described in the last chapter as a form of resistance. Why should not failure to do work on time or properly or sneaking extra breaks or simply complaining frequently be seen as an employee attempt to limit the power of management to effect its ends?

I do not think it is best understood this way and I do not think NEC employees think so either. Stealing a rabbit from a wealthy landowner to feed one's family or stealing a break from factory management may seem like expropriation; stealing a rabbit from a neighbor or a break from a coworker does not. Those who discuss "everyday resistance" try to make a sharp distinction between the two. The first is resistance, the second is "beggar-thy-neighbor."[54] But the line between the two is often not very clear. Consider the following incident:

One time when I was working production I refused to dump any more mills, because the boy I was sharing the job with, I would have to go find him every time I wanted to pull a mill out, so I just said to the foreman, "I'm not doing it." And of course, later I found out you're not allowed to say this to a foreman. When the foreman tells you to do something, you're supposed to do it. But I just got so sick and tired of this young boy always goofing off, I mean having to go find him, that I refused. Everybody got hysterical. And then the next day everybody was patting me on the back, saying "Good, *[name]*, good."

Who was the resister here? From the view of resistance described above, all the possibilities are open: both, one or the other, or neither. Because so much of the work in a factory is a collective endeavor, it is difficult (although not completely impossible) to make claims on time and effort from the company that do not make more work for others, essentially "beggaring thy fellow employees." Even in cases where no more work is actually shifted to others, if an employee is indifferent to that happening and/or has no knowledge of whether that happens, it is hard to credit that employee with expropriating rather than beggaring.

There is another reason why I would hesitate to attach the label "resistance" to any attempt to do less work or to take back time from the company. It is one thing to argue that "negative attitudes" pose a problem for management, as they certainly do.[55] It is another to see them as an asset or even a tactical ploy for workers in opposing factory authoritarianism. As suggested in the discussion of "criticism of negative attitudes" in chapter 5, people try to find standards and norms that allow them to find some meaning in their work, even when it might seem to the outside observer there is no possibility of finding any. Thus, in the example above, the woman who refused to dump the mills was viewed more favorably by coworkers than the employee who hid out. (I would not describe either act as resistance.) But what if mill dumping had been a one-person job? The answer to that question comes fairly directly from the unrecorded section of all four re-interviews. These were people who—as we have already seen—were at least tolerant of, and in Jill's case positively exuberant about, acts that bordered on collective sabotage. But in each case, I first inquired about resistance by asking about the "battle over time."[56] The question was always some variation on this theme:

Wherever I worked, there was always a contest with the company over control of time. How much was yours, how much was theirs? People always tried to reclaim time for themselves, even if just in little ways. Does that kind of thing go on at NEC?

I think the reader will agree that this is not a question worded in such a way as to elicit disparaging remarks about the activity in question. It certainly was not intended that way. If anything, I was trying to signal the respondents that I used to goof off at work too, so it was all right to level with me. But all four re-interviewees used the "critique of negative attitudes" framework in answering the question.

Jill: Oh, yes. That kind of thing goes on all the time, all the time, everyday. People make a game out of it, seeing how much they can get away with. I think it's silly.

Tony: The guys take care of it themselves. If there's an employee who's abusing the breaks, then the employees take care of that guy. Nobody gets more than the other.

John: Yes, it goes on all the time, in every building, all day. That's what I was talking about work ethics. *[He had previously criticized some work habits he saw.]* People always seem to want to get away with things.

Paul: Of course there are people like that there, there are people like that everywhere. It's just part of human nature. Sure there are people like that. The kind of people who don't take pride in their job, they probably don't take pride in what they do at home. They don't accomplish nothing.

While these four people are obviously not a representative sample, they are very far from being among the most complacent or compliant workers at NEC. But they drew my attention sharply to the difference that they saw between resistance and goofing off. Hiding in bathrooms, cutting corners, taking extra breaks, and evading work happens all the time. Certainly I took part in it. Probably these four did also. But in doing so, they saw themselves and others as abandoning a certain moral high ground. They would probably agree with this characterization by Pfeffer of such "resistance" as an unfortunate by-product of factory life. Pfeffer quoted Balzer's observation that "being able to do something illegal can be very satisfying" and went on:

> So much has "personal freedom" been degraded! It is hardly surprising, then, that to the extent the company is successful in manipulating workers' behavior to superficially satisfy these "needs not to feel powerless" [Balzer], major breaches of rules in the plant are infrequent. *The company protects its real interests in part by facilitating in a complex way rule violations that do not affect those interests.*[57] [emphases in the original]

What has been described in these pages is similar to what Richard Sennett called "disobedient dependence," rebelling not against authority but within authority.[58] If this were the only form of opposition one could find historically, there might appear to be nothing significant about such a state of affairs. But there have been times—rarer than most Marxists have expected, more often than conventional political science can account for—when relations of domination themselves have been called into question. These are the times Lefebvre described as containing "an explosion of consciousness," and Zolberg called "moments of madness."[59] No discussion of coercion, compliance, acquiescence, and resistance is complete without consideration of such moments. Chapter 8 makes a brief approach to this question. But NEC is not a factory where such moments have occurred. It has a relatively placid strike history; there have been no huge layoffs, nor has there been any threat to close the whole operation. Management, while certainly not exploring any new frontiers in industrial relations, seems reasonably careful in avoiding confrontation when the results might be counterproductive. The uses of power on both sides discussed in this chapter have taken place beneath a calm surface. That appearance we have seen to be simultaneously deceptive and revealing. NEC employees assert their interests vigorously in some areas, but within boundaries both sides understand well and do not lightly transgress.

Notes

1. Stanley Elkins, "Slavery and Ideology," p. 359.
2. Stanley Elkins, *Slavery: A Problem in American Institutional and Intellectual Life.*
3. Robert Fogel and Stanley Engerman, *Time on the Cross.*
4. Herbert Aptheker, *American Negro Slave Revolts.*
5. Earl Thorpe, "Chattel Slavery and Concentration Camps"; Sterling Stuckey, "Through the Prism of Folklore: The Black Ethos in Slavery."
6. Eugene Genovese, "American Slaves and Their History," p. 294.
7. Robert Nozick, "Coercion."
8. The various forceful means of preventing unionization and other forms of labor activity are chronicled in Robert Justin Goldstein, *Political Repression in Modern America,* particularly chapters 1 and 2.
9. Robert Dahl, *Dilemmas of Pluralist Democracy,* p. 29.
10. Companies are becoming more adept at preventing unionization. Michael Goldfield, in *The Decline of Organized Labor in the United States,* discusses the increasing sophistication of anti-union consulting agencies as the principal reason.
11. This agreement was transacted quickly and quietly in 1974. A group of steelworkers opposed to the ENA filed suit. Charles Spencer, in *Blue Collar,* told of the disposition: "The judge was convinced when he asked the international union president why this new provision hadn't been discussed beforehand with the union members or in the columns of its monthly journal, and the president I. W. Abel answered that it might have been rejected had it received advanced publicity" (p. 119).
12. *NLRB* v. *Mackay Radio and Telegraph Co.,* quoted in James Atleson, *Values and Assumptions in American Labor Law,* p. 23.
13. Ibid., p. 30. This is not at all a victimless proposition. Many of the well-known strikes of the 1980s have had as their centerpiece the immediate hiring of permanent replacements. This has been at the heart of the Hormel strike in Minnesota, the Jay Maine Paper strike, and the four-year Colt Manufacturing strike in Connecticut (al-

though in this last instance, the NLRB has been asked to consider it an unfair labor practice strike, in which case the company would have to reinstate all the strikers).

14. Reinhard Bendix, *Work and Authority in Industry: Ideologies of Management in the Course of Industrialization;* T. H. Marshall, *Class, Citizenship and Social Development.* The industrial sociologists of the 1950s maintained that class conflict within factories was potentially present, but that it could be diffused by representation of interests and incremental resolution of demands.

15. Richard Emerson, "Power-Dependence Relations." Emerson specifically mentioned subordination in a factory as an example, arguing that "identification with the aggressor"—the dominant class—is a painless method of cost reduction.

16. Claus Offe, "Two Logics of Collective Action: Theoretical Notes on Social Class and Organizational Form," p. 76.

17. Robert Dahl, *Dilemmas of Pluralist Democracy,* p. 19. Dahl also says there that it is possible to treat structure "as in some sense an actor."

18. Michael Burawoy, *Politics of Production,* p. 34.

19. Nicholas Abercrombie, Steven Hill, and Bryan Turner, *The Dominant Ideology Thesis,* p. 154.

20. Adam Przeworski, "Material Bases of Consent: Economics and Politics in a Hegemonic System," p. 26.

21. Charles Lindblom (*Politics and Markets,* p. 172), says this about the privileged position of business—dependence on a society-wide basis (emphases added): "Constitutional rules—especially the law of private property—specify that, although governments can forbid certain kinds of activity, they *cannot* command business to perform. They *must* induce rather than command. They *must* therefore offer benefits to businessmen in order to stimulate the required performance." I should add that Lindblom is chiefly interested in the relationship of political and economic authority. This relationship is not one of dependence but, as he explains, of rivalry. It is the citizenry as a whole that is dependent.

22. For instance, Agnes Heller (*Everyday Life,* p. 217) points to the teacher-student relationship as hierarchy without dependence. Students may disagree.

23. Samuel Bowles, David Gordon, and Thomas Weisskopf captured the clash between rationality within the limits imposed by the logic of profit and the dictates of moral economy. They pointed out that job security is not efficient, but is a "defensive demand in a hostile economic environment." But it is also a "natural worker response in an unstable market economy" (*Beyond the Waste Land,* p. 275). This is precisely Paul's dilemma; he resolved it by ignoring his previous criterion of profitability.

24. I think this is similar to Przeworski's formulation that "appropriation of profit is a necessary but not sufficient condition for the future realization of the interests of any group" ("Material Bases," p. 27).

25. Huw Beynon, *Working for Ford,* p. 318.

26. Studs Terkel, *Working,* p. xxxi.

27. Barrington Moore, *Injustice: The Social Bases of Obedience and Revolt,* p. 203.

28. The rule applied to many who were never in areas where respirators were worn. In addition, some people felt that NEC relied excessively on respirators, which imposed a burden on employees, as opposed to engineering controls, which imposed a burden on the company. This point was mentioned in a union-sponsored safety report. This does not mean that the company was unreasonable in instituting the facial hair policy, only that the employees were also not unreasonable in objecting to it.

29. When I asked the LRS why he thought there had been only two strikes in the Lockland plant's history, he singled out the notion of "mature labor relations."

30. Michael Crozier, *The Bureaucratic Phenomenon,* p. 185.

31. Fogel and Engerman, *Time on the Cross,* p. 146: "Most [slavemasters] accepted it

[whipping], but recognized that to be effective whipping had to be used with restraint and in a cooly calculated manner."

32. Herbert Gutman and Richard Sutch, "Sambo Makes Good, or Were Slaves Imbued with the Protestant Work Ethic?" p. 59. In making this point, Gutman and Sutch temporarily suspend disbelief in the veracity of the Fogel and Engerman statistical methods, in order to highlight the use of coercion more forcefully. Fogel and Engerman interestingly use their research on whipping to make a point similar to the point about "dependency-as-coercion" that I make above: "With the rise of capitalism, impersonal and indirect sanctions were increasingly substituted for direct, personal ones. The hiring of the free workers in the market-place provided management of labor with a powerful new disciplinary weapon. Workers who were lazy, indifferent, or otherwise shirked their duties could be fired—left to starve beyond the eyesight or expense of employers" (*Time on the Cross*, p. 147). That argument does not reinforce their point about whipping as much as it does mine. In *both* settings, superordinates (generally) employ such force as is required to accomplish their ends.

33. The importance of people being awarded (or awarding themselves) the right to *legal* violence was pointed out in Augustine's famous example of a confrontation between King Alexander and a pirate: "The king asked the fellow, 'What is your idea in infesting the sea?' And the pirate answered, 'The same as yours, in infesting the earth! But because I do it with a tiny craft, I'm called a pirate: because you have a mighty navy, you're called an emperor' "(*City of God*, p. 139).

34. Lest this appear too fanciful even as an abstraction, consider the MOVE episode in Philadelphia in May 1985. The first set of charges against the inhabitants involved build-ing code violations and delinquent payments on utilities. In the confrontation, eleven people died and virtually a whole city block was burned down. Of course the code violations were not the real issue; that is precisely my point. What this does demonstrate is the ability of an established order to enforce even minor laws with maximal strength.

35. It would be inappropriate in a book written in this country to fail to point out that those generals had the help and probably the direction of the United States government.

36. Thomas Murton, *The Dilemmas of Prison Reform:* "The fact that picking 300 pounds of cotton a day will result in parole and that not picking 300 pounds of cotton a day will result in being beaten, is easily understood" (p. 92).

37. Thomas Murton and Joe Hyams, *Accomplices to the Crime: The Arkansas Prison Scandal.* These arguments are not Murton's, although they seem to follow fairly directly from the logic and case history he presents.

38. Michael Burawoy, *Manufacturing Consent*, pp. 86, 93. The "we" here refers to employees; Burawoy worked in the company for a year.

39. Ervand Abrahamian, "The Non-violent Peasantry of Modern Iran."

40. Ian Lustick, *Arabs in the Jewish State.*

41. Craig Jenkins and Charles Perrow, "Insurgency of the Powerless: Farm Worker Movements (1946–1972)."

42. John Gaventa, *Power and Powerlessness: Quiescence and Rebellion in an Appa-lachian Valley*, p. 143. Gaventa does not base his whole argument on vulnerability. Nor, for that matter, do any of the previously cited authors.

43. Bertell Ollman, "Toward Class Consciousness Next Time," p. 8. Ollman several times mentions "some" or "many" workers; he certainly knows that many were also not so tame.

44. My original phrase was "class oppression without Armageddon." But vulnerabil-ity in its strongest form would also suppress the incremental "democratic class struggle" for redistribution of wealth.

45. Sabel, *Work and Politics*, p. 15; see also Kenneth Roberts, F. G. Cook, S. C. Clark, and Elizabeth Semeonoff, *The Fragmentary Class Structure*, p. 90.

46. While a few people may have answered by telling me the first thing they thought of, the fact that eight people answered no suggests that most people understood the intent of the question. Here, for example, is one of the "no" answers: "I would say I've never seen anything that was *grossly* unjust or unethical. There have been cases where something happens where I say, 'Oh, that's not quite right.' " I should also mention that one of the twenty-five yes people gave as his answer, "the last strike. We should never have gone out." This was the only instance of a "yes" answer that did not pinpoint the company.

47. James Scott, *Weapons of the Weak: Everyday Forms of Peasant Resistance.*

48. James Scott, "Everyday Forms of Peasant Resistance."

49. I mean to describe that relationship in exactly the way the sentence reads. Employee opposition does not eliminate or limit managerial prerogatives. The rules that would allow them to discipline remain in force. It does raise the cost of enforcing those rules without challenging their existence.

50. I have been describing "coercion-in-dependence" as a purely impersonal "market and private enterprise" phenomenon, but some very real people fight hard when attempts are made to mitigate the effects of dependency—as, for instance, in the virtually unanimous disapproval by industrial leaders of "plant-closing" legislation. See Lawrence Rothstein, *Plant Closings: Myths, Power, Politics.*

51. This is a condensation of lists made in Scott, *Weapons of the Weak*, p. 350, and "Everyday Resistance," p. 6.

52. Scott, *Weapons of the Weak*, p. 296.

53. Scott, "Everyday Resistance," p. 31. This definition is not so much Scott's own as it is an attempt to find agreement among those from various *genres* who discuss everyday resistance.

54. Scott, "Everyday Resistance."

55. See, for instance, Bowles, Gordon, and Weisskopf, *Beyond the Waste Land,* for a look at declining productivity, which places employee attitudes at center stage. Or any of the "blue-collar blues" literature of the early 1970s, of which the study by the U.S. Department of Health, Education, and Welfare *(Work in America)* is an overview.

56. I wish I could say that this was a prescient way of eliciting information useful to discussing this point. Actually it was a watered-down way of asking about more intentional forms of resistance. It was the employees themselves who insisted that I draw the distinction.

57. While I obviously agree with the thrust of Pfeffer's observation, he implies more conscious planning on the part of the company than I think is necessary to sustain the point. On the other hand, see L. R. Zeitlin, "A Little Larceny Can Do a Lot for Employee Morale," who advocates managerial toleration and even encouragement of employee theft.

58. Richard Sennett, *Authority*, p. 33.

59. Henry Lefebvre, *The Explosion: Marxism and the French Revolution;* Aristide Zolberg, "Moments of Madness."

7

Preference and Interest, Redux

All ran to meet their chains thinking they had secured their freedom.
—Jean Jacques Rousseau[1]

How do I know what I've missed? Can't you see? I ain't here.
—Georgetown basketball player Eric Smith, answering reporters
who asked whether he missed the excitement of the Final Four in
New Orleans, due to his coach keeping the team in Biloxi

The last matter I will address I approach with caution for it is both highly contentious and somewhat amorphous in nature. In the first chapter, I indicated that the origins of the "power" debates turned at least in part into consideration of some epistemological questions. Stephen Lukes found the "most effective and insidious" use of power to be to its role in affecting the preferences of those over whom power is exercised; thus, no empirical examination that looked at contestation over resources could be complete in documenting the existence and exercise of power. The responses to Lukes have generally claimed not just that such manipulated preferences do not exist but that they *could* not exist; that is, that "stated preferences" are the extent of our knowledge about the needs of others.[2] There could be no interest separate from preference, and preferences are revealed in the act of choosing. Put more simply, the recent discussions of "power" have taken place in the framework of the old concepts of "false consciousness" and "objective interest." It is that can of worms that must now be opened.[3]

The purpose of my examination of these questions is not to provide definitive answers to them, which I do not do. Since this is a subject that flows and eddies in a number of directions, at times tangential arguments are relegated to notes. But I feel compelled to address the problem of preference and interest (and the relation between them) for two reasons: first, there are some lessons to be drawn from my interview material that bear on those questions; second, and even more compelling, my account would clearly be incomplete without taking note of such an important critique of what I have already presented. So far, I have compared

161

employees' comments to each other, to such "objective" evidence as was available to me, to theorists who propose different work relationships (as in the chapter on participation), to statements made by the LRS on behalf of the company, and to other subordinate groups. At times I have given reasons why I would expect to find some point of view that did not appear; at other times, I have described a range of opinions that seemed narrow or constrained. In discussing workplace populism, I noted the seeming paradox of those who were most critical using the company's central goal (profitability) as the standard by which they measured policy. But—as anyone might have asked—who am I to say any of this? That is, would it not be better simply to say that people have different values that they go about trying to achieve as best they can in a hard world? By what right does anyone assume that someone else's stated preference is not a complete record of that person's interest? In short, the charge could be made that what I have found is simply that people trade off some values for others in a situation of scarce resources. Rousseau himself, immediately after this chapter's opening quotation, proposed this counterargument:

> [E]ven the wise saw the necessity of resolving to sacrifice one part of their freedom for the preservation of the other, just as a wounded man has his arm cut off to save the rest of his body.[4]

If I were not to engage that position in some discussion, many of my interpretations would simply rest uneasily on the assumption that interest can be separated from preference, or worse, on the hope that the reader will not pursue that question. This chapter is more argumentative than the others, drawing heavily from other writers, particularly those who argue against separating interest from preferences. While I make less use of the interview material, toward the end I present discussions that I regard as the dramatic highlights of the whole interview process.

De Gustibus

I first outline what I see as the strongest possible argument against separation of the concepts "preference" and "interest."[5] I am sure that proponents of this view could make the case stronger and better than I can, one reason among many that this chapter cannot settle the issues raised. But by trying to construct a strong argument rather than a made-to-order straw man, I hope that my evaluation addresses rather than evades issues. I draw principally upon the arguments of Pareto and recent ones of Polsby.[6] A few counterarguments are introduced to strengthen their case; my own will wait.

The center of gravity of this position lies in three concepts: tastes, trades, and judges. Taste is beyond argument and beyond explanation, subject only to the generalization that people differ and tastes vary. Pareto tried to create an impenetrability around taste:

[A]n agreeable or disagreeable sensation is a primitive fact, which cannot be deduced by reasoning. When a man experiences one sensation, it is absurd to want to demonstrate to him that he is experiencing a different one.[7]

Taste is also not amenable to change by appeal. Elsewhere, in another celebrated passage, Pareto writes:

Take a man who is eating a chicken; someone wishes to demonstrate to him that he would experience more pleasure if he ate only half of it and gave the other half to his neighbor. He replies, "Certainly not; I have already tried that and I assure you that I experience more pleasure by eating the whole thing than by giving half of it to my neighbor." You can call him wicked, you can insult him, but you cannot prove to him logically that he does not experience that sensation.[8]

Finally, tastes are also not comparable. There is no "objective" basis for assigning a value to two unique sensations, hence there is no way to estimate a rate at which they should be exchanged for each other:

The ophelimity, or its index [the sum of pleasing sensations] for one individual, and the ophelimity, or its index for another individual, are heterogeneous quantities. We can neither add them together nor compare them.[9]

For the time being, I am allowing "taste," "want," and "preference" to be equivalents. If Pareto is right in this elementary formulation, there is no reason to expect members of a subordinate class to react to similar conditions in similar ways. People have their own reactions. Further, if someone were to say that NEC is a "good place to work," it would be incoherent to argue with him or her or to entertain the possibility that he or she is mistaken. Guenther Lewy, defending the position that preferences should be regarded as idiosyncratic and noncomparable, draws the following lesson in regard to the possibility of the existence of "false consciousness":

The lowly clerk or secretary or young worker whose ambition it is to become the owner of his own business may have a realistic or unrealistic understanding of his chances for social advancement, but unless he lives in a static society where social mobility is completely foreclosed, he cannot be said to be acting irrationally or contrary to the "real" interests of his class. There are no true ideologies appropriate for a given class; there are no such things as "correct class interests." What is best for one's class can always be the subject of rational argument.[10]

Polsby concentrated less on the inscrutability of interests for his argument against external determination of interest than on the individual nature of trade-offs through which actors try to maximize their values. I have described a variety of hardships faced by people at NEC, and situations in which people are left with very narrow choice ranges between relatively unpalatable alternatives. Should an employee work swing shift to stay on the relatively interesting Production Repair job or be bored on steady shifts? Should Wendy and Thelma be bored and aggravated for the rest of their working lives ("forty hours of dues") "to do something nice for me and the kids on weekends?" Should people be so accepting of the system of factory authoritarianism? Polsby would argue that if an analyst finds people's attitudes toward these and other such questions shortsighted or even wrongheaded, they should be interpreted as involving "a complex set of trade-offs that for one reason or another are of more interest to a given set of actors than to a particular analyst."[11] Even if the actors involved have previously specified values that their choices do not seem to maximize, the strongest possibility is that they are "simply involved in trade-offs disagreed with (or not understood) by analysts."[12] In other words, an observer cannot know the relative weights an actor gives to different values in making decisions; and, further, any decision entails costs, meaning that the actor will have to trade some values for some others. This could potentially explain, to use a very specific example, why people would tolerate working with OSHA-listed carcinogens, as well as and also why people who worked at NEC and lived in Lockland were hostile to the environmental group's criticisms of NEC.[13]

Pareto, and more recently Nozick, have proposed a more absolutist interpretation of trade-offs than that of Polsby to eliminate any conceivable separation of preference from interest.[14] When *any* exchange is made—including, for example, labor (power) for wages—the result must be understood as mutually beneficial to both parties (assuming no force was used), because the alternatives to the exchange must have been worse for both parties. The proof is simply that the uncoerced exchange took place—if it had not been beneficial to both, there could be no explanation for why it occurred.[15] Preferences can only be understood by an observer after a decision has been reached. The outcome of a decision regarding trade-offs reveals what those preferences had been.

The other area of criticism of those who consider interest separate from stated preference is contained in the question, "Who judges?" One can be agnostic on the above two points and still regard this question as sufficient grounds for challenging those (such as myself) who argue otherwise. There are actually two claims in the "who judges" criticism. First, who has the capacity to know what specific combination of values represents an individual's actual wants and therefore the type of trade-offs he or she will want to make? Only the person involved is so qualified. Polsby, for instance, pointed out that interests cannot be estimated as one would read a gas meter.[16] Pareto again used a food metaphor to argue his case:

The individual is the sole judge of what pleases or displeases him; and if, for example, a man does not like spinach, it is the height of ridiculousness and absurdity to want to show him, in the same way that one proves the Pythagorean theorem, that it does please him.[17]

Second, who has the *right* to judge and what are the consequences of awarding that right to some person or body other than the individual involved? Stipulate for a moment that one could define a need that might be different than a want, or at a minimum that the relation is in dispute. Who arbitrates? Arbitration by anyone else—particularly an award of the *right* to arbitrate to anyone else—seems to have authoritarian implications.[18] Here are descriptions of this problem, the first from Polsby, and the second two from Lewy:

> If such knowledge [to choose in accordance with interests] exists at all, we must conclude it is in the possession of self-proclaimed "radicals" or third dimensionalists [Lukes] (or even reactionaries) who know enough to be able to tell when it is appropriate to reject the choices of ordinary citizens as insufficiently enlightened to reflect their real interests.[19]

> What is there to be done about social groups that do not experience dissatisfaction with their condition? How will the social critic get them to participate in and accept enlightenment?[20]

> [I]t is important to note that the potential for repression is present in the very idea of false consciousness. He who has found the truth not infrequently considers it his moral obligation to benefit others who are less fortunate and less enlightened.[21]

These are the outlines of the free market theory of preference "formation" (more accurately, discovery) and articulation. One frequent criticism of this theory is that market theories work on the assumption of full information and such information is not always available. Preferences are formed in relation to information that people have; they might be different if more information were available. This is one of William Connolly's arguments[22] and a common line of attack on the "preference" position. If person 1 chooses between alternatives A through D and person 2 chooses between A through Z, and if the only reason for the difference is that person 1 is unaware of E through Z, how can we assume that what person 1 chooses is in his or her interest? That is, how can we assume that person 1 would not have chosen M had he or she known about its existence? As quoted in chapter 4, a worker told John Witte, "Authority is the way we are used to working." Perhaps this worker might have chosen differently if he had been exposed to alternative forms of workplace organization.

While this does pose problems for the "preference" position, there is an answer that adds considerably to the force of that formulation; this answer makes use of Anthony Downs's concept of information costs. Obtaining any information requires time and effort. Thus, each increment of information results from a trade, in which a person believes that the information obtained will prove worth the resources it took to acquire it, or as Downs explains, "By definition, any cost is a deflection of scarce resources from some utility-producing use; it is a foregone conclusion."[23] He is primarily concerned with information pertaining to voting decisions and uses examples appropriate to that concern. But there is no reason why this concept should not be considered in relation to the decisions discussed in this investigation. The "alternative" argument might be challenged on this ground: every trade-off involves as one of the traded values the time and effort needed to learn about and consider each alternative. For person 1 above, learning about E through Z would require more time and the fact that the person has chosen not to make that investment reveals that it was in his or her interest not to do so. Perhaps NEC workers do not want to make the additional effort required to consider alternatives to factory authoritarianism (other than "team Taylorism"). To gather all the needed information, they might have to, variously, read additional newspapers, go back to school, go to graduate school, read Marx, or Gramsci, or Habermas. Of course I am not suggesting seriously that this argument is tied to the assumption that people actually consider each alternative course of action and reject it, but that people achieve a certain level of satisfaction and then reject new information costs. That the cost of information might be used in this way is not entirely hypothetical. Polsby used the essentials of this argument to explain why people might choose not to act on questions that seem obviously to concern them:

> [P]luralists presume that there are certain costs to taking any action at all. This refers not simply to the possibility of losing, or making political enemies, and so on, but also to the costs in personal time and effort, in lobbying or campaigning, and in taking the trouble to vote.[24]

For this reason, according to Polsby, one should make a "presumption of inertia," particularly for the lower classes. The presumption is not merely that people from those classes will not act when one might expect them to, but that one should not expect them to, that to act would require paying an information cost they are not prepared to pay.

Neither Polsby nor Lewy takes an absolutist position on the question of the inseparability of preference and interest. They both specify rigorous conditions under which they might be willing to consider that an actor decided against his or her best interest. I call this the "pure preference" position, not to set up a straw man or to attribute to them positions they do not take, but primarily for reasons of convenience. I say "primarily" because there are aspects of their own arguments that do tend toward the absolutist (Paretian) position. There is an inexorable logic in the position that there is *no conceivable* situation in which one may claim to know that a person is mistaken in regard to his or her interest.

Using that argument against others (such as Lukes) while finding selective exceptions is something like trying to ride a rhinoceros carefully; it tends to go where *it* pleases rather than where *you* please.[25] This is the "of course" problem. As an illustration, consider these qualifications Raymond Wolfinger added to a critique of the "neo-elitist" practice of alleging interest different from preference:

> [S]ome examples of false consciousness are indisputable, e.g., the long period of feeble protest by southern Negroes. . . . Almost any social scientist would agree that the blacks had been manipulated because almost any social scientist's view of rational political behavior, irrespective of their specific character, would attribute certain goals to southern Negroes.[26]

But by what right can this conclusion be reached? Is the proper criterion for selecting times when preference and interest are different to be agreement by "almost any social scientist"? Lewy, for example, would not agree with the characterization of "false consciousness" that is said to be incontrovertible here; he explicitly called acquiescence to slavery a form of pain reduction in a situation of unavoidable suffering.[27] Polsby does attempt to specify very carefully what criteria might be used to review stated preferences to find instances where they might not reflect real interest, but what he comes up with is not very much different from Wolfinger. The filter for finding potential cases would be the "fireside induction," about which "hardly anyone entertains serious doubts."[28] The arbitration would be by "very widely shared agreement about causes and effects in the political world."[29]

This characterization of some cases as "indisputable" to "almost any social scientist" is clearly a *deus ex machina*. There is no theory to explain how a mistaken judgment could have occurred, especially if the cost of information is taken into account. Nor is there any general explanation of who is specifically charged with judging (surely not a convocation of social scientists).[30] The charges they make against others can be—must logically be—turned back on them. A theory with ad hoc "of courses" will be more defensible but less rigorous and less persuasive. By focusing attention on an idealized "pure preference" theory, to which the previous arguments belong by convenience and logical direction, I am testing my previous conclusions against the strongest counterargument.

Disputandum Est

The above argument is crucial because its general outlines seem applicable to the choices made by employees at NEC (as just a specific example of factory workers as a whole). No one is forced to seek employment at NEC and no one is forced to stay once there. Neither anyone who works there nor NEC itself has unlimited resources and people throughout these pages have expressed a willingness to tolerate inconveniences and hardships in some areas for the achievement of goals in others. While I have considered some of these objections previously, I look at them more broadly here, focusing my attention on adaptation and on the pervasive effects of privilege on adaptation.

Even if we restricted the scope of the examination of choice to that of the classic taste, food, there are problems in describing the reasons for choice as completely mysterious to outsiders. Tastes are not nearly as unfathomable as Pareto indicated, nor are they completely without causality. People do have different tastes and aspects of taste appear to be unexplainable. Nothing need deny that; that is my "of course." But, contrary to Pareto, even the liking or disliking of spinach occurs with some degree of predictability.

In *All Manners of Food*, Stephen Mennell writes that food tastes cannot be seen as a matter of "purely individual and random variation," and that innate instincts play only a small part in explaining likes:

> Tastes in food, like tastes in music, literature or the visual arts, are socially shaped, and the major forces which have shaped them are religions, classes and nations. In European history, religion has been a relatively weak influence on food, class overwhelmingly the strongest.[31]

Mennell goes on to describe the process by which the lower classes accommodated the lack of available foodstuffs by learning to *like* the nonnutritious and repetitive diet they were able to obtain.[32] If tastes in food vary over time, and vary at any one time between classes, they cannot be methodologically impenetrable. It may not be possible to specify what causal factors combine to create variation in taste, but it is inescapable that there *are* causal factors. The fact that there is also some randomness cannot be used, and would never be used in other contexts, to argue that no variables explain or predict taste. Pareto himself, a few pages after the chicken and spinach arguments, noted and bemoaned the "decay" of faith and morals—both of which are "tastes" *par excellence*. How can there be a massive nonrandom change in faith and morals if there are no causal factors operating, even if they operate "behind the backs" of those whose tastes are changing?[33] This is not intended to be a counterintuitive interpretation. Ron Eyerman, exploring the "false consciousness" question, made the same point this way:

> A frustrated suburban housewife in California is more likely to be attracted to "Primal Scream" to explain her experienced frustration than a woman factory worker in Alabama.[34]

There may be no disputing taste, but there may be predicting it and explaining it retrospectively in aggregate. If this is so, there also may be grounds for disputing what social conditions and conditioning lead to what tastes. This is what

Mennell was trying to do for taste in food. Whether his answers are sufficient is less important than whether the project is legitimate. Tastes are not exogenous to social systems.[35]

In creating the "pure preference" argument, I temporarily considered taste and preference to be synonyms. But it is certainly the case that the questions to which NEC workers were responding involved choices of a different sort than whether they liked nouvelle cuisine or ham and cheese sandwiches. The importance of the choice is not the principal difference but the nature of the criteria used to arrive at the choice. In fact, there can only be such a category as "nondisputandum" tastes if there are no criteria used at all. There can be much less controversy about the types of decisions, aspirations, goals, and trade-offs described in previous pages. These choices are influenced by the system of variables in which they are made. Lindblom argues that tastes cannot be decided upon, that they must be discovered.[36] When information about matters about which one can theoretically be mistaken is needed for judgment, it is hard to sustain an argument that the choices are simply discovered. Wildavsky writes that more attention must be paid to "preference formation."[37] He separates preferences from taste and suggests that preferences are formed in part by cultural factors. Lindblom separates preference *and* taste from more sophisticated political judgments he calls "volitions," and suggests that they are in part formed by polyarchy (where it exists).[38] My argument above would add that even the simplest tastes can in some measure be said to be "formed."

In earlier chapters, particularly chapter 3, I discussed a form of choice built explicitly on considered judgment—what I informally called an "evaluative category." Some workers volunteered the information that NEC was "a good place to work," in spite of having misgivings about many aspects of the job. In fact, people volunteered the category, not just the judgment, since it was not among my questions. I interpret that as a choice about rank. Some factors—hard place to get fired from, not many layoffs—simply "counted" more than others toward the overall summary. Hardships in some other categories did not count at all. This was particularly noticeable for those employees who were thoroughly dissatisfied but who still found NEC a "good place to work," such as the employee (quoted in chapter 3) who said, directly after giving the unsolicited "good" evaluation, that as far as what he was doing with his life, "This is nowhere."

Another illustration of the existence of minimal standards for evaluating the category of "good job" comes from Paul, who worked previously at another large factory I called Apex. He was effusive in his praise of that company, ending the first interview by telling me, "No greater pleasure have I had than to work for Apex." But as I listened to that interview, I realized that one could take the same material and describe it as a horror show. I will mainly paraphrase here because this compresses over an hour of information—and Paul wanders. He gave several examples from Apex to illustrate his strongly held conviction that companies do not listen to their employees. He told me that he had "seen the handwriting on the wall,'' in its de-emphasis of quality (Apex's business has declined sharply). He said that his only training came from a summer employee and was completely inadequate. There were also two situations he did not raise as criticisms of Apex that have had devastating consequences for him. In response to the "Absolutely Wrong" question, he told me that he hurt his back there in an incident he blamed on company safety practices. Months after I finished the interviews, I was informed that Paul had to take a long leave of absence from NEC due to pain from that back injury, which doctors have advised him might be permanent. Also, he was laid off for three lengthy periods when he worked at Apex and by the time of the interview knew he would not be called back. I decided to see what Paul would say if I noted the incongruity. The reader should keep in mind Paul's emotional recital of the difficulties of unemployment:[39]

Q. This came from something you said the first time. You mentioned a lot of very positive things about Apex. But, you also were laid off several times for long periods of time, you mentioned one or several incidents where you were hurt on the job, and you also said that you saw the handwriting on the wall as far as bad-quality products being put out and what it might lead to. So the question I had was, how do you look at all those things and still tell me that you found Apex a very good company to work for?

A. Well, okay. *[pause, sigh]* Let's look at probably number one, which is going back to benefits, wages. It assures any individual that worked there that they will have a certain standard of living. That they know financially that they're going to be in good shape, not only now but in future years. Versus, for example, a calamity because they have an excellent health plan. Versus retirement, because they have a good pension. Versus sickness because they have a good accident and sickness plan.

His answer is revealing in two ways. Most of what the company "assures" simply did not benefit Paul, because he cannot work there any more and perhaps was injured there too seriously to work at all. But more important (because presumably there are healthy employees who still work there), he simply did not count these hardships in coming to his judgment. Such matters do not seem to be in the set of things one estimates in making an overall evaluation of a job. He is accustomed to not weighing some factors. The evaluative category "good place to work" is a social construct.

There was an even more powerful example of how some information is separated from socially derived evaluative criteria. I have mentioned the accident that killed two employees at NEC about twenty years ago. In my interviews, there were a number of vivid descriptions of that accident and a minimum of conflicting stories. People were not reading from a prepared script; several of the speakers were critical of NEC for not making a fuller accounting of the accident. The following is Tony's detailed account, which serves as the context for the next respondent, whose answer is the one of substantive interest:

That's one thing that never should have happened. There was a tank wagon that was dirty and our normal procedure has always been that if it comes in dirty, it's theirs. But it's the weekend, the terminal was closed, the load had to go out, the foreman calls, the guy says, "Send our people in to wipe it out." We have procedures for going into tank wagons. Our people didn't follow those procedures. The people who went in on the first shift wore safety equipment. They found they didn't have to wear the mask so they went in without it. Shift change came. The foreman told them to put in an air hose to dry it out. This group of people went home, the other group came in and—this is just speculation on my part—the workers in the lunchroom talk to each other and said, "Hey we're in with no masks on." The new foreman comes in and says to his crew, "They got air inside the tank drying it out. Go in and check, make sure it's dry and we'll load it." They go and the first guy jumps in with no equipment. What they thought was an air line turned out to be inert gas. It was just a fiasco, a real bad fiasco. The color codes were off, two foremen not realizing it was inert. He wrote right on his shift log, "Air in Truck." If he wrote "Inert," somebody might have picked it up.

Six people, two of whom had not been in the plant at the time, gave this incident as their answer to the "Absolutely Wrong" question. The most interesting case was one interviewee who did not. In order to highlight some of the implications of this exchange, I will retell it backwards: first the story, then the earlier evidence which points to the lessons it may have for a study of legitimation. The speaker is a plant guard with over thirty years at NEC. I asked several employees about the accident and did not have any reason to think he knew anything more than anyone else. This story cannot be changed and clearly identifies the person involved, but because of its importance and because it involved facts that are already documented, I have not altered events as I did in all other cases. One other important fact that is not explicit in Tony's account: inert gas in an enclosed area kills instantly.

Q. Were you on the security job when the incident happened where two men were killed?

A. Yes. I was there.
Q. You were—somewhere near it?
A. I was right at the scene.
Q. Could you describe from your point of view what happened?
A. *[pause]* It was my first night coming in as sergeant of the gatehouse. I just got to work at midnight shift. All of a sudden I found I was out of cigarettes. So I went down and got a pack of cigarettes and a can of soda and came back out to the gatehouse. Just then the alarm went off. Then we got the word there was two guys in the tank that might be—*bad.* So I said, "*[name],* would you mind staying over while I go to the scene?" So myself and the other guard, we hopped in the car and went down to where the emergency was. As a matter of fact I went up on the landing and I got filled in that there was the two men in the tank. I said, "Oh my god." *[pause]* At first I didn't know what happened or why they passed out or what. And I started to go down in the tank. And *[name],* he was the superintendent, as I was going down the ladder into the tank, he grabbed me by the collar and lifted me off the ladder. He grabbed me and said, "No you don't. We don't need another one." And I says, "There's two guys down there." He says, "I know it." And he pulled the hose out and he put it up to his nose and he said, "Oh my god. They're dead." It was inert gas. That takes the oxygen right out of the air. I was there the whole night, throughout the whole ordeal. As a matter of fact I went back to the gatehouse and I was working on the report when one of the women called, one of the wives. Somebody had called her and told her there was a big accident and that her husband was in the middle of it. She called up and she demanded to talk to somebody, she heard her husband was very bad. I was already told by the bosses not to say anything to anybody outside, especially the families. I notified my boss and told him I had her on hold. He said, "Tell her that we'll get back to her as soon as we can." She wouldn't accept that either. It was an experience I don't want to go through again. I was—some scared. I was right there and I'll never forget that night.

The question and response immediately before this story were these:

Q. During the time you've been there, has anything ever happened where you said to yourself, "This is a situation which is simply wrong," whether to you or to someone else you saw—"This shouldn't have happened this way, this is totally wrong?"
A. I'm not out in the plant much. Maybe seventy, eighty percent of

the time I'm sitting there by myself taking care of the trucks. I don't really see what's going on in the plant. The majority of time I think the company's treated us fair and I can't complain about anything.

Several things stand out about the story and its place in this employee's thinking. His recall of detail—cigarettes and soda *before* the alarm—is remarkable for an incident that happened twenty years ago. It was certainly the accident that fixed the details in his memory; he did not reveal unusual recall in the rest of the interview.[40] His retelling was generally nonrecriminatory, although he was slightly more upset about having to put off the widow than about his own considerable danger. Finally, and of course the lesson I am trying to draw, when I asked him this "Absolutely Wrong" question, he brought up neither the fact that he came within a few seconds of dying in an accident that was widely seen as the company's fault, nor the brief cover-up that he had to handle while he was still "some scared." The fact that he did not bring up the accident in response to the question could not have been simply an unease with the intentionally moralistic "totally wrong" phraseology of the question. The employee himself had used phrases such as "all out wrong" or similar terms three times previous to any of these questions. In fact, he was one of the few respondents who introduced moral terminology before I did. This incident—which left *me* shaken when I heard it recounted, let alone the person recounting it—also did not count for him in estimating the rights and wrongs of industrial authority at NEC.

In other chapters, I have tried to create categories of responses to serve as an approximate spectrum of views in the work force as a whole, but my purpose here is not to draw a broad picture. There were people who did give the accident as their answer to the "Absolutely Wrong" question. The issue underlying this chapter is the plausibility of a claim that preferences and interests can be different, and the point directly at hand is whether people can exclude crucial information from judgments. This speaker has certainly done that. Each successive step away from unexplainable taste—tastes that can be partially explained, preferences in Wildavsky's sense, volitions in Lindblom's, and the sort of line-drawing I encouraged people to make—makes it more difficult to sustain a "pure preference" perspective. Each level of choice described increases the degree to which the choice is endogenous to some system of allocated resources. The "choices" made in the two situations above—which would better be described as "verdicts"—are conditioned by available resources, available information, estimation of life chances, and the cost of alternatives (i.e., the cost of not working at NEC). While the weight assigned to each of these may be up to the individual, the value of each is set largely by the nature of the specific system within which the individual makes a choice. What appears to be simple choice is an estimation of interest.

Preference and Perception

If the theoretical door to establishing some difference between preference and interest has opened a crack, what might affect the choices people make and what conclusions can be drawn from that? More specifically, how might it affect subordinates in comprehending and responding to the system of domination to which they are subordinate?

The simplest problem is factual error—misperception of empirical information. Some would rule this out as an interesting subject; since factual errors are clearly widespread, they are theoretically trivial.[41] I would not dismiss them quite this easily. In theory, a want informed by factual errors is still a want, and "pure preference" theory must still honor it as synonymous with interest. For example, if a person mistakenly thinks that formaldehyde is harmless and wants a first-shift job working extensively with it, which is open because other people do not want to expose themselves, there are no grounds for saying that it is not in his or her interest to take the job (so long as OSHA and NEC have not concealed the dangers). The fact that market theories always stipulate perfect information is not a serious counterargument, since those stipulations are not meant to approximate actual situations. The practice of getting facts wrong—even readily available facts—has been so widely noted by political scientists that no one can seriously doubt that it is commonplace. If a factual assessment is necessary to make a judgment, a misassessment can create a gap between preference and interest. The best that can be said here in defense of the "pure preference" theory is that misperception is a relatively benign problem and nothing close to the problems created by claims of "false consciousness."

But is it? Claus Offe asks whether it is possible to argue seriously that misperception occurs randomly.[42] If there is a larger pile of misperceptions at the lower ends of the social hierarchy than at the top, they begin to look less benign. This observation can be useful in considering the problem of information costs. If our hypothetical employee above had wanted to know more about formaldehyde, the argument goes, he or she would have done what was needed to get the information. Since he didn't want to, he didn't do so. That is the model; a down-and-dirty way of saying the same thing is that employees find it more to their liking to spend the time boating than reading OSHA reports. But information costs are not distributed equally. When Downs proposed the concept, he understood it to imply important and unresolvable inequalities in political power. People have different incomes and educational backgrounds; apart from every other advantage that affords them, Downs argued, it simplifies and cheapens the process of obtaining information: "The president of a giant firm often receives information of national political significance in chats with colleagues; whereas a dishwasher may never hear politics discussed at all."[43] While Downs argued that there would be inequalities due to different ways of obtaining information even among citizens equal in every other respect, he added this qualification which is especially pertinent to my argument:

> Furthermore, to be at all realistic, we must add to the aforementioned differentiating forces the unequal distribution of income. All information is costly; therefore those with high incomes can better afford to procure it than those with low incomes.[44]

Benjamin Page developed Downs's theory into an explanation of how the ambiguities inherent in political campaigns made information more accessible to "the well educated, the wealthy, organized groups, large corporations."[45] Page analyzed information costs as playing a substantial role in creating and maintaining inequality. I am proposing unequal information costs as an important argument against "pure preference" theory. Several NEC workers mentioned that they wished they knew more about the chemicals with which they worked. Three employees told me that they had tried to find out more about particular situations and were thwarted not because information was withheld but because it was presented in technical jargon. Here is how Wendy characterized this problem:

Factory workers, the blue-collar workers, a lot of times, their education level is not—college. When they publish reports of how much fiber and whatever and the dust and everything, they do it in kilograms and milligrams and all this stuff—you know, I want to—Yah, they do give you the information. Yes. And they did give you the safety meeting on how this is supposed to be read, but, fifteen minutes? It's totally foreign to you. How the hell am I supposed to know what it means?

The problem of information costs is more serious even than Downs's demonstration that wealth buys more of this resource just as it buys others, although that in itself is a serious problem. The acquisition of additional information is more costly per unit for subordinates since it is the primacy of deep background factors such as education and social circles that is decisive here. Offe and Wiesenthal summarized this point well: "[I]n order to achieve an equal amount of accuracy in awareness of their respective interests, vastly different efforts are required on both sides of the major dividing line of social class."[46]

There is another element that must be added to the now growing list of difficulties in accepting as "interest" people's estimations of it. In addition to the unequal distribution of misperception and the unequal cost of information, there is an actual disincentive for people to seek out better information. Particularly in an authoritarian institution such as a factory, the possession of such information cannot always change the situation in any significant way. If Wendy were to learn that a number of chemicals she works with could cause serious long-term problems, it would not sharply increase her chances of avoiding exposure. There are relatively few times when the union can make a major issue of a long-term health problem and OSHA intervenes even more seldom. Even when one of these organizations takes a strong stand and makes a compelling case for greater health and safety protection, they are not necessarily successful. This leaves the incentive for any employee to seek bad news near zero while making even minimal costs seem high.

The disincentive to obtain information leads directly to the possibility of adaptive preference formation. That is the process of bringing wants into alignment with the set of feasible alternatives, what Jon Elster called the "sour grapes" adaptation.[47] Workers who consider NEC a "good place to work" are certainly not comparing factory work at NEC with the set of jobs in society but with the much smaller set that they see as open to people with their qualifications. When people describe their views on decision making, they are dealing with a similarly restricted set. Even those who advocate the "team Taylorist" alternative take for granted that a chemical plant "is not a debating society."[48] When Balzer and Pfeffer were shocked by the noise, physical demands, and repetition of factory life (as recounted in chapter 3), they were told that they would get used to it, which meant that they would begin comparing factory jobs to each other, rather than to other circumstances.

The adaptation process need not be instantaneous, nor completely divorced from coercion, and it can even be that it begins as resignation, not adaptation. Two authors who interviewed employees in another chemical plant reported this comment about working with toxic substances: "What you can't change, you accept, so we kid about it. 'Cyanide is good for your health.' "[49] The authors called this "resigned compliance and passive adaptation." Of course behavior that is resigned and passive may be different from values that are compliant and adaptive. But over a period of time the first may become the second, precisely because there is no choice. When I asked a very new employee if he had ever encountered people who told him (as they told me), "I've been working here twenty years and look at me, I'm healthy," he replied, "They all say that." Wendy told me that when she worked in a new building, she asked what a particularly pungent smell was. She was told it was toluene, and was also told to keep away from it.[50] Toluene is a widely used solvent with known toxic effects. Of course it was impossible for her to avoid it, since it was everywhere in the building. She explained her own process of adaptation.

Wendy: I don't know what it is *[the toluene]* because I worked as a janitor in the building. They just told me, that's what the smell is. It's toluene, try to avoid it. But by the third day I didn't even smell it anymore.

Q. Do you ever worry that you don't know what you're working with?
A. Me personally? I accept it as a fact of life. There are certain things that you just can't—you can be made more aware. Each individual has his choice. I don't think that anybody really wants to give up the end product, so therefore it's good enough.

Adaptive preference formation implies the construction of wants. But it is possible to argue that such an adaptation is a positive and helpful adjustment for people in subordinate positions. Elster points out that some conceptions of freedom are compatible with either the satisfaction of wants or the elimination of most of them.[51] Sisyphus might be a "free" man if his only desire were to roll rocks up and down hills. Emerson in his discussion of dependence called "identification with the aggressor" a costless sedative for a subordinate.[52] He was making an observation, not a case. But Lewy did make a case for adaptive preferences in situations where oppression is inescapable:

> An escapist religion may be the only way to prevent utter demoralization. For example, according to the Hindu doctrine of karma, the law of action and retribution, membership in a caste was determined by the virtues or sins of a previous existence, and misfortune and distress were considered the result of one's own doing. This religious belief not only justified the manifest social inequalities of the Aryan community but provided a credible explanation of human suffering. To call such beliefs "false consciousness" would seem to ignore the extent to which they are rooted in people's existential needs.[53]

In other words, interest and preference are still the same because it is in the interest of a suffering person not to know that the explanation for his or her suffering may be fraudulent. This seems to me to be an odd argument for supporters of "pure preference" theory because if self-deception can be socially useful, deception must be as well. In fact, at times it should be mandated to superordinates that one of the tasks of domination is to provide and disseminate arguments that will provide solace for those below them.

The possibility of defining elimination of wants as freedom, and of finding virtues in solace would create a virtually airtight case for "pure preference" theory. There are two possible lines of counterargument. One is to object on normative grounds.[54] That is how Elster answered the problem after he himself had posed it:

> [I]ntuition tells us that it is perverse to say of a man that he is free simply because he is made to content himself with little, by manipulation or adaptive preference formation.[55]

Larry Spence offered another such verdict:

These functions of reconciling men and women to the status quo while limiting their aspirations to the results of available practice are contrary to the social functions of a productive science.[56]

While I am inclined to agree with both of these comments, there is another approach to the problem of solace, which will require an excursion into my second line of criticism of "pure preference" theory.

Preference and Privilege

The range of choices for everyone is finite, but for some, it is more finite than for others. No one denies that rewards are unequally distributed in a capitalist society, not even those who might want to argue that such inequality reflects the justice of such societies. The range of choices is very different for different groups and individuals. If the range of wants is also very different through adaptive preference formation, this might be thought of as making the best of a bad deal. When people trade values (for instance, health or satisfaction or democracy for continued employment), they have to estimate their own resources. Acceptance of an unpleasant consequence, according to this reasoning, can be explained by referring to what must have been an even more unpleasant previous state of affairs. Here are two examples of such trades; the first is from Nelkin and Brown's interviews with chemical workers, referring to the uncertainties inherent in working with chemicals:

> While professionals told us "It's worth the risk," production workers said, "We have no choice. You can never balance the wage against the risk; you balance the wage against the alternative. The alternative is starving."[57]

>During my probationary period at Procter and Gamble, the company decided to eliminate the bonuses that had paid some employees up to 30 percent over base pay based on performance. The "bonus" did not feel like piecework pay since performance varied mainly with line speed. Obviously, this caused a great deal of discussion. It also raised fears that this might be a prelude to more general cutbacks in benefits. During this period, one worker came into a lunchroom and announced jokingly, "Guys, I heard this straight from the top. If we don't kick up a fuss about the bonuses, they won't cut our medical."< PG, PO

The terms of trade-offs are dictated not simply by the presence or absence of resources but by position in a given hierarchy. Place in the hierarchy conditions every aspect of choice. The higher up, the greater the range of choice; the less cost, the more accurate and cheaper the information. The lower, the more choice becomes a matter of picking one's poison. Wendy, for instance, said that the desire to make the "final product"—which for her was not a chemical product but a job—made the conditions "good enough," not "good."

But "good enough" may be good enough, because satisfaction with the outcome of a trade may be contoured to fit the choice made. Runciman, Gallie, and Hyman and Brough documented the overwhelming tendency of blue-collar workers to use other blue-collar workers as a reference group.[58] The use of a reference group is not necessarily important in the process of coming to a decision, but is crucial in evaluating a choice once made. Mann and Blackburn found and described a hierarchical blue-collar labor market in an English city in which the choices were between "more or less unpleasant jobs, demanding little or no skill." But they found that the very sameness of jobs made the one distinguishing feature—relatively small differences in pay—take on increased importance: "Thus, paradoxically, the neo-classical theory of the labour market has some validity because constraint facilitates 'choice.' "[59]

If constraint does not lead directly to the suppression of a want, it can do so indirectly through the vehicle of compartmentalization. In a study of second generation Eastern European immigrants to Johnstown, Pennsylvania, Ewa Morawska discusses a process she calls their "segmentation of reality into two spheres: the dominant American world and the ethnic community, each 'ruled' by different perceptions."[60] People are capable of simultaneously holding the views that job A and job B are hot, hard, dirty, and low-paid, *and* that job B pays a little more. But if those two pieces of information are kept separate and if it is the second that dominates employees' discourse once the decision to work at B is made, the importance of the first set diminishes. As I did with the other re-interviewees, I asked Tony why people would say that NEC was a good place to work even when they expressed dissatisfaction with it:

It's a *good* place to work. The reason it's a good place to work is that it's easy work. I don't think there's a job down there that's physically demanding. It ain't like construction work. Don't get me wrong, it's manual work, and you'll have a bad day or two. But it's not like—what do I want to say?—it's not like being a roofer.

He voluntarily returned to the subject later in the interview to reemphasize his point:

That's another thing when people say NEC is a good company to work for. They *are* a good company to work for. If you make a big mistake and you go to them and say, "Hey, I made a mistake—." I know a guy who ruined a million pounds of product. *[gives details]*

He was honest. He went to them and said, "I made a mistake. I didn't really know." They gave him three days off with no pay. Any other company, I don't care where it is, he would have been gone.

>*I can only speak from my own experience on that point, but I am fairly sure that the assumption that "at any other company he would be gone" is not true. I committed some whoppers myself, including wrecking (unintentionally and maybe even unavoidably) a print cylinder at Diamond worth several thousand dollars. Employees at each place I worked told me that the bosses at that place were especially fair, or at least especially complacent.<* DI, PA

These are similar to comments in Tony's first interview. But after the first interview was over and the tape recorder off, he told me this:

It's not a bad place if you're going to punch a clock. My only complaint is, I wish I had an education. Then I wouldn't have to work at a place like that. Once you've been there ten, fifteen years, you know, you're kind of set.

And in answer to the question about advice would he give his children about working "at a place like NEC":

I've already given it to them. They won't work at NEC. They'll both be in business for themselves. They'll be their own boss. Why should you work for somebody else?

These two sets of observations are kept separate. Tony is able to specify both the terms he finds acceptable for factory employment and the unfreedoms inherent in subordination. The two views did not interpenetrate, despite my pleadings and insistence that he consider both at the same time. They are separate statements of preferences, one confined to the set of available alternatives, the other critical of the limitations of the set. There are no grounds for describing the second as his "real" preference. Tony had every opportunity to work elements of this more critical stance into an evaluation of the job, and he would not do so.[61] But is does show us that his first statements cannot be read as simple taste. They are wants refracted through the lens of subordination.

Polsby directly took on the question of trade-offs in which the alternatives are both unpleasant. He admits that such situations occur, but:

The argument that rich is better does not imply that promoting equality is a method for getting rich—it may be a device merely to impoverish everybody. And insofar as this is true, it is clearly not a device for escaping unpleasant trade-offs and hence fails as an argument in support of the notion that people in the community are falsely conscious when they make these trade-offs.[62]

There are two arguments welded together here. The first is the undeniable claim that every choice is an economic one; that is, one that entails costs. The second is that we should pay no special theoretical attention to costs that are higher and benefits that are smaller at the lower end of the socioeconomic spectrum. But consider the extreme case: if person A trades the possibility of a vacation in Monte Carlo for a BMW, and person B trades information about hazardous chemicals for an average of one hour of free time after work for a month, and if both people express satisfaction because the alternative was worse, should we not look for the role privilege may be playing in the formation of preferences? The fact that other systems of distribution *might* fail to solve the problem of privilege does not explain why people would be satisfied with current inequalities. There is no reason, for instance, why democracy at work should be a costly preference, except that there are those with the authority to make it so. It is not a persuasive argument to say that the present system of inequality and distribution of authority, whether at work or more generally, is a precise balance of efficiency and equality such that any move toward greater equality would be self-defeating. It is even less convincing to base an argument on the premise that people understand the situation in this way. If people do not express displeasure at the outcome of distasteful trade-offs, some explanation is required.

I will put my case even more provocatively. A few NEC employees whom we have already met *have* argued that further demands on a precarious system might mean losses for everyone. Some of Paul's comments can be read that way. Such statements are not realistic appraisals of an imperfect world of scarce resources but are of a species that Marx and others called "reification." That is a grandiose (and sometimes pretentious) name for what has become conventional wisdom in sociology—that concrete, physically existing organization has "an apparent solidity" that obscures its contingent and manmade nature:

> It is probable that for much of the time most men do not perceive the conventional and arbitrary nature of many of the social arrangements under which they live and suppose them to be the only possible ones given "the nature of things."[63]

Preferences are formed in situations in which there is an unavoidable bias toward the status quo. Not one NEC employee found hierarchical work organization *strange;* of course, I did not expect them to. Those who are privileged by that status quo certainly do their part to perpetuate that bias, but that is not what I have been describing. The origins of the belief s .ctures of the employees I have presented is a separate topic. No doubt would have to add indoctrination to those other factors that have lurke .nroughout this account: rational choice, moral economy, adaptation. B the "conservative bias" toward awarding existing institutions legitim ;y is something employees are capable of developing on their own.[64] Th > final NEC employees to speak for themselves are Wendy and Thelma, who were only interviewed once and have been introduced by name, along with the re-interviewees, because they were interviewed together. The two are close friends. Although Wendy did the bulk of the talking, they discussed ideas between themselves, thought about each other's statements, and fine-tuned their points through that process with less need for my intervention than there was in other interviews. These comments show very powerfully what a conservative bias is, how it legitimates hierarchy and how that is possible when the employees are intelligent, clear-headed, and even slightly cynical people. This discussion followed Wendy's discussion of toluene by about ten minutes. Both Wendy and Thelma had used the phrase "That's just a fact of life" in the interview and I wanted to find out about the influence of the "apparent solidity" of factory life on their conception of what those facts were and were not:

Q. It's interesting, you mentioned that you smelled toluene when you went in and then you got used to it. Do you find that you get used to things that you probably shouldn't get used to *?*
Wendy: I don't know, because I don't know the hazards of it. I walked in figuring, hey they know what they're doing, and they tell you this toluene's no problem. Now I'm not sure whether it is or isn't. Nobody else is making a fuss, why should I?
Thelma: Have you ever ridden a bus?
Me: Sure.
Thelma: When you got on that bus, did you ever think about whether that bus driver knew where he was going?
Me: [pause] No.
Wendy: [laughs] Very good. I like that. That's good.
Thelma: You know when they found out? Probably the last coffee stop they made. You have to assume. We assume a lot of things in our life. We get on trains and airplanes and we assume the pilots know where they're going. We go to work and we assume people who are in charge of a given area know what they're doing.
Wendy: You assume that even though they tell you it's carcinogenic, when you go in as an entry-level factory worker, you kind of hope that these people know what they're doing.

This section began as an attempt to find some way other than normative claims to reject the description of restricted wants as freedom. Solace certainly does have a functional value, smoothing the workings of any system or subsystem of hier̄ ̄al authority. But advocates of the value of solace rest their argum ̄ ̄ ̄ncomfortably on the proposition that whatever exists is in all likelihood the best that can be achieved at the time. Solace for subordinates may reduce the cost of maintaining such a system but it may also reduce the possibility of changing it, or even of allowing people to choose whether or not a change is desirable.

False Consciousness

Polsby says that people who claim that the preferences of others can be "misguided by their own lights" bear a heavy responsibility for proving such a claim.[65] This is a fair challenge, particularly given some historical uses of that claim. I have tried in this chapter to assume that responsibility in one lump sum rather than on a case-by-case basis. To recapitulate: even simple taste is not so simple; it is influenced by the extent of exposure to alternatives. More complicated choice, involving judgment, is open to error based on lack of information or the dissemination of misinformation; these misperceptions are exacerbated by the existence of class divisions (or stratification of any kind, such as ownership-workers in a factory). Dominant institutions do more than provide vast resources for superordinates; by their very existence they provide an argument (if not in every instance a clinching one) for their own legitimacy. Finally, it is a perversion of the concept of freedom to equate it with adaptation. The argument in this chapter has not been an empirical one, as in the previous four chapters. Rather, I have sought to justify the comparisons made throughout between opinions and "objective" evidence, or between opinions and the set of possible alternative opinions.

To these arguments for separation of preference and interest I add one more, suggested not by my interviews but by research on mass beliefs and values. This last argument is that some beliefs act as an intervening variable in "determining" (in a loose sense) others. "Social values"—which is another name for conventional wisdom—can distort people's perceptions. An extreme instance of this occurred during interviews conducted by Lillian Rubin. Rubin received comments from many working-class women who said that they did not like the "libbers." A common reason given was, "I like a man to open the car door and light my cigarettes." After hearing that several times, Rubin asked one respondent when that had last happened. Her answer: "I've gotta admit, I don't know why I said that. I don't even smoke."[66]

While this is somewhat comical, recent research has produced many more serious examples of misperceptions driven by other beliefs. The focus of this literature has been the centrality of a belief in individual responsibility for place in the social and economic order, even among those whose place is low. Two sets of writers—Huber and Form, and Kluegel and Smith—call this the principal culturally specific form of dominant ideology.[67] Robert Lane provided an overview of this literature that assessed the massive evidence of this point.[68] Halle took note of this core belief among chemical workers and described it concisely and well:

> It is important to note that like most Americans these workers typically believe that their position in the class structure is of their own doing. They are factory workers because they want to be or, if they do not want to be, because "they missed the boat." They "had their chances." If they regret their position they tend to blame not their class origins but themselves.[69]

These studies are part of what could be called the American Daydream literature. This is a slightly ironic interpretation of those values as disenabling people from correctly perceiving cause and effect in the political world. Schlozman and Verba carefully documented in the case of the unemployed how the principle of individual responsibility "took the edge off potential discontent" and "built a barrier between unhappy experience with the economic system and beliefs about the essential justice of the order which produced those experiences."[70] Robert Lane, adding another core belief, the fairness of market distribution,[71] to the discussion of individual responsibility, pointed out one potential result for derivative beliefs (ones that are sometimes held to be unexplainable preferences):

> These two forms of attribution require a person to believe that if he is unemployed it is through some discretionary act of his own, but that if a firm lays him off it is because it could not do otherwise.[72]

There is another core belief that has received less attention (including, for instance, my own failure to devise questions about it) but may function in a similar way: this is Albert Hirschman's contention that Americans prefer exit to voice. Hirschman suggested that the "curious conformism of Americans" could be partly due to the neatness of exit and its high rank as a national symbol as opposed to the messiness of voice.[73] He also argued that a high exit price would suppress both exit and voice. Within a factory like NEC, exit is mainly a myth, since there is an enormous price to be paid for leaving. But myths have a real influence. Here is a task for future American Dream research: if the preference for exit may explain the "curious conformism," the *myth* of exit among subordinates may account for the peculiarity of acquiescence taking the form of rebellious ("rugged") individualism.[74]

>*I worked at Diamond during one contract negotiation. During the period prior to the contract vote, I worked with a few people in my department to put out a leaflet. We handed it out one day at break*

time. The next day management brought everybody who handed out the leaflet into the office, reprimanded me, and warned the rest of the department not to talk to me "because of the confusion." Some people had fun, holding up signs saying "Hi" or "My name is Roger." When the next shift came in, I explained what had happened to a young employee I knew. He shrugged it off. "They can't tell me who to talk to. I'll just go home." This distanced him somewhat from the subterranean battle going on. He repeated that on a few other occasions—"They know they can't push me around. I'll walk out the door." Some years after I left Diamond, I met him at a fair. He told me angrily that he had been fired. "I got an order to move a skid from another department. I told them I wouldn't do it and I went home. They told me to stay there."< DI, PA

The arguments and the evidence show both that a disjuncture between preference and interest can be theoretically sustained and that in fact in some cases it does exist. This brings the discussion to a point I have been tiptoeing around softly: the usefulness of the term "false consciousness." That phrase is derived from the Marxist tradition, specifically the Marxist-Leninist tradition (if Lukacs is included in that category).[75] At times it has taken on one very specific meaning: that those workers who do not identify the capitalist system as their enemy and do not want to abolish it and replace it with socialism are falsely conscious. That is not the contention of this investigation. But the term has a looser meaning; it suggests that there are times when a system of domination appears to be legitimate to those whom it affects adversely.[76] Some recent writers have tried to capture that meaning while avoiding the term. Lukes spoke of "manipulated preferences," Lindblom of "constrained volitions," Gaventa of "false consensus," and Elster, as I have already indicated, of adaptive preference formation. While I am not highly committed to the term "false consciousness," and consider Gaventa accurate in saying that it is not possible to speak of a state of mind as being "true" or "false,"[77] I still consider it possible for states of mind to reflect external circumstances more or less accurately. This is what is contested, and because that is where the real issue lies, I do not want to wave the white flag on the term "false consciousness," despite its liabilities.[78] There is, however, one claim usually associated with "false consciousness" that I need to address because it is always a target for critics, although not always a claim by adherents: this is that "false consciousness" always means the practice of putting short-term interests ahead of long-term ones. While false consciousness certainly can mean that, as in the frequently cited problem of addiction, it can also mean a distortion of both sets of interests. In addition to his description of his own life in a concentration camp, Bruno Bettelheim wrote a critical and perceptive article on the "Anne Frank" phenomenon.[79] What was so appealing to many people about Anne Frank's diary was the Frank family's insistence on maintaining the norms of living as closely as possible. Bettelheim pointed out the futility and illusory character of that course. Unlike many Jews in Holland (for example), the Frank's did not even have escape routes in their hiding places. Bettelheim was less critical of the Franks themselves, whom he saw as dealing as best they could with a terror-filled situation, than he was of those who made a virtue out of the choice of self-delusion. In this admittedly extreme case, Bettelheim concluded that both the long- and short-term interests of the Frank family suffered because of the path they chose.

Objective Interest

Since I have been wading in shark-infested waters in this chapter, I may as well plunge all the way in. An even more problematic concept than false consciousness is "objective interest." The two phrases share the problem of unfavorable past associations. The view that some interests are objective has enabled those who claim they know which are and which are not to discount any costs or real opposition to the imposition of plans based on those "interests." At times, "objective interest" has been used as a synonym for "historical inevitability." But "objective interest" has no monopoly on misuse. The term "free markets" has been used to justify the Chilean regime, and "democracy" to justify the attempt to overthrow the government of Nicaragua. This is not to say that "objective interest" does not have severe conceptual problems on its own. How is one to know what an "objective interest" looks like? Would such a concept mean that people should have no choice in goals and values? Who decides, if not the person whose "interest" is alleged?

Thus far, every use of the term "objective" has been enclosed in quotation marks, so that I might hold the validity of the concept in abeyance until I could address it directly. It might have been easier to leave the question alone, particularly since what I have to say will be sketchy. But any claim that people can misjudge must ultimately include some objective referent; if it does not, the "pure preference" theorists can convincingly point to inconsistencies. The formulation that people would choose differently if they had more information or more alternatives (roughly the arguments of Gaventa, Lindblom, Connolly, and Lukes) is vulnerable on this point. A person may have developed want X based on one set of facts. He or she sets about trying to achieve that want. Why is anyone entitled to say that if the person had additional or more accurate information, want Y would be better for him or her? If X and Y are both achievable (say, for example, a two-cents-an-hour increase in wages and a comprehensive health plan that requires extensive testing of and dissemination of information about chemicals), how could an observer maintain that the person is better off with Y than with X? The intuitive answer is that the observer can see what is coming—that Y offers more of benefit to the chooser (and not just necessarily in the long run) than X. These are footprints leading toward objective interest.

Let me give one more example of the difficulties of making an argument that simultaneously describes manipulated preferences and denies objective interest. In a review of Lukes, Ted Benton carefully demonstrated some inconsistencies inherent in such a position.[80] Lukes has only two methods, Benton points out, by which to judge a preference to be manipulated. One would be an *ex cathedra* judgment by a third person. But how could that person have avoided whatever mechanisms produced the manipulation and how could we know if he or she had successfully avoided them? The second would be comparison of choices made under optimal conditions with those made under conditions of incomplete information. The chooser would still be the ultimate arbiter. Benton plausibly points to a problem with this method:

> The judgment that has to be made is how the actor would feel or behave under conditions which do not now hold, and may never have, or never will hold. No matter how well-intentioned the observer, this is still other-ascription of interests, and not self-ascription.[81]

Benton then goes on to try himself to build a case for manipulated preferences without other-ascribed interests. What he builds around is the contention of Gramsci that hegemony is more complete in the sphere of ideas than in the sphere of action. This would raise the possibility that evidence of unmanipulated preferences can be found in people's practical activity, which can be contrasted with verbal expressions of wants. Social practice, Benton claims (that Gramsci claims), is "*relatively* [his emphasis] impervious to the cultural and intellectual labour of the hegemonic group or class." But if practice is only *relatively* impervious to hegemonic devices, which forms of practice represent the "alternative conception in its embryonic form," and which do not? How can that decision be made in some way that is not other-ascribed?[82] Benton cannot escape the terms of his own critique of Lukes.

The purpose of reviewing these debates has been to demonstrate the difficulty I would have, as others have had, in avoiding an approach to other-ascribed interest. Of course, the logic here could as easily be used to question the rest of my project—that is, to affirm the "pure preference" formulation. But my own evidence and that of others suggests too strongly that preferences can be constrained, manipulated, adaptive, and "false." I will therefore offer a few thoughts on the possible objectivity of interests, beginning with what is probably the least controversial. At times, I have referred to "objective evidence," meaning evidence taken not from a distillation of attitudes, opinions, or values, but from external scientific examination. Because I have been looking at a chemical plant, some of that evidence concerned the problems of shift rotation and health and safety. I have used this evidence to compare employees' assessments of sets of facts with externally derived scientific information. The relevant element is that there is information available independent of employee judgment. Further, the employees can be affected adversely (in some cases) by a set of conditions whether or not they are cognizant of that happening. There is certainly a long leap from this tame assertion to a tight determination of interests, but I am not making a case for that kind of determination.

The admissibility of objective evidence is actually a more respectable appearing subset of the wider and more debated category of needs. The contention has been made that there are broadly definable human needs, and when people act in ways contrary to those needs, they act contrary to their interest. The most immediate challenge to a needs-based concept of interest is that needs must be defined in a way that is either contestable or trivial. It is true, in regard to contestability, that needs are not easily derived from the multiplicity of human experience and wants. But it would be harder to create a convincing case that there is no such category at all. Barrington Moore, for instance, tried to locate some common needs in a cross-cultural and transhistorical examination. His method was to look at need in its absence—to answer the question by looking at what is always noxious to humans. He concluded that at least these were candidates: physical deprivations (absence of food, water, shelter, among others) and psychic deprivations (including lack of love and respect, and boredom). Moore's purpose was not to draw an inclusive list but to provide a rationale for making this examination, and to avoid the "curious counsel of scientific perfectionism" that would prevent anyone from addressing the question of needs.[83] The argument that any description of needs must be trivial also has some validity. Polsby pointed out that any description of needs must leave unanswered the great bulk of questions on which choice must be exercised.[84] But the significance of the triviality argument is that it admits into existence a category of needs, however unimportant that seems to be. There can be debate over triviality. In the situation under investigation, I would include the following as needs: not to die in a Bhopal-type disaster; not to be continuously exposed to chemical X (the OSHA-listed carcinogen); not to have the plant close and leave everyone without a job. I can agree that most questions involve a cost-benefit decision in which the goals of the individual (however derived) are crucial, and still maintain that there is a degree of objectivity involved—some set of inputs that are accessible to both to the observer as to the chooser.

This does not lead, to anticipate the next objection, directly to authoritarian conclusions about the arbitration of interests. My purpose here is to see whether there can be any standards of objectivity to use in deciding whether people's preferences are in every instance to their own benefit. This does not necessarily imply awarding the right of arbitration of that decision to anyone else. One can for the purposes of discussion and debate argue that employees would be better off with (for example) more autonomy at work, without denying that those employees have the right to make that decision. It is also worth pointing out that those who are scandalized by such an assertion should not overlook the fact that currently employees do *not* have the right to make such a decision and that the thrust of this and other research cited is that there are obstacles to even forming a preference for that as a goal.

It also seems fair to say that people have an objective interest in equal costs of information. If misperception can be explained by a desire not to gather further information, and if this whole bundle can be called a preference and used as an argument that people maximize values that are important to them and trade off those that are less important, it cannot be consistent to argue that anyone lower in a hierarchy could have an interest in unequally distributed information costs. While this may seem reasonably intuitive, it is difficult to demonstrate and the objective interest with the broadest implications. It is certainly rational for someone to want to achieve more free time and keep commitment to work minimal and "instrumental," but it would still not be in that person's interest that exposure to various alternatives be more costly than it is for someone higher on the hierarchical ladder. In a previous section I built on Offe's argument that subordination itself increased information costs. If so, superordinates may be doubly comforted; first, because they have the resources to be successful in the parceling out of rewards; second, because they are able to point to the disproportionate inattention of subordinates (Polsby's "presumption of inertia") to activity that might challenge the distribution of rewards.

There is enough basis for some categories of "other-ascribed," or objective, interest to warrant the arguments made throughout the first six chapters that people's ideas about social structures are in some degree molded to fit the contours of those structures. The defense of objective interest has not been the bottom line of this project, or even of this chapter, and I have approached it with some trepidation. My purpose has been to address what I consider the very compelling criticisms raised by "pure preference" theory of most theories of hegemony or dominant ideologies. My findings and interpretations generally fall into that latter group. Bringing into relief the criticisms such strongly opposing views make of each other carries risks, but at least I have been able to clarify the components of my case. In this last section I have sought to develop a modest case for distinctly immodest and controversial concepts. Neither the interpretation of the interview material nor the arguments of this chapter can stand alone. Together, they portray the influence that a system of subordination and the dominant institutions that organize that subordination can have in placing constraints on the judgment of subjects about the legitimacy of that system.

Notes

1. Jean Jacques Rousseau, "Second Discourse," in *First and Second Discourses*, p. 159.

2. For instance, Barry Hindess, "On Three-Dimensional Power"; Guenter Lewy, *False Consciousness: An Essay on Mystification;* Nelson Polsby, *Community Power and Political Theory: A Further Look at Problems of Evidence and Inference.*

3. Steven Lukes, *Power: A Radical View.* While it was Lukes's short book that first raised the "manipulated preferences" argument, there is no doubt that the argument would have been raised in some form. In another vernacular, the appearance of Lukes's argument at this time was historically determined. One reason people began to look at the nature and significance of preferences was exogenous to the "power" debates—the diffuse influence of "dominant ideology" formulations. The criticism by Nicholas Abercrombie, Steven Hill, and Bryan Turner *(The Dominant Ideology Thesis)* of such writings is precisely a recognition of their growing influence. For others, the pluralist-described political world of dispersed and widespread access to power simply did not square with the existence and intractability of social and economic inequalities in those same systems. While the existence of the second did not disprove the pluralist findings, it is not in comfortable harmony with them. For those not impressed with historical inevitability, one might say that if Lukes had not made his case, it would have had to be invented.

4. Rousseau, *First and Second Discourses*, p. 160.

5. It may puzzle the reader that I am only now introducing what I consider "the strongest argument" against any notion of manipulated preferences, since I have been discussing throughout the arguments of Abercrombie, Scott, and Hill, who are also critical of dominant ideology theories. I do not consider one set of opponents more worthy than the other, but they are very different from each other. If it has not been made clear by now, I will make it explicit: there are *three* positions, not two, on the issues at hand. Abercrombie and Scott do not build their case around epistemological objections to separating preference from interest, but around evidence that convinces them that subordinates do not in fact adopt the values of the dominant classes. See the discussion of reciprocity theorists in chapter 1 for the suggestion of some similarities between Scott's case and "pure preference" theory; in most respects, however, the positions are sharply different.

6. Vilfredo Pareto, *Manual of Political Economy*; Polsby, *Community Power.* I am well aware that when Polsby addresses these issues in chapter 12, he specifically attempts to include criteria for determining cases where expressed preference and interest might vary. How his own case *against* "false consciousness" would invalidate those exceptions is explained below. Polsby's arguments appear more than others because his manner of arriving at these questions was the same as mine—he used an empirical examination of power while fending off a variety of counterarguments. While it will be apparent that I do not agree with Polsby's position, I do believe that he poses the issues in an especially clear and sharp way.

7. Pareto, *Manual of Political Economy*, p. 44.

8. Ibid., p. 45. In this paragraph, Pareto is arguing against Herbert Spencer on the pleasures of altruism. In relation to the general conceptualization of taste, the same position would result from the reverse structure—that is, if the man had given away half the chicken and the neighbor had suggested he eat it all himself.

9. Ibid., p. 192.

10. Lewy, *False Consciousness*, p. 114.

11. Polsby, *Community Power*, p. 229.

12. Ibid., p. 230.

13. Polsby came very close to making this last point himself: "Many people trade off air pollution against employment, and it is not necessarily the case that they do so unwittingly" (*Community Power*, p. 217).

14. See Robert Nozick on "Having a Say over What Affects You," in *Anarchy, State and Utopia*, especially p. 269.

15. I am not trying to create a straw man. This argument is clearly based on market norms of preference formation and exchange and that certainly is a criticism that must be handled seriously. Further, it has a certain appeal to common sense, despite its counterintuitive appearance. It has some "bitter truth" similarity to a comment about the relation of talent to winning basketball games delivered by former Boston Celtic player Paul Silas: "The better team wins. The better team always wins. If you don't believe it, just look at the final score."

16. Polsby, *Community Power*, p. 222.

17. Pareto, *Manual of Political Economy*, p. 45.

18. And in fact has been used this way. I would not agree that Marxism or Leninism rests completely on Platonist foundations, but they have taken on some of those aspects, and not so benign ones. This is from a tape of a speech given in 1979 by the chairman of the Revolutionary Communist Party of the United States:

> I was talking to this dude in my home town Chicago the other day. And he said, "Well, you know, they told me when I started working at the plant"—he's been working there thirteen years—"and they said if I worked hard, I could have a lot of good things." This is the land of opportunity, even the working people. Where else but in America could working people have all these good things—nice car, maybe even a boat, maybe even a house. Shit—you can own your own home—the *American Dream!* And then do what? Sit behind locked doors afraid to go outside your own home because of what's out on the street. That's the American Dream.
>
> I'd rather live in a society where the dream wasn't to have your own home, but where people could go out on the streets together and change the world and make revolution and advance mankind. I'd much rather have a society like that.

Of course what he would "much rather have" is up to him. But there is a fairly pronounced implication that what other people would "much rather have" is not up to them. The most flagrant case imaginable of deciding and then dictating what other people's preferences should be was the alleged remark of a Khmer Rouge official about the difference between the methods of socialist construction in his country, Cambodia (Kampuchea), and Vietnam. The official said that the Vietnamese erred by trying to pick the rotten fruit out of the basket without tipping it over; the Khmer approach was to tip over the basket and select only those fruits that satisfied them completely. See Gavan McCormack, "The Kampuchean Revolution, 1975–1978: The Problem of Knowing the Truth," p. 8→, for discussion of whether this remark was reported accurately.

19. Polsby, *Community Power*, p. 224.

20. Lewy, *False Consciousness*, p. 116.

21. Ibid., pp. 126–27.

22. William Connolly, "On 'Interests' in Politics."

23. Anthony Downs, *An Economic Theory of Democracy*, p. 211, but in general, part III, "Specific Effects of Information Costs."

24. Polsby, *Community Power*, p. 211.

25. The logic and the rhino ride are on display in the preface to Nozick's *Anarchy, State and Utopia* (p. ix): "[M]any persons will reject our conclusions instantly, knowing they don't *want* to believe anything so apparently callous toward the needs and suffering of others. I know the reaction; it was mine when I first began to consider such views. With reluctance, I found myself becoming convinced of (as they are now often called) libertarian views, due to various considerations and arguments."

26. Raymond Wolfinger, "Nondecisions and the Study of Local Politics," p. 1077. I must take note here of the fact that Wolfinger has inferred consciousness from action. While I might agree with the characterization, and agree that it creates a problem for "pure preference" theory, Scott and Abercrombie et al. would probably object.

27. Lewy, *False Consciousness*, p. 117.

28. Polsby, *Community Power*, p. 228.

29. Ibid., p. 230.

30. Nor do they say what they would do about the mistaken judgment. But neither will I. I mention this here only because Polsby said that Connolly and Lukes would logically try to "jam their ideas down actors' throats" (*Community Power*, p. 222, n. 7).

31. Stephen Mennell, *All Manners of Food: Eating and Taste in England and France from the Middle Ages to the Present*, p. 17.

32. Ibid., p. 227.

33. Pareto himself is ambiguous in trying to answer this question: "Investigating whether moral sentiments have an individual or social origin is useless. The man who does not live in society is a very unusual man, one who is almost, or rather entirely, unknown to us. And a society distinct from individuals is an abstraction which does not correspond to anything real" (*Manual of Political Economy*, p. 71). I think this is not in keeping with his earlier absolutist position on taste.

34. Ron Eyerman, *False Consciousness and Ideology in Marxist Theory*, p. 21.

35. Pareto does not actually argue that they are exogenous, only that they are noncomparable. But then they must be exogenous. If some part of tastes X and Y can be explained by the same variable, then to that extent they are comparable. Even if the variable is not known, but there is the *potential* for explaining common variation if it were, the tastes cannot be said to be noncomparable by definition.

36. Charles Lindblom, *Politics and Markets: The World's Political-Economic Systems*, pp. 135–36. While I was thinking about the status of different choices, I saw an incident on an episode of "Miami Vice" that illustrated the discordant, jarring feel of equating simple taste with choices of other kinds. An American spy for the Soviets was pursuing the Miami lieutenant, Castillo, and a woman who was a KGB defector and the wife of a dead friend of his (who had been pursued in a hostile way by the CIA). The agent came with a machine gun into a field where Castillo and the woman were hiding, unarmed, behind separate trees. He gave Castillo this choice, expressed in "preference" language: "Okay, we've got to wrap this thing up. We can end it in two flavors. Either I blow you all away or you [Castillo] come out. I kill you, and take the woman back to Moscow. I won't harm her, I give you my word on that." Castillo was being asked to weigh professional duty, friendship, fear, loyalty, national security, and trust, and to announce which flavor he preferred. The outcome, not relevant here, is that the two Miami Vice heroes, Crockett and Tubbs, acted as exogenous variables, jumping out from behind another tree and expanding the set of available alternatives by blasting the agent.

37. Aaron Wildavsky, "Choosing Preferences by Constructing Institutions: A Cultural Theory of Preference Formation."

38. Lindblom, *Politics and Markets*, p. 136.

39. In a pause in the first interview, Paul said to me, "You talk about working

conditions—looking for a job is one of the hardest things in this day and age. I'd be appreciative if you'd put that in there somewhere.''

40. Kai Erickson noted the same phenomenon after the Buffalo Creek flood of 1972—that people retained precise immediate pre-flood recollections (*Everything in its Path*, especially the chapter, ''Looking for Scars'').

41. David Miller, ''Ideology and the Problem of False Consciousness.''

42. Claus Offe, ''Two Logics of Collective Action: Theoretical Notes on Social Class and Organizational Form,'' p. 90.

43. Downs, *An Economic Theory of Democracy*, p. 229.

44. Ibid., p. 236.

45. Benjamin Page, *Choices and Echoes in Presidential Elections*, p. 190.

46. Offe and Wiesenthal, ''Two Logics,'' p. 92.

47. The language and a number of arguments in this section are influenced by Jon Elster's *Sour Grapes (Studies in the Subversion of Rationality)*, particularly chapter 3, p. 109: ''Why should individual satisfaction be the criterion of justice and social choice when individual wants themselves may be shaped by a process that preempts the choice?''

48. Charles Spencer, *Blue Collar*, p. 83.

49. Dorothy Nelkin and Michael Brown, *Workers at Risk*, p. 181.

50. >*Supervisors often operate with a cold hypocrisy in telling workers to avoid things they cannot avoid. A department manager at P and G showed us a film on how back pain is caused and how to avoid it. Since my job required quick and heavy lifting, I asked him how we were supposed to use the careful motions suggested in the film. "Do the best you can," he told me. In another department, the foreman showed me how a large machine had become jammed with cans. He looked at me, plainly wanting me to stick my hand in and unjam it, an act that involved a fifty-fifty chance of my losing my arm. "Well, I shouldn't go after this by hand, should I?" I asked. "Good Lord, no," he replied, disappointed.* < PG, PO

51. Elster, *Sour Grapes*, p. 127.

52. Richard Emerson, ''Power-Dependence Relations,'' p. 33.

53. Lewy, *False Consciousness*, pp. 117–18.

54. The normative aspects of deciding this question were reinforced by a finding by James Kluegel and Eliot Smith in *Beliefs about Inequality*. They found that a number of ''positive emotions''—pride, happiness, confidence—were positively correlated with ''internal control''—that is, with the belief that one decides one's own fate. That is so, the authors found, even if that fate ''is objectively a poor position, and even if the belief is objectively inaccurate'' (p. 285). This seems to substantiate Lewy's contention, although the authors do not draw the same conclusion.

55. Elster, *Sour Grapes*, p. 128.

56. Larry Spence, *The Politics of Social Knowledge*, p. 21.

57. Nelkin and Brown, *Workers at Risk*, p. 180.

58. W. G. Runciman, *Relative Deprivation and Social Justice;* Duncan Gallie, *Social Inequality and Class Radicalism in France and Britain;* Richard Hyman and Ian Brough, *Social Values and Industrial Relations: A Study of Fairness and Equality*. Although these authors are British, Hyman and Brough devote a considerable amount of space to reviewing the evidence from the United States and find little difference. (See chapter 2.)

59. Robert Blackburn and Michael Mann, *The Working Class in the Labour Market*, p. 290.

60. Ewa Morawska, *For Bread with Butter*. While compartmentalization is my own choice of terms, and seems suited for describing the division of information into nonoverlapping categories, it certainly bears a resemblance to Robert Lane's ''morselization'' in

Political Ideology, with the only slight difference that my compartments seem larger and more internally coherent than his morsels.

61. See Jennifer Hochschild, *What's Fair?*, for another set of interviews in which responses fell into categories with different organizing principles that the respondents would not compare with each other.

62. Polsby, *Community Power*, p. 231.

63. Peter Berger and Thomas Luckmann, *The Social Construction of Reality*. See also Stephen Hill, *Competition and Control at Work*, p. 44; and Spence, *The Politics of Social Knowledge*, p. 129. Tony and John both used the phrase, "just like a solid rock," to describe NEC's appearance as part of Lockland's landscape.

64. See also Elster, *Sour Grapes*, p. 147: "It *is* a massive fact of history that the values and beliefs of the subjects tend to support the rule of the dominant groups, but I believe that in general this occurs through the spontaneous invention of an ideology by the subjects themselves, by way of dissonance-reduction, or through their illusionary perception of social causality."

65. Polsby, *Community Power*, p. 230. "I believe that a heavy responsibility rests upon analysts in such situations to justify the claim that actors are in fact unaware of what they are doing and are genuinely misguided by their own lights, rather than simply involved in trade-offs disagreed with (or not understood) by analysts."

66. Lillian Rubin, *Worlds of Pain: Life in the Working-Class Family*, p. 131.

67. Joan Huber and William Form, *Income and Ideology*; Kluegel and Smith, *Beliefs*.

68. Robert Lane, "Market Justice, Political Justice," p. 386.

69. David Halle, *America's Working Man*, p. 169.

70. Kay Schlozman and Sidney Verba, *Insult to Injury: Unemployment, Class and Political Response*, p. 198.

71. On this point, see also Hochschild, *What's Fair?*, on the "norm of differentiation" in the economic sphere.

72. Lane, "Market Justice," p. 392.

73. Albert Hirschman, *Exit, Voice and Loyalty: Responses to Decline in Firms, Organizations, and States*, p. 106.

74. There are indications of this rebellious subservience also in Paul Willis's *Learning to Labour*, perhaps indicating this is not American exceptionalism. In Willis's account, the anti-intellectual "lads" mock authority in their school and have a great time thumbing their noses at it—a process that leads them to leave at the earliest possible moment and go to work in a factory. In both cases, there is an element of macho posturing which may help explain the oxymoron.

75. It has been widely documented that Marx never used the term "false consciousness" and that Engels used it once, in 1893, in a letter to Franz Mehring. What Engels meant by the term was consonant with what he and Marx thought generally about mistaken ideas—that they were the special property of intellectuals. Marx did not discuss the consciousness of the workers a great deal and seemed to assume that the whole raft of "nonproletarian" ideas would diminish over time. The charge that Marx and Engels relied heavily on the notion of "false consciousness" is untrue.

76. Another loose and useful definition is John Witte's: "uncertainty that biases belief in favor of the status quo" (*Democracy, Authority, and Alienation at Work*, p. 41).

77. John Gaventa, *Power and Powerlessness: Quiescence and Rebellion in an Appalachian Valley*, p. 29.

78. I should also point out that the criticism of "false consciousness" from Abercrombie et al. and Scott is criticism of the looser versions. That is, they do not attack "false consciousness" by demonizing it; they present and criticize various forms of dominant ideology theory.

79. Bruno Bettelheim, "The Ignored Lesson of Anne Frank."

80. Ted Benton, " 'Objective' Interests and the Sociology of Power."

81. Ibid., p. 167.

82. In a review of Benton's article, Jeffrey Isaac pointed out that the problem is basically one for Benton, not for Gramsci, for whom power and class domination were ascertained through previous analysis and were relatively unproblematical ("On Benton's 'Objective Interests and the Sociology of Power': A Critique").

83. Barrington Moore, *Injustice: The Social Bases of Obedience and Revolt,* pp. 5–15.

84. Polsby, *Community Power,* p. 225.

8

Conclusion

I keep my nose to the grindstone, work hard every day
I might get a little tired on the weekend, after I draw my pay
But I'll go on working
Come Monday morning I'm right back on the crew
I'll drink a little beer that evening, cry a little bit of these workingman's blues.
—Merle Haggard[1]

Now some guys they just give up living and start dying little by little,
piece by piece
Some guys come home from work and wash up and go racing in the streets.
—Bruce Springsteen[2]

When dealing with a human spirit that has produced both passive submission and the Warsaw Ghetto uprising, one is ill advised to claim finality for any conclusions about acquiescence and rebellion. My own conclusions are limited by the specificity of the situation through which I have looked at powerlessness (hourly factory workers) and the case through which I have examined it (NEC). There are some issues on which I did not have enough evidence to generalize and others that, quite frankly, I simply have not resolved in my own thinking. I have not spoken the final word on *any* of the matters raised, but there are some areas that warrant discussion in which I could see the questions without being in a position to provide the answers. Rather than summarizing what has appeared already, I want to point out a few questions that remain.

It is now widely accepted to say that control of the terms of political discourse and/or the agenda for political action has an effect on both those who support and those who oppose particular outcomes. The most compelling feature of the rightward push of American politics in the late 1970s, culminating with the first election of Ronald Reagan, may not have been the election to office of conservatives, but the pull on Democrats, even liberal Democrats, toward budget cutting and muscle flexing. A similar process unfolded in debates around policy toward

Nicaragua. The debates did not produce consensus on aid to the Contras, but were conducted in terms increasingly helpful to those who promote that program. Neither the position that the Sandinista government might have been a positive development for Nicaragua, nor the position that the United States has no right to decide what is positive and what is not for countries in Central America was considered to be respectable. To avoid being considered fringe actors, most members of Congress who formerly held those positions had to draw in their horns. The ability to dictate the terms of discussion may be more visible and significant in its impact on what is held to be reasonable and legitimate opposition than on the determination of immediate outcome. The legitimating principles of a system or subsystem can be seen most clearly in what an opposition chooses not to discuss, or what is removed from the category of choice.[3]

For this reason I have been particularly interested in examining the composition of seemingly oppositional thinking and acting at NEC. Those who are relatively uncomplaining about a given state of affairs—for instance, about nonparticipation or the safety and health program—do not need to argue for their position or create a rationale for it.[4] Although here and there employees were forthcoming and precise about positive features they saw in the work environment, for the most part expressions of satisfaction took the form of "I got no problem with it." When people saw defects in some aspect of NEC work life, they had to work at constructing an explanation for the defect and some pattern into which the defect might fit, and had to work even harder to pose any alternative. What they came up with forms the content of the oppositional "mini-ideologies" that have appeared in each chapter: "team Taylorism," "criticism of negative attitudes," "workplace populism," and "defense of the everyday conception."[5]

In the course of discussing these ideologies, I have tried to indicate which prerogatives of NEC management and of industrial authority as a whole they challenged and which they did not. Some broad questions, such as private property and hierarchical internal structure, were hardly raised at all. Others, including market relations ("competitiveness"), and the *right* to manage (although, as Jill said, "They could leave a little spot open where people could use their imagination and intelligence"), were largely affirmed even by those with critical positions. What was subject to challenge were the outcomes that seem to follow from these arrangements. There was contention over individuality, control of daily routines, and the worth of work ("criticism of negative attitudes").

If even the "opposition" is loyal to this extent, industrial authority would seem to be quite secure. But legitimating symbols lend themselves to several interpretations. We have seen, for instance, "workplace populism" as a call for more participation in order to increase a company's competitive position. We have seen blame for "negative attitudes" being placed everywhere. While "team Taylorism" is a timid alternative to factory authoritarianism, as well as seeming to rest more on criteria of, or speculation about, efficiency rather than right, it nevertheless presents a case for collective intervention by employees in some aspects of production. I do not want to be ambiguous; I think people mean what they say. But it is at least possible that they do not say what they mean. "Workplace populism" may be more important because of its presentation as a critique than because of any specifics it may encompass. Those specifics may be particularly susceptible to conventional wisdom and available vocabularies.[6] In other words, one aspect of the exercise of power might be the creation of a language from which the powerless draw without fully understanding its content. It would take observation and study over a protracted period and through different situations in which different vocabularies might emerge to be able to make finer distinctions between vocabulary and meaning. Whatever more complete answer might come out of such a study, my working hypothesis would be that the tendency for oppositional thinking (and activity) to be expressed in terms that include the legitimacy of existing structures must give at least some aid and comfort to those institutions.

A second unsettled question concerns the direction in which the American Dream moves people to think and act. The literature discussed in chapter 7 often describes those core values as an opiate. Huntington, on the other hand, sees them as an amphetamine—constantly setting impossibly high standards to which institutions are expected to conform.[7] Morawska, based on her Johnstown, Pennsylvania research, found both impulses at work, with people torn between them:

> Evaluating their experience and American society in general, the immigrant children had been unable to separate the sense of accomplishment and frustration, achievement and failure. The two had been inextricably enmeshed in their lives, at the same time legitimating and delegitimating the social order in which they evolved.[8]

The American Dream, as I have been using it, is not simply a collection of nationally shared values, but the national form in which a dominant ideology appears. As with any set of ideas that legitimate existing institutions and processes, the American Dream must contain promises as well as counsels of acceptance. Scott points out that any legitimating ideology promotes standards by which it can be judged, providing its own definitions of "dirty linen."[9] The thrust of chapter 3 was that the promises that served as the basis for industrial authority are almost absurdly small. But they are satisfactory because the "promise" contained in the central legitimating principle of the larger society is that everyone will be given a fair chance in the free market. Those who wind up at NEC deserve to be there.[10] The problem that emerges is whether people can come to question the unfreedoms of factory authoritarianism *on the basis of* the dominant American ideology, or whether those elements of resignation implicit in "individual responsibility" depress expectations to a point where the only possible challenge would be a counter-ideology. In short, are the "promises" held out by the American Dream leading people—specifically the lower classes—down blind alleys, forcing opposition to take the principle form of demands to "let capitalism be capitalism?"[11] While my study proceeded from questions about power and subordination, it has produced information mainly about a subsystem, albeit a very important one. I cannot claim that it provides any precise answer to that question, although insofar as it does, it tends toward answering in the affirmative.

It might have been possible to answer both of these questions more fully, as well as some others that remain underexplored, were it not for the relatively placid history of labor relations at NEC. At the end of chapter 6, I referred briefly to Zolberg's description of "moments of madness": times when authority relations are called into question and people envision alternatives that were previously beyond their conceptual horizon. "Everything is possible," Zolberg says of such times.[12] His description of their attributes makes them necessarily rare, evanescent, and highly unlikely to be applicable to any industrial situation in the United States. They are the by-product of a revolutionary challenge to authority and the temporary euphoria is the product of the initial successes of that challenge. The 1968 May-June uprising in France is an often discussed example of such an occurrence.

It is important methodologically (for purposes for comparison) to point out that such moments do occur. Recent research on the Russian Revolution has centered on sharp changes in the working class that led to the ascendancy of the Bolsheviks. Victoria Bonnell established that the Russian working class underwent a change in consciousness in 1905 notable for its "abruptness and totality."[13] When the central political authority that provided the legal and coercive backing of factory management disintegrated, workers quickly moved to assert forms of self-rule. Steven Smith described the practice of "carting out" supervisors in worker-controlled factories in 1917: Workers put their supervisors in wheelbarrows and pushed them around the plant, occasionally dumping them in a river.[14]

The main characteristic of such moments is that people question subjects that had previously been considered settled or even taboo: the emperor's new clothes are exposed. While such a tumultuous world of new visions has not been part of the political landscape for American workers at least since the 1930s, there have been and are times when "normal" authority is called into question in ways different from the loyal opposition of everyday struggle. The precipitating factor might be a company violation of the informal "contract," such as a plant closing or an especially hard-fought strike, particularly one in which coercive pressures are mobilized (arrests, injunctions, mass firings, strikebreakers, decertification). There can be dramatic situations in otherwise nondramatic times.

What such incidents have in common with Zolberg's "moments" is the suddenness of change in the balance of forces and the primacy of collective redefinition of goals. Several writers point out that "collective enthusiasms" are typical of the original stages of union organization, both over time (from the nineteenth to the twentieth centuries) and in compressed form in current situations.[15] In time, collective goals and collective debate as a means of formulating those goals give way to individual calculation. Craig Calhoun argued that social scientists need to differentiate between two sets of assumptions in viewing popular activity in these two situations: " 'Disturbance theorists' do best at explaining millenial movements, 'social choice' theorists at explaining stable groupings with defined objectives."[16] It is possible that some such jolting event as a plant closing could reestablish the "collective enthusiasm." While "enthusiasm" might seem an inappropriate word, or "collective definition of interest" might seem better (given that a reaction to such a development would be defensive), one can look for new understandings of the "possible" even in collective retreat. Staughton Lynd, the lawyer hired by the Ecumenical Counsel of Youngstown when three steel mills shut down, recounted the rapid transformation of employees' attitudes and activity. The employees of the Youngstown Works, for example, engaged in brief occupations of U.S. Steel headquarters (the parent company) in both Youngstown and Pittsburgh.[17]

But no such situation has developed at NEC, and it is unfortunate that my case study will not help in interpreting these "moments." There are legitimate questions about the after-effect of such outbursts of spontaneous energy. Lynd pointed out in the Youngstown case that even as collective activity was being planned, people were already beginning to make individual adjustment primary:

> As time goes on, collective outrage dims and personal survival takes over. The failure to produce a quick change in the company's decision leads to a mood of resignation and a focus on looking after oneself. The rhetoric of struggle is replaced by a rhetoric of benefits. Since each union member is slightly differently situated with respect to the benefits available, the pain of the plant closing becomes privatized.
>
> . . . The lesson appears to be this: *It is humanly very difficult to "start behaving as if a shutdown is coming," and at the same time take daring action with unpredictable consequences, to try to stop the shutdown.* People calculating their benefits are unlikely to chain themselves to their machines. [emphases in original][18]

Christopher Hill, who wrote an account of the way in which the norms of British society had been thrown open to question during the English Revolution, provided the best description of the reimposition of normalcy: "For some at least," Hill wrote, "the revolutionary decades had been a period of intense strain: for such the fear of freedom was removed by the return to old familiar values."[19]

It was not my original intention to approach such an important question as these "moments of madness" only through other people's work. As noted in chapter 2, I tried and failed to gain entry to two factories prior to the interviews at NEC. My first attempt was at a factory that would have provided information on "nonnormal" times, and my failure to gain entry was closely linked to the reason the interviews would have been so useful. The circumstances of my attempt themselves give some evidence that the effects of such times do not fade quickly. That plant was the site of a long, bitter, and ultimately unsuccessful strike in the early 1970s. A number of developments occurred that ranged from unusual to extraordinary: strikebreakers were immediately called in; there were repeated confrontations between strikers and strikebreakers, including fistfights and slingshot attacks; dozens of strikers were arrested, many several times; the strikers welcomed support from openly leftist students (many of whom were also arrested); and toward the end of the strike, someone made an unsuccessful attempt to kidnap the son of a company official. The strike was resolved in 1971 with the total defeat and decertification of the union. Most of the strikers were permitted to return to work, but with seniority beginning from the day of their return—meaning, with less seniority than the strikebreakers. Out of this caldron of resistance, coercion, and humiliation would certainly have emerged useful information on the after-effects of collective struggle. But that was precisely why I could not get permission to do interviews there. One former employee, whom I knew through other connections, told me when he heard of my plans, "You have to remember, in that place it's like the strike just ended yesterday." When I discussed this project with the current union president, he was also cautious: "You got guys that have sat next to each other for fifteen years in the lunchroom and haven't said a word to each other and ain't never going to." He also said that people would never agree to tape recording: "The company has people tape recording us in the bathrooms." Even though he was personally interested, he found when he asked others that too many people were hesitant. When he finally rejected my request, he said that the consensus among people he talked to was, "We got a contract coming up pretty soon and nobody wants somebody running around raking up old coals." Certainly, there is no precise way to gauge how hot those old fires were or to know how to interpret them. The point of the interviews would have been to do exactly that. But what comes through from simply the attempt is that this fifteen-year-old confrontation created a lasting atmosphere that was distinctly different from that at NEC.[20]

I have presented throughout two interpretations of resistance and quiescence that compete in some ways with mine—those of Abercrombie and Scott on the one hand, and "pure preference" theory on the other. Each of the three positions could be consistent with these "moments of madness." To Scott and Abercrombie, such times would enable the powerless to show what their real sentiments were all along. Remove the coercion and you will see that people were always able to envision many alternatives to subordination. To "pure preference" theorists, the circumstances brought about by new relations between actors—such as the faltering ability of a dominant class to maintain order—mean new calculations and therefore new estimates of interest. When the situation changes, the situation changes. My proposed explanation is that the breakup of an old order (even a temporary breakup) shakes loose the social constraints that prevented people from seeing clearly those relations of domination that always existed, and leads toward new alternatives because the old ones are no longer seen as natural. While my case study offers no evidence in favor of or against any of these explanations, the issue is important and warrants further research.

There is one more form "madness" may take; this is the complete rejection of subordination in "normal" times. Genovese discussed the character of some of the leaders of slave rebellions in the South as "fanatic, millenarian, and possibly mad":

> If so, the question presents itself: What judgment should be rendered on a society the evils of which reach such proportions that only madmen are sane enough to challenge them?[21]

On a plane somewhat below the leaders of slave rebellions are those whose "rebellion" takes the form of flaunting individuality in contradistinction to the homogenizing dictates of subordination:

> Oppressed people cannot avoid admiring their own nihilists, who are the ones most dramatically saying "No!" and reminding others that there are worse things than death. No people wholly lacking such an attitude can expect to survive.[22]

In the less harsh world of industrial subordination, such people are the "characters" about whom stories are told, people who simply never are made to fit in to the smooth flow of orders given and received. Frequently the stories are told in their absence, because "not fitting in" is a constant provocation to management. I did not encounter any such people or stories at NEC, but in this instance, I have to conclude that it was because of my outsider status, or because I was using a tape recorder. At each of my jobs, stories circulated about people who were regarded as "mad." The stories were half-approving, but *only* half— even workers who had the least use for industrial authority had trouble knowing how to interpret nihilistic rebellion against authority. The first story was about someone I knew well, although I was not on the shift when the incident happened; the second was an obviously well-travelled story about someone long gone:

> *"Bill," a young employee at P and G, would always bellow out people's names several times at them when they walked by. Nobody paid much attention, since it got to be part of the background noise in the department. Because he was a general goof-off and*

usually high, he was regarded as somewhat off-center. One day, somebody told me that Bill had been working the previous afternoon when "Jerry," the building superintendent, went past the line where Bill was working. In a perfectly consistent but outrageously equalizing way, Bill shouted, "Jerry, Jerry, JERRY!" People talked about that for weeks.< PG, PA

>After I had become involved in some of the activity I described in chapter 7 around the contract, a Diamond employee told me the following story in a bar: "Did you ever hear anybody talk about Charlie? [I hadn't.] He was some character. Too bad you didn't know him. He was a nut. He would never stop arguing, not with his foreman or anybody. If they told him it was day, he'd swear it was night. If his boss told him to do a job one way, he'd do it the other, even if it was harder, just to piss him off. He was always in trouble. One day they were going to fire him and they had a big meeting. He walks in with a suit and tie and carrying a brief case and everybody thinks, 'What's he up to?' He didn't say a word the whole meeting, just sits there with his briefcase on the table. Finally they asked him if he had anything to say. He gets up and opens the briefcase and dumps a whole bunch of oranges and bananas on the table, and says, 'I think you're all a bunch of fruits' and just walks out."< DI, PA

When I began thinking about the subject of this research, another graduate student who was familiar with some of this literature asked me, ''The question I've always had is, what do you expect out of these guys? What are they supposed to do?'' On one level, there would be some tangible differences. If people did not come to grant some legitimacy to relations of domination, their answers to some of my questions would probably be different. They also might act differently—be more assertive of their rights, be more active in demanding changes of various magnitudes in industrial structure. They might demand more information about the dangers of work with toxic material and more protection from it. They might even question the sacred cows of capitalist industry—the *efficiency* of capitalist production[23] and the basis in *right* for private ownership.

But while some things might conceivably be different, I am not suggesting that I would expect them to be. I have not argued anywhere that NEC workers are mindless; on the basis of much of what I have quoted, I imagine that readers would take exception if I had. The pulls toward adaptation and acceptance are pervasive and are reinforced (in the case of factories) by the coercive aspects of dependence and by real live coercion. While workers at NEC did not create the present industrial system, they must live with it, and to resent it constantly might not be the most satisfying alternative. Elizabeth Janeway convincingly described the adaptation process of even the most skeptical:

> [E]ven the most revolutionary of us believes that quite a lot of what is, is right. Political rebels have found it easy to go along with sex inequity; economic reformers set up production systems that parallel ones they attack. . . . We have absorbed the language we were taught, with all the logical or illogical connections among ideas that it carries with it. . . . We love our own landscape, our own climate. And we have all invested a great deal of effort and ingenuity in adjusting ourselves to what we take to be inescapable, continuing circumstances in the life around us.[24]

Of course, the ''life around us'' for the NEC employees who have appeared here is one of workday subordination. Several employees pointed out emphatically that NEC was not a sweatshop, and according to normal standards, that is an accurate assessment.

> *When I started at Diamond and on several occasions after that, my foreman told me that he enjoyed it there; that I would too; that people got along well, horsed around and that time passed quickly. Sometime later, after the big blowup around the contract described in chapter 7, he learned that I had already graduated from college. I had lied about this, since I never would have been hired if I had not. He called me into his office and said, "What I really don't understand is, why would you want to work in a damn hole like this anyway?"[25] < DI, PA*

Employees can understand the difference between NEC and contemporary sweatshops, let alone those between current industrial conditions and those of Dickensian England. It is hard to imagine human beings working in the conditions of those times. But in the future—and not necessarily a utopian future—it might be equally hard to imagine how anyone could have worked in a situation such as that at NEC and the other ''damn holes'' that constitute modern factory times. This investigation has been an attempt to clarify how people come to live with the ''stones'' (in Oglesby's phrase) of hierarchy, inequality, and non-democracy that characterize their own times.

Notes

1. Merle Haggard, ''Workingman's Blues,'' copyright 1972, Merle Haggard reprinted by permission.

2. Bruce Springsteen, "Racing in the Streets," copyright 1981, Bruce Springsteen, reprinted by permission.

3. See Charles Lindblom, *Politics and Markets,* pp. 142–43 on grand issues, on which all parties agree, and secondary issues, on which there may be disagreement.

4. "The weight of social influences involved falls overwhelmingly on the side of conservatism. That every wage bargain must be 'fair' or 'reasonable' now goes without saying. Also unspoken—though for a different reason—is the rubric by which the fair and reasonable is defined. That is where conservatism comes to the rescue. Change—always, everywhere, in everything—requires justification. The strength of conservatism is that it is held to justify itself" (Barbara Wooten, quoted in Richard Hyman and Ian Brough, *Social Values and Industrial Relations: A Study of Fairness and Equality,* p. 231).

5. I want to make it as clear as I can that the sets of people who held these views or took part in this activity were different according to the issue at hand. Not only am I restrained by numbers and the representativeness of the sample from translating these mini-ideologies into categories firm enough to serve as variables, but my sense is that even with a larger number of respondents, different people would be advocates of each of these positions. The exception is the group of "alienated instrumentalists," who fairly consistently hold to each of the mini-ideologies.

6. Michael Emmison, "Class Images of 'The Economy': Opposition and Ideological Incorporation within Working Class Consciousness," did a survey of shop stewards in Australia and found that they departed from "dominant managerial perspectives" if, and only if, they were offered such an alternative as one answer in a forced-choice questionnaire. His conclusion was that the stewards adopted whatever language seemed to be conventional, but that this should not be understood as an expression of their "real" understandings. Similarly, Jean Grossholtz of Mt. Holyoke College explained to me that until recently women had trouble understanding date rape as *rape,* since the vocabulary did not exist to describe rape occurring when there was no male jumping out from behind a tree.

7. Samuel Huntington, *American Politics: The Promise of Disharmony.* Paul Sniderman raises similar points in *A Question of Loyalty,* p. 122. Sniderman's finding is strengthened by the fact that his research on the alienated was done in the San Francisco Bay Area in the early 1970s when there was unquestionably a high concentration of unusually disaffected types. Seymour Martin Lipset and William Schneider, in *The Confidence Gap* (especially chapter 12), affirm this pattern for the population as a whole.

8. Ewa Morawska, "East European Laborers in an American Mill Town, 1890–1940: The Deferential-Proletarian-Privatized Workers."

9. James Scott, "False Consciousness or Laying It on Thick."

10. The dominance of the "same starting line" criterion for evaluating fairness is so ingrained that the main problem with it is not the acceptance of the unequal finish line, it is that people often overlook manifestly unequal starting positions. Almost any element of impartiality is enough to establish the "same starting line."

11. I want to explain here why I have quoted the lines from Bruce Springsteen's "Racing in the Streets" at the beginning of this chapter, and possibly convince unbelievers of the subtlety and sweep of his vision. Springsteen exposes dead-end alternatives, especially when they come packaged as escape. His protagonist in this song—clearly not himself—"rebels" against a deadening life by "racing in the streets," which he sees as the only alternative to the sad resignation of those around him, who are "dying little by little, piece by piece." But Springsteen sees neither of these as productive or life-affirming. Racing and resigning are two sides of the American Dream, both leading nowhere. In the middle of the song, the protagonist comes

to the same conclusion. His wife, whom he "won" in a race, loses hope of finding satisfaction in this macho, postured rebellion:

> She sits on the porch of her daddy's house
> But all her pretty dreams are torn
> She stares off alone into the night
> With the eyes of one who hates for just being born
>
> For all the shut-down strangers and hot rod angels
> Rumbling through this promised land
> Tonight my baby and me we're gonna ride to the sea
> And wash these sins off our hands.

—Bruce Springsteen, copyright 1981, reprinted by permission

Early industrialization in England had its William Blake; late capitalism in America has its poet also.

12. Aristide Zolberg, "Moments of Madness."

13. Victoria Bonnell, *Roots of Rebellion*, p. 447. Bonnell also documented a decisive move toward the Bolsheviks before the war.

14. Steven A. Smith, *Red Petrograd: Revolution in the Factories 1917–18*, pp. 55–60.

15. For example, Agnes Heller, *Everyday Life*, p. 98 and Alessandro Pizzorno, quoted in Charles Sabel, *Work and Politics*, p. 8.

16. Craig Calhoun, *The Question of Class Struggle: Social Foundations of Popular Radicalism during the Industrial Revolution*, p. 212.

17. Staughton Lynd, *The Fight against Shutdowns*.

18. Ibid., p. 123

19. Christopher Hill, *The World Turned Upside Down*, p. 354. Hill is so persuasive that I quote him again on the process of the re-routinization of life: "There was inevitable pressure on all sects to seek some support from some men of property; and this in time exacted its price. The insidious pressures of the world bore down on the children of light even as they organized to turn the world upside down" (p. 374).

20. Another example of long-lasting lessons of a different sort is the account of the famous Gastonia millworkers strike by Liston Pope (*Millhands and Preachers: A Study of Gastonia*, p. 312): the communist leader of the strike was still regarded as a folk hero by many employees fifteen years after he was gone, even though he had been sharply red-baited, even though the strike was unsuccessful, and even though in the intervening years he had, unbeknownst to the employees, turned anticommunist.

21. Eugene Genovese, *Roll, Jordan, Roll*, p. 595.

22. Ibid., p. 629. See again Hill, *The World Turned Upside Down*, p. 279: "A partial lapse from 'sanity' may have been the price to be paid for certain insights."

23. Herbert McClosky and John Zaller, *The American Ethos: Public Attitudes toward Capitalism and Democracy*, p. 122: "Arguments of this kind [the kind that attribute maximum efficiency to capitalism] have become so commonplace in American society that many may be unaware that they are, after all, only arguments—and that their empirical status and normative warranty are by no means beyond dispute."

24. Elizabeth Janeway, *Powers of the Weak*, p. 152.

25. James Scott, with whom I have had occasion to differ in these pages, has proposed the important notion of an "official" transcript which is the product of open transactions between powerful and powerless and an "off-stage" transcript that reflects their actual attitudes. This transcript, he argues, principally reflects the desire on the part of both parties to pretend that little antagonism exists. The exchange I related does seem to illustrate the distance between public pose and real attitude on the part of superordinates.

Appendix A

The questions that formed the heart of the interviews, or were repeated verbatim, were:

1. How long have you worked here? What kind of work do you do now? What have you done here before?

2. Tell me in your own words what it's like to work here.

3. When there's a decision to be made, whether it's about a job you do, or what gets produced, or how fast, who makes those decisions? Do you ever get asked your opinion? Do they keep you informed?

4. Can you imagine any other way decisions could be made?

5. [Expect] What do you expect from the company? What do they expect from you?

6. [Absolutely Wrong] In the time you've been here, has anything happened to you or to anyone around you where you said to yourself at the time, "This is wrong, this is absolutely wrong"? What did you do about it?

7. Is there much conflict at work—with other employees, with the union, with management? What usually happens?

8. [One Thing] If you were to get a call from New York [company headquarters] and they told you that you could change one thing here—anything at all from the biggest to the smallest—what would it be?

Appendix B

The following questionnaire formed the heart of the re-interviews:

1. [Asked for more biographical information—age, children, education, previous jobs.]

2. What were you looking for when you applied to work at NEC? Has it met your expectations?

3. Compare NEC to other job experiences. [I would specify, depending on the person.] Try to think of both positives and negatives of working here.

4. One of the answers I got from almost everybody in the original interview was that NEC was a good place to work. Some people would tell me that even if they then went on to criticize a lot about it. So I decided to ask people during these re-interviews why they thought that was, why I got that answer from so many people. Why do you think that happened?

5. [At this point, I would turn off the tape recorder.] I'll turn this thing off before I ask this. You might feel more comfortable answering if your words aren't recorded. Wherever I worked there was always a constant battle over time—how much would be mine, how much would belong to the company. It went on in little ways, people trying to cut corners, the company always trying to take back your free time. Does that kind of thing happen here?

6. [Recorder back on.] Would you say that in this country there is a great deal of opportunity for everyone to move as far as their ability takes them? Has it been that way for you?

7. I'm going to characterize the industrial system in this country and I want to

hear your comments on it. The industrial system of the United States is made up of privately owned corporations which compete with each other in the market and set their own rules for internal organization, modified only slightly by unions. Does this lead to fulfilling work? Is the paycheck enough compensation? Do you think NEC gives you the chance to use your talents?

8. Imagine your children being high school age [or, imagine you had children and they were]; what advice would you give them about working at a place like NEC?

Bibliography

Abercrombie, Nicholas; Hill, Steven; and Turner, Bryan. *The Dominant Ideology Thesis.* London: Allen and Unwin, 1980.

Abrahamian, Ervand. "The Non-violent Peasantry of Modern Iran." *Iranian Studies* 11 (1978): 254–303.

Adas, Michael. "From Avoidance to Confrontation: Peasant Protest in Precolonial and Colonial Southeast Asia." *Comparative Studies in Society and History* 23, 2 (1981): 217–47.

———. "From Footdragging to Flight: The Evasive History of Peasant Avoidance Protest in South and Southeast Asia." *Journal of Peasant Studies* 13, 2 (1986): 64–86.

Alier, Juan Martinez. *Labourers and Landowners in Southern Spain.* London: Allen and Unwin, 1971.

Aptheker, Herbert. *American Negro Slave Revolts.* New York: International Publishers, 1974.

Aristotle. *Politics.* New York: Penguin, 1981.

Arjomand, Said. "Iran's Islamic Revolution in Comparative Perspective." *World Politics* 38, 3 (1986): 383–414.

Aronowitz, Stanley. *False Promises: The Shaping of the American Working Class.* New York: McGraw-Hill, 1973.

———. *Working Class Hero: Evolution of the American Labor Movement.* New York: Pilgrim Press, 1983.

Atleson, James. *Values and Assumptions in American Labor Law.* Amherst: University of Massachusetts Press, 1983.

Augustine. *City of God,* ed. David Knowles. New York: Penguin Books, 1972.

Avakian, Bob. *For a Harvest of Dragons.* Chicago: RCP Publications, 1983.

Bachrach, Peter, and Baratz, Morton. "The Two Faces of Power." *American Political Science Review* 56 (1962): 947–52.

Balzer, Richard. *Clockwork: Life in and outside an American Factory.* Garden City, NY: Doubleday, 1976.

Batstone, Eric. "Systems of Domination, Accommodation, and Industrial Democracy." In *Work and Power,* ed. Tom Burns and Veljko Rus. Beverly Hills, CA: Sage Publications, 1979.

Bendix, Reinhard. *Work and Authority in Industry: Ideologies of Management in the Course of Industrialization.* New York: John Wiley, 1956.

Benton, Ted. " 'Objective' Interests and the Sociology of Power." *Sociology* 15, 2 (1981): 161–84. (1981).

Berg, David. "Failure at Entry." In *Failures in Organization and Development and Change: Cases and Essays for Learning,* ed. David Berg and Philip Mirvis. New York: Wiley, 1977.

Berger, Peter, and Luckmann, Thomas. *The Social Construction of Reality.* New York: Doubleday, 1966.

Bettelheim, Bruno. "The Ignored Lesson of Anne Frank." In *Surviving.* New York: Alfred A. Knopf, 1979.

————. *The Informed Heart.* New York: Free Press, 1960.

Beynon, Huw. *Working for Ford.* London: Allen Lane, 1973.

Blackburn, Robert, and Mann, Michael. *The Working Class in the Labour Market.* London: Cambridge University Press, 1979.

Blackburn, Robin. "The Unequal Society." In *The Incompatibles: Trade Union Militancy and the Consensus,* ed. Robin Blackburn and Alexander Cockburn. Harmondsworthy, England: Penguin, 1967.

Blauner, Robert. *Alienation and Freedom.* Chicago: University of Chicago Press, 1964.

Bluestone, Barry, and Harrison, Bennet. *Capital and Communities: The Causes and Consequences of Private Disinvestment.* Washington, DC: Progressive Alliance, 1980.

————. *The Deindustrialization of America.* New York: Basic Books, 1982.

Blumberg, Paul. *Industrial Democracy.* New York: Schocken, 1969.

Bonnell, Victoria. *Roots of Rebellion.* Berkeley and Los Angeles: University of California Press, 1983.

Bowles, Samuel; Gordon, David; and Weisskopf, Thomas. *Beyond the Waste Land.* Garden City, NJ: Anchor Press, 1983.

Bradley, Keith, and Gelb, Alan. "The Radical Potential of Cash Nexus Breaks." *British Journal of Sociology* 31 (1980): 188–201.

————. *Worker Capitalism: The New Industrial Relations.* Cambridge, MA: MIT Press, 1983.

Braverman, Harry. *Labor and Monopoly Capital.* New York: Monthly Review Press, 1974.

Brecher, Jeremy. *Common Sense for Hard Times.* New York: Two Continents/Institute for Policy Studies, 1976.

————. *Strike!* San Francisco: Straight Arrow Books, 1972.

Bulmer, Martin, ed. *Working Class Images of Society.* London: Routledge and Kegan Paul, 1975.

Burawoy, Michael. *Manufacturing Consent.* Chicago: University of Chicago Press, 1979.

————. *Politics of Production.* London: Verso, 1985.

Calhoun, Craig. *The Question of Class Struggle: Social Foundations of Popular Radicalism during the Industrial Revolution.* Chicago: University of Chicago Press, 1982.

Chinoy, Eli. *Automobile Workers and the American Dream.* Boston: Beacon Press, 1965.

Clawson, Dan. *Bureaucracy and the Labor Process.* New York: Monthly Review Press, 1980.

Clayre, Alisdair. *Work and Play: Ideas and Experience of Work and Leisure.* London: Weidenfeld and Nicolson, 1974.

Cohen, Bernard. *The Press and Foreign Policy.* Princeton: Princeton University Press, 1963.

Cohen, Joshua, and Rogers, Joel. *On Democracy: Toward a Transformation of American Society.* New York: Penguin Books, 1983.

Cole, Robert. *Work, Mobility, and Participation.* Berkeley and Los Angeles: University of California Press, 1979.

Connolly, William. "On 'Interests' in Politics," *Politics and Society* 2 (1972): 459–77.

Converse, Philip. "The Nature of Belief Systems in Mass Publics." In *Ideology and Discontent,* ed. David Apter. New York: Free Press, 1964.

Crosby, Faye. *Relative Deprivation and Working Women.* New York: Oxford University Press, 1982.

Crozier, Michael. *The Bureaucratic Phenomenon.* Chicago: University of Chicago Press, 1964.

Dahl, Robert. *After the Revolution?* New Haven, CT: Yale University Press, 1970.

———. *Dilemmas of Pluralist Democracy.* New Haven, CT: Yale University Press, 1982.

———. *Preface to Economic Democracy.* Berkeley and Los Angeles: University of California Press, 1985.

———. *Who Governs?* New Haven, CT: Yale University Press, 1961.

Dahrendorf, Ralf. *Class and Class Conflict in Industrial Society.* Stanford: Stanford University Press, 1959.

David, Paul, ed. *Reckoning with Slavery: A Critical Study in the Quantitative History of American Negro Slavery.* New York: Oxford University Press, 1976.

Davies, James. "Toward a Theory of Revolution." *American Sociological Review* 27 (1962): 5–19.

Della Fave, Richard. "The Meek Shall Not Inherit the Earth: Self-evaluation and the Legitimacy of Stratification." *American Sociological Review* 45 (1980): 955–71.

Downs, Anthony. *An Economic Theory of Democracy.* New York: Harper and Row, 1957.

Easton, David. "The New Revolution in Political Science." *American Political Science Review* 43, 4 (1969): 1051–61.

Edelman, Murray. *Political Language.* New York: Academic Press, 1977.

Eisenman, Robert. "Working Class Consciousness." Unpublished doctoral dissertation, Yale University, 1976.

Elkins, Stanley. *Slavery: A Problem in American Institutional and Intellectual Life.* Chicago: University of Chicago Press, 1959.

———. "Slavery and Ideology." In *The Debate Over Slavery,* ed. Ann Lane. Urbana: University of Illinois Press, 1971.

Ellerman, David. "The Employment Relation, Property Rights and Organizational Democracy." In *International Yearbook of Organizational Democracy,* ed. Colin Crouch. New York: J. Wiley & Sons, 1983: 265–77.

Elster, Jon. *Making Sense of Marx.* Cambridge: Cambridge University Press, 1985.

———. *Sour Grapes (Studies in the Subversion of Rationality).* Cambridge: Cambridge University Press, 1983.

Emerson, Richard. "Power-Dependence Relations." *American Sociological Review* 27 (1962): 31–40.

Emmison, Michael. "Class Images of 'The Economy': Opposition and Ideological Incorporation Within Working Class Consciousness." *Sociology* 19, 1 (1985) 19–38.

Engels, Friedrich. *The Condition of the Working Class in England.* Moscow: Progress Publishers, 1973.

———. "Letter to Mehring." In *Karl Marx and Friedrich Engels, Selected Works.* New York: International Publishers, 1968.

Erickson, Kai. *Everything in its Path.* New York: Simon and Schuster, 1976.

Ewing, David. *Freedom inside the Organization.* New York: Dutton, 1977.

Eyerman, Ron. *False Consciousness and Ideology in Marxist Theory.* Stockholm: Almquist and Wiksell International, 1981.

Fanon, Frantz. *The Wretched of the Earth.* New York: Evergreen Press, 1962.

Fantasia, Rick. *Cultures of Solidarity.* Berkeley and Los Angeles: University of California Press, 1988.

Finn, Peter. "The Effects of Shift Work on the Lives of Employees." *Monthly Labor Review* 104, 10 (October 1981): 31–35.

Fogel, Robert, and Engerman, Stanley. *Time on the Cross.* Boston: Little, Brown, 1974.

Form, William. *Divided We Stand: Working Class Stratification in America.* Chicago: University of Illinois Press, 1985.

Fox, Alan. *Beyond Contract: Work, Power and Trust Relations.* London: Faber and Faber, 1974.

Frankl, Viktor. *Man's Search for Meaning.* New York: Pocket Books, 1963.

Gallie, Duncan. *In Search of the New Working Class.* Cambridge: Cambridge University Press, 1978.

————. *Social Inequality and Class Radicalism in France and Britain.* Cambridge: Cambridge University Press, 1983.

Garson, Barbara. *All the Livelong Day.* New York: Penguin, 1977.

Garson, David. "Automobile Workers and the Radical Dream." *Politics and Society* (Winter 1973): 163–77.

Gaventa, John. *Power and Powerlessness: Quiescence and Rebellion in an Appalachian Valley.* Urbana: University of Illinois Press, 1980.

Genovese, Eugene. *Roll, Jordan, Roll.* New York: Random House, 1974.

————. "American Slaves and Their History." In *The Debate Over Slavery,* ed. Ann Lane. Urbana: University of Illinois Press, 1971.

Geuss, Raymond. *The Idea of a Critical Theory: Habermas and the Frankfurt School.* Cambridge: Cambridge University Press, 1981.

Gibson, Mary. *Workers' Rights.* Totowa, NJ: Rowman and Allanheld, 1983.

Goffman, Erving. *Asylums.* New York: Anchor Books, 1961.

Goldfield, Michael. *The Decline of Organized Labor in the United States.* Chicago: University of Chicago Press, 1987.

————. "Labor in American Politics." *Journal of Politics* 8 (February 1986): 2–29.

Goldstein, Robert. *Political Repression in Modern America.* Cambridge: Schenkman, 1978.

Goldthorpe, J. H., and Lockwood, David. *The Affluent Worker in the Class Structure.* Cambridge: University of Cambridge Press, 1968.

————. *The Affluent Worker: Industrial Attitudes and Behaviour.* Cambridge: University of Cambridge Press, 1968.

————. *The Affluent Worker: Political Attitudes and Behaviour.* Cambridge: University of Cambridge Press, 1968.

Gorz, Andre. *Farewell to the Working Class: An Essay on Post-industrial Socialism.* London: Pluto Press, 1982.

Gouldner, Alvin. "The Norm of Reciprocity: A Preliminary Statement." *American Sociological Review* 25 (April 1960): 161–78.

————. *Patterns of Industrial Bureaucracy.* New York: Free Press, 1954.

————. *Wildcat Strike: A Study in Worker-Management Relationships.* New York: Harper and Row, 1954.

Gramsci, Antonio. *Selections from Prison Notebooks,* ed. Quentin Hoare and Geoffrey Nowell Smith. London: Lawrence and Wishart, 1971.

Greenberg, Edward. *Workplace Democracy.* Ithaca, NY: Cornell University Press, 1986.

Greenberg, Stanley. "Democratic Defection Revisited." Unpublished paper, 1986.

Gunn, Christopher. *Workers' Self-Management in the United States.* Ithaca, NY: Cornell University Press, 1984.

Gurn, Ted. *Why Men Rebel.* Princeton: Princeton University Press, 1970.

Gutman, Herbert, and Sutch, Richard. "Sambo Makes Good, or Were Slaves Imbued with the Protestant Work Ethic?" In *Reckoning with Slavery,* ed. Paul David. New York: Oxford University Press, 1976.

Haimson, Leopold. "The Problem of Social Stability in Urban Russia, 1905–1917 (Part 1)." *Slavic Review* 23, 4 (1964): 614–41.

Halle, David. *America's Working Man.* Chicago: University of Chicago Press, 1984.

Hamilton, Richard, and Wright, James. *The State of the Masses*. New York: Aldine, 1986.

Hanagan, Michael. *The Logic of Solidarity: Artisans and Industrial Workers in Three French Towns 1871–1914*. Chicago: University of Illinois Press, 1980.

Hay, Douglas, ed. *Albion's Fatal Tree: Crime and Society in Eighteenth Century England*. New York: Pantheon Books, 1975.

Hearn, Francis. *Domination, Legitimation and Resistance*. Westport, CT: Greenwood, 1978.

Hegel, Georg. *The Philosophy of Hegel*, trans. and ed. Carl Friedrich. New York: Modern Library, 1954.

Heller, Agnes. *Everyday Life*. London: Routledge and Kegan Paul, 1984.

Herman, Edward. *Corporate Control, Corporate Power*. New York: Cambridge University Press, 1981.

Herzberg, Frederick. *Work and the Nature of Man*. New York: World Publishing, 1966.

Hill, Christopher. *The World Turned Upside Down*. Middlesex: Penguin Books, 1972.

Hill, Stephen. *Competition and Control at Work*. London: Heineman, 1981.

Hindess, Barry. "On Three-Dimensional Power." *Political Studies* 24 (1976): 329–33.

Hirschman, Albert. *Exit, Voice, and Loyalty: Responses to Decline in Firms, Organizations, and States*. Cambridge, MA: Harvard University Press, 1970.

Hobsbawm, Eric. *Laboring Men*. New York: Basic Books, 1964.

———. *Pre-Capitalist Economic Formations*. New York: International Publishers, 1964.

Hobsbawm, Eric, and Rude, George. *Captain Swing*. New York: W. W. Norton, 1968.

Hochschild, Jennifer. *What's Fair?* Cambridge, MA: Harvard University Press, 1981.

Hoggart, Richard. *The Uses of Literacy*. Oxford: Oxford University Press, 1958.

Huber, Joan, and Form, William. *Income and Ideology*. New York: Free Press, 1973.

Hunnius, Gerald. "On the Nature of Capitalist-Initiated Innovations in the Workplace." In *Work and Power*, ed. Tom Burns, Lars Karlsson, and Veljco Rus. Beverly Hills, CA: Sage Publications, 1979.

Hunnius, Gerald; Garson, David; and Case, John, eds. *Workers' Control: A Reader on Labor and Social Change*. New York: Random House, 1973.

Huntington, Samuel. *American Politics: The Promise of Disharmony*. Cambridge: Harvard University Press, 1981.

Hyman, Richard. "Andre Gorz and His Disappearing Proletariat," *Socialist Register* (1983): 272–95.

———. *Marxism and the Sociology of Trade Unions*. London: Pluto Press, 1971.

Hyman, Richard, and Brough, Ian. *Social Values and Industrial Relations: A Study of Fairness and Equality*. Oxford: Blackwell, 1975.

Isaac, Jeffrey. "On Benton's 'Objective Interests and the Sociology of Power': A Critique." *Sociology* 16, 2 (1982): 430–44.

Jackman, Mary, and Jackman, Robert. *Class Awareness in the United States*. Berkeley and Los Angeles: University of California Press, 1983.

Janeway, Elizabeth. *Powers of the Weak*. New York: Morrow Quill Paperbacks, 1980.

Jenkins, Craig, and Perrow, Charles. "Insurgency of the Powerless: Farm Worker Movements (1946–1972)," *American Sociological Review* 42, 2 (1977): 249–67.

Jepperson, Ron. "Consensus, Dissensus, and the Condition of Political Knowledge." Unpublished paper, 1984.

Jessop, Robert. *Traditionalism, Conservatism and the British Political Culture*. London: Allen and Unwin, 1974.

Katznelson, Ira. *City Trenches: Urban Politics and the Patterning of Class in the United States*. New York: Pantheon, 1981.

Kluegel, James, and Smith, Eliot. *Beliefs about Inequality*. New York: Aldine De Gruyter, 1986.

Kohn, Melvin. *Class and Conformity*. Homewood, IL: Dorsey Press, 1969.

Kusteror, Ken. *Know-how on the Job: The Important Working Knowledge of "Unskilled Workers."* Boulder, CO: Westview Press, 1978.

Landtmann, Gunnar. *The Origin of the Inequality of the Social Classes*. London: Routledge and Kegan Paul, 1938.

Lane, Ann, ed. *The Debate over Slavery: Stanley Elkins and His Critics*. Urbana: University of Illinois Press, 1971.

Lane, Anthony, and Roberts, Kenneth. *Strike at Pilkington's*. London: Fontana Press, 1972.

Lane, Robert. "From Political to Industrial Democracy." *Polity* 17, 4 (1985): 623–48.

———. "Market Justice, Political Justice." *American Political Science Review* 80, 2 (1986): 383–401.

———. *Political Ideology*. New York: Free Press, 1962.

Lazonick, William. "The Subjugation of Labour to Capital: The Rise of the Capitalist System." *Review of Radical Political Economy* 10, 1 (1978): 1–32.

Lefebvre, Henri. *Everyday Life in the Modern World*. New York: Harper and Row, 1971.

———. *The Explosion: Marxism and the French Revolution*. New York: Monthly Review Press, 1969.

Leggett, John. *Class, Race and Labor: Working-Class Consciousness in Detroit*. New York: Oxford University Press, 1968.

Levi, Margaret. "Weapons of the Strong and How the Weak Resist Them." Paper delivered to the American Political Science Association convention, 1987.

Levi, Primo. *The Reawakening*. New York: Summit Books, 1986.

———. *Survival in Auschwitz*. New York: Summit Books, 1986.

Lewy, Guenther. *False Consciousness: An Essay on Mystification*. New Brunswick, New Jersey: Transaction Books, 1982.

Lindblom, Charles. "The Market as Prison." *Journal of Politics* 44 (1982): 329–33.

———. *Politics and Markets: The World's Political-Economic Systems*. New York: Basic Books, 1977.

Lipset, Seymour Martin, and Schneider, William. *The Confidence Gap*. Baltimore: Johns Hopkins University Press, 1987.

Littler, Craig, ed. *The Experience of Work*. Hampshire, England: Gower, 1985.

Locke, John. *Two Treatises of Government*, ed. Peter Laslett. New York: Cambridge University Press, 1963.

Lockwood, David. *The Blackcoated Worker: A Study in Class Consciousness*. London: Allen and Unwin, 1958.

———. "Sources of Variation in Working Class Images of Society," *Sociological Review* 14 (1966): 249–67.

Lukacs, Georg. *History and Class Consciousness*. Cambridge, MA: MIT Press, 1971.

Lukes, Steven. *Power: A Radical View*. London: Macmillan, 1974.

Lustick, Ian. *Arabs in the Jewish State*. Austin: University of Texas Press, 1980.

Lynd, Staughton. *The Fight against Shutdowns*. San Pedro, CA: Singlejack Books, 1982.

McCaffrey, David, ed. *OSHA and the Politics of Health Regulation*. New York: Plenum, 1982.

McCloskey, Herbert, and Zaller, John. *The American Ethos: Public Attitudes toward Capitalism and Democracy*. Cambridge, MA: Harvard University Press, 1984.

McCormack, Gavan. "The Kampuchean Revolution, 1975–1978: The Problem of Knowing the Truth," *Journal of Contemporary Asia* 10, 1/2 (1980): 75–118.

Machiavelli, Niccolo. *The Prince and the Discourses*. New York: Random House, 1950.

McKenzie, Robert, and Silver, Allan. *Angels in Marble: Working Class Conservatives in Urban England*. Chicago: University of Chicago Press, 1968.

MacLeod, Jay. *Ain't No Makin' It*. Boulder, CO: Westview, 1987.

MacPherson, C. B. *The Political Theory of Possessive Individualism.* Oxford: Oxford University Press, 1962.

Mallet, Serge. "The Class Struggle: Death and Transformation at Caltex." In *Work and Community in the West,* ed. Edward Shorter. New York: Harper and Row, 1973.

Mann, Michael. *Consciousness and Action among the Western Working Class.* London: Macmillan, 1973.

———. "The Social Cohesion of Liberal Democracy." *American Sociological Review* 35, 3 (1970): 423–39.

Mansbridge, Jane. *Beyond Adversary Democracy.* Chicago: University of Chicago Press, 1983.

Marcus, Steven. *Engels, Manchester, and the Working Class.* New York: Random House, 1974.

Marglin, Stephen. "What Do Bosses Do?" *Review of Radical Political Economy* 6, 2 (1974): 60–112.

Marshall, T. H. *Class, Citizenship and Social Development.* Garden City, NY: Doubleday, 1964.

Marx, Karl. *Capital.* New York: International Publishers, 1967.

———. *The Communist Manifesto.* In *The Marx-Engels Reader,* ed. R. C. Tucker. New York: W. W. Norton, 1978.

———. *The German Ideology.* In *The Marx-Engels Reader,* ed. R. C. Tucker. New York: W. W. Norton, 1978.

———. *The Grundrisse.* In *The Marx-Engels Reader,* ed. R. C. Tucker. New York: W. W. Norton, 1978.

———. *The Poverty of Philosophy.* In *Selected Writings,* ed. David McLellan. Oxford: Oxford University Press, 1977.

———. *Value, Price, and Profit.* New York: International Publishers, 1933.

Mason, Ronald. *Participatory and Workplace Democracy.* Carbondale: Southern Illinois University Press, 1982.

Meissner, Martin. "The Long Arm of the Job: A Study of Work and Leisure." *Industrial Relations* 10 (October 1971): 239–60.

Mennell, Stephen. *All Manners of Food: Eating and Taste in England and France from the Middle Ages to the Present.* Oxford: Basil Blackwell, 1985.

Miller, David. "Ideology and the Problem of False Consciousness." *Political Studies* 20, 4 (1973): 432–47.

Moberg, David. "No More Junk: Lordstown Workers and the Demand for Quality." *Insurgent Sociologist* 8, 2 and 3 (1978): 63–69.

Montgomery, David. *Workers' Control in America.* London: Cambridge University Press, 1979.

———. "Workers' Control of Machine Production in the Nineteenth Century." *Labor History* 17, 4 (1976): 485–509.

Moore, Barrington. *Injustice: The Social Bases of Obedience and Revolt.* White Plains, NY: M. E. Sharpe, 1978.

———. *Reflections on the Causes of Human Misery and on Certain Proposals to Eliminate Them.* Boston: Beacon Press, 1972.

Moorehouse, H. F., and Chamberlain, C. "Lower Class Attitudes to Property." *Sociology* 8, 3 (1973): 387–405.

Morawska, Ewa. "East European Laborers in an American Mill Town, 1890–1940: The Defererential-Proletarian-Privatized Workers." *Sociology* 19, 3 (1985): 364–83.

———. *For Bread with Butter.* Cambridge: Cambridge University Press, 1986.

Murton, Thomas. *The Dilemma of Prison Reform.* New York: Holt, Rinehart and Winston, 1982.

Murton, Thomas, and Hyams, Joe. *Accomplices to the Crime: The Arkansas Prison Scandal.* New York: Grove Press, 1969.

Nelkin, Dorothy, and Brown, Michael. *Workers at Risk.* Chicago: University of Chicago Press, 1984.

Newby, Howard. "The Deferential Dialectic." *Comparative Studies in Society and History* 17, 2 (1975): 139–64.

Noble, David. "Social Choice in Machine Design: The Case of Automatically Controlled Machine Tools." In *Case Studies of the Labor Process*, ed. Andrew Zimbalist. New York: Monthly Review Press, 1979.

Nozick, Robert. *Anarchy, State and Utopia.* New York: Basic Books, 1974.

———. "Coercion." In *Philosophy, Politics and Society*, 4th series, ed. Peter Laslett, W. G. Runciman, and Quentin Skinner. New York: Harper and Row, 1972.

Oglesby, Carl. *Containment and Change.* New York: Macmillan, 1967.

Offe, Claus. "Two Logics of Collective Action: Theoretical Notes on Social Class and Organizational Form." In *Political Power and Social Theory*, ed. Maurice Zeitlin. Greenwich, CT: JAI Press, 1980.

Ollman, Bertell. "Toward Class Consciousness Next Time: Marx and the Working Class." *Politics and Society* (Fall 1972): 1–25.

Page, Benjamin, *Choices and Echoes in Presidential Elections.* Chicago: University of Chicago Press, 1978.

Pareto, Vilfredo. *Manual of Political Economy*, ed. Ann Schwein and Alfred Page. New York: M. Kelley, 1971.

Parkin, Frank. *Class Inequality and Political Order.* New York: Praeger, 1972.

———. *Marxism and Class Theory: A Bourgeois Critique.* New York: Columbia University Press, 1979.

Pateman, Carol. *Participation and Democratic Theory.* Cambridge: Cambridge University Press, 1970.

Perrow, Charles. *Normal Accidents: Living with High-Risk Technologies.* New York: Basic Books, 1984.

Pfeffer, Richard. *Working for Capitalism.* New York: Columbia University Press, 1979.

Polsby, Nelson. *Community Power and Political Theory: A Further Look at Problems of Evidence and Inference*, 2d ed. New Haven, CT: Yale University Press, 1980.

Pope, Liston. *Millhands and Preachers: A Study of Gastonia.* New Haven, CT: Yale University Press, 1965.

Popkin, Samuel. *The Rational Peasant.* Berkeley and Los Angeles: University of California Press, 1979.

Poulantzas, Nicos. *Classes in Contemporary Democracy.* London: New Left Books, 1975.

Przeworski, Adam. "Material Bases of Consent: Economics and Politics in a Hegemonic System." In *Political Power and Social Theory*, ed. Maurice Zeitlin. Greenwich, CT: JAI Press, 1980.

Rae, Douglas. *Equalities.* Cambridge, MA: Harvard University Press, 1981.

Reinarman, Craig. *American States of Mind.* New Haven, CT: Yale University Press, 1987.

Roberts, Kenneth; Cook, F. G.; Clark, S. C.; and Semeonoff, Elizabeth. *The Fragmentary Class Structure.* London: Heineman, 1977.

Rothstein, Lawrence. *Plant Closings: Myths, Power, Politics.* Dover: Auburn House, 1986.

Rousseau, Jean Jacques. *First and Second Discourses*, ed. Roger D. Masters. New York: St. Martin's Press, 1964.

———. *On the Social Contract*, ed. Roger D. Masters. New York: St. Martin's Press, 1978.

Rubin, Lillian. *Worlds of Pain: Life in the Working-Class Family*. New York: Basic Books, 1976.

Runciman, W. G. *Relative Deprivation and Social Justice*. Berkeley and Los Angeles: University of California Press, 1966.

Rustow, Alexander. *Freedom and Domination: A Historical Critique of Civilization*. Princeton, NJ: Princeton University Press, 1980.

Sabel, Charles. *Work and Politics*. Cambridge: Cambridge University Press, 1982.

Sartre, Jean-Paul. Preface to Frantz Fanon, *The Wretched of the Earth*. New York: Evergreen Press, 1962.

Schiller, Nina Glick. "Management by Participation: The Division of Labor, Ideology, and Contradiction." Presented to American Anthropological Association, 1983.

Schlozman, Kay, and Verba, Sidney. *Insult to Injury: Unemployment, Class and Political Response*. Cambridge, MA: Harvard University Press, 1979.

Schrank, Robert. *American Workers Abroad: A Report to the Ford Foundation*. Cambridge, MA: MIT Press, 1979.

———. *Ten Thousand Working Days*. Cambridge, MA: MIT Press, 1978.

Schwartz, Nancy. "The Time of Our Being Together: An Inquiry into the Meaning of Marx's Labor Theory of Value." *New Political Science* 8 (1982): 73–87.

Scott, James. "Everyday Forms of Peasant Resistance." *Journal of Peasant Studies* 13, 2 (1986): 5–31.

———. "False Consciousness or Laying It on Thick." Paper presented to American Political Science Association convention, 1987.

———. *The Moral Economy of the Peasant*. New Haven, CT: Yale University Press, 1976.

———. "Resistance without Protest and without Organization: Peasant Opposition to the Islamic *Zakat* and the Christian Tithe." *Comparative Studies in History and Society* 29, 1 (1987): 417–52.

———. *Weapons of the Weak: Everyday Forms of Peasant Resistance*. New Haven, CT: Yale University Press, 1985.

Sennett, Richard. *Authority*. New York: Random House, 1972.

Sennett, Richard, and Cobb, Jonathan. *The Hidden Injuries of Class*. New York: Random House, 1972.

Shanin, Teodor. "Class, State and Revolution: Substitutes and Reality." In *Sociology of Developing Societies*, ed. Hamza Alavi and Teodor Shanin. New York: Monthly Review Press, 1982.

———. *Late Marx and the Russian Road*. New York: Monthly Review Press, 1983.

Simmons, John, and Mares, William. *Working Together*. New York: Alfred A. Knopf, 1983.

Sirianni, Carmen. "Production and Power in a Classless Society: A Critical Analysis of the Utopian Dimensions of Marxist Theory." *Socialist Review* 59 (1981): 33–81.

———. *Workers' Control and Socialist Democracy: The Soviet Experience*. London: Verso, 1982.

Smith, Steven A. *Red Petrograd: Revolution in the Factories 1917–18*. New York: Cambridge University Press, 1983.

Sniderman, Paul. *A Question of Loyalty*. Berkeley and Los Angeles: University of California Press, 1981.

Spence, Larry. *The Politics of Social Knowledge*. University Park: Pennsylvania State University Press, 1978.

Spencer, Charles. *Blue Collar*. Chicago: Vanguard Press, 1977.

Stigler, George, and Becker, Gary. "De Gustibus Non Est Disputandum." *The American Economic Review* 67 (March 1977): 76–90.

Stone, Lawrence. "Theories of Revolution." *World Politics* 18 (1966): 159–76.

Stuckey, Sterling. "Through the Prism of Folklore: The Black Ethos in Slavery." In *The Debate Over Slavery*, ed. Ann Lane. Urbana: University of Illinois Press, 1971.

Tannenbaum, Arnold. *Hierarchy in Organizations*. San Francisco: Jossey-Bass, 1974.

Taussig, Michael. *The Devil and Commodity Fetishism in South America*. Chapel Hill: University of North Carolina Press, 1980.

Terkel, Studs. *Working*. New York: Pantheon, 1972.

Thomas, Henk, and Logan, Chris. *Mondragon: An Economic Analysis*. London: Allen and Unwin, 1982.

Thompson, E. P. *The Making of the English Working Class*. London: Gollancz, 1963.

————. "The Moral Economy of the English Crowd in the Eighteenth Century." *Past and Present* 38 (1967): 76–136.

Thorpe, Earl. "Chattel Slavery and Concentration Camps." In *The Debate Over Slavery*, ed. Ann Lane. Urbana: University of Illinois Press, 1971.

Truman, David. *The Governmental Process: Political Interests and Public Opinion*. New York: Alfred A. Knopf, 1971.

U.S. Department of Health, Education, and Welfare. *Work in America*. Cambridge, MA: MIT Press, 1973.

Vanneman, Reeve, and Cannon, Lynne. *The American Perception of Class*. Philadelphia: Temple University Press, 1987.

Walker, Charles, and Guest, Robert. *The Man on the Assembly Line*. Cambridge, MA: Harvard University Press, 1952.

Watson, Bill. "Counter Planning on the Shop Floor." *Radical America* 5, 3 (1971): 77–85.

Wertheim, Willem. *Evolution and Revolution: The Rising Tide of Emancipation*. Hamondsworth: Penguin Books, 1974.

Westergaard, John, and Resler, Henrietta. *Class in a Capitalist Society*. New York: Basic Books, 1975.

White, Christine. "Everyday Resistance, Socialist Revolution and Rural Development: The Vietnamese Case." *Journal of Peasant Studies* 13, 2 (1986): 49–63.

Wildavsky, Aaron. "Choosing Preferences by Constructing Institutions: A Cultural Theory of Preference Formation." *American Political Science Review* 81, 1 (1987): 3–22.

Willis, Paul. *Learning to Labour*. Westmead: Saxonhouse, 1977.

Winget, Charles; Hughes, Lewis; and Ladou, Joseph. "Physiological Effects of Rotational Work Shifting: A Review." *Journal of Occupational Medicine* 20, 3 (March 1978): 204–210.

Witte, John. *Democracy, Authority, and Alienation in Work*. Chicago: University of Chicago Press, 1980.

Wolfinger, Raymond. "Nondecisions and the Study of Local Politics." *American Political Science Review* 65 (1971): 1063–80.

Wood, Stephen. "The Cooperative Labour Strategy in the U.S. Auto Industry." *Economic and Social Democracy* 17, 4 (1985): 415–47.

Wright, Eric Olin. *Class, Crisis and the State*. London: New Left Review Books, 1976.

Zeitlin, L. R. "A Little Larceny Can Do a Lot for Employee Morale." In *The Experience of Work*, ed. Craig Littler. London: Gower, 1985.

Zolberg, Aristide. "Moments of Madness." *Politics and Society* 2 (Winter 1972): 183–207.

Index

Marc Lendler received his B.A. from Antioch University in 1970. For the next eight years he worked in a variety of factories in Cincinatti, Ohio. He then went on to receive his M.A. and Ph.D. in Political Science from Yale University. Professor Lendler has taught at Connecticut College, Mount Holyoke, and the University of Pennsylvania. He now teaches Political Science in the Social Science division at Bennington College.